INDEPENDENCE DAY

INDEPENDENCE DAY

JIM KEEBLE

An *Abacus* Book

First published in Great Britain in 2000 by Abacus
This edition published in 2001

Copyright © Jim Keeble 2000

The moral right of the author has been asserted.

A CIP catalogue record for this book
is available from the British Library.

ISBN 0 349 11294 0

Typeset by
Palimpsest Book Production Limited,
Polmont, Stirlingshire
Printed and bound in Great Britain by
Clays Ltd, St Ives plc.

Abacus
A Division of
Little, Brown and Company (UK)
Brettenham House
Lancaster Place
London WC2E 7EN

www.littlebrown.co.uk

To my parents for a lifetime of dedication, cash and love.
To all my friends for listening.
And to LGC for all that I now know.
Let me know.

CONTENTS

'The human heart is vast enough to contain the whole world.'

Joseph Conrad

'America is a vast conspiracy to make you happy.'
John Updike

1

Angie – A Niagara Falls Ending

She dumped me in the Honeymoon Capital of the World. It was March, the month when nothing good happens. Outside it was cold enough to shatter steel, windscreens and hearts. Mine stopped beating, cracked, split and shattered into shards, like a porcelain globe dropped from the Empire State Building. Or a melon on a motorway.

'No.'

One syllable, a bullet to the core.

'No.'

A breath, just.

Who was it that said, 'It's better to have loved and lost than never to have loved at all'? Either they never truly loved or never truly lost.

I'd rather lose anything than love.

An FA Cup Final. A major limb, say a leg, hand or head. Control of my bowels. A million in crisp red fifty-pound notes. My sanity. A world war, my autographed Kevin Keegan photo, my job (if I had one), my house (if I had one), my Yamaha Clavinova PF p100 (I have one, it's expensive, and I'd miss it very much).

All of these would I have gladly forgone if I could have won the Canadian's heart.

I had asked her to marry me.

She looked at me with pity but not love and said, 'No.'

At least she had the decency to cry.

Unlike men, when it comes to crying, women are always decent.

It had started magically seven years ago, in the south of France, where everything seems romantic because it's hot and sunny and beautiful, but mainly because most of the time you're drunk on cheap rosé. We met, hit it off, had more fun than is usually allowed when you first start going out with someone.

Angie was beautiful, funny, caring. She was tall, dark, of Italian descent, and had the sort of curly hair that I first drew when I was five. She made me laugh a lot. I made her laugh sometimes. We both liked Al Pacino, basketball and watching the sun set with alcohol in hand.

Everything about her was new, strange, and enticing. She talked of a world I'd only dreamed of, of snowstorms and baseball, of drive-in cinemas and bears that lived in the woods. Her references were baffling – Howdy Doody, Hundred Grand chocolate bars, Oatmeal Cream Pies, the Toronto Maple Leafs. I was swept up, wrapped up, laid to bed and ravished by her exoticness.

In return, I tried to be cool and detached because I thought that would intrigue her, but I blew it when I cancelled a round-the-world trip to go and see her when she returned to Canada. I fell in love with Canada as I fell in love with her – the space, the extremes of climate, the maple syrup.

It was a wonderful time. We agreed we were made for each other. Small happy birds sang around our heads.

Then things started to go wrong. She decided to move to London to be with me, which I didn't think much of at the time, but afterwards, when it was too late, I realised it was a huge step on her part, since she knew no one there and had no money. She came, I convinced myself at the time, to study photography, but really she came because she loved me and wanted to be with me.

She had a bad time in London, partly because it was cold and damp and unfriendly, but mainly because I was cold and damp and unfriendly.

Because I'd decided to be a writer. And to write you had to be tormented, which meant, I thought, much self-pitying introspection, added to a blatant disregard for the feelings and thoughts of those closest to you.

So she returned to Canada and gradually I realised torment only produces great works of art when allied with great talent. Looking back on it, her return to the frozen north was probably the turning point. I had rejected her love. And that, I now know, is something you should try to avoid doing if you want to end up marrying someone.

For the next three years we carried on a trans-Atlantic relationship involving constant heart-ache and lots of air miles. Then, finally, I got the courage, after a couple of false starts, to ask her to marry me. I had never been so excited. Not only was I a Titanium Mileage Plus member of Canadian Airlines, but I knew for the first time where I wanted to be when I was seventy.

Sipping frozen margaritas, watching the sun set with Angie by my side.

All those doubts – you'll never again be able to date other women, never know what it's like to wake up next to Uma Thurman, never be able to feed Emmanuelle Béart asparagus tips with your toes – these delusions had ceased. Suddenly they seemed bygone testosterone dreams of twenties adolescence. I had finally grown up.

I wanted to sleep with Angie until eternity. I wanted only her. Of that, and only that, I was utterly certain.

She was caring, good, talented and heart-warmingly gorgeous in a way reminiscent of the Italian women in Cornetto advertisements. There is a scene in *Butch Cassidy and the Sundance Kid* in which Sundance (Robert Redford) goes off to find a woman who turns out to be Etta Place (Katharine Ross).

'Shouldn't be too hard,' says Redford. 'I'm not picky. Just so she's pretty and sweet and gentle and soft and quiet and smart and refined.'

Angie was my Etta Place. And she made me feel like the Sundance Kid.

In some ways we were opposites. She was bubbly, outgoing, vivacious, a born optimist who always saw beauty in the world. I am quiet, and sometimes introverted. If she was Italianate, I was, well, English. I expect the worst, so as not to be disappointed.

'Will you marry me?'

The cornerstones of the English language. You, me. Will. Marry.

'No.'

The worst. I was more than disappointed.

I couldn't really blame her. She'd been waiting three years for me to pop the question, while I dithered, anxious about my writing, about whether I could live in Canada, about my inability to ice-skate, the pro-democracy movement in China, world peace in general and my own immaturity in particular.

By the time I'd stopped worrying and realised she was the one thing in my confused little life that mattered, she'd moved on.

Timing, as they say in Switzerland, is everything.

The location was perfect, in a Stephen King sort of a way. It was her home town, the city of Niagara Falls, Canada, otherwise known as the 'Honeymoon Capital of the World'.

Even in the depths of winter, the city was full of Japanese couples clutching certificates saying they'd consummated marriage on a heart-shaped water-bed beside the world's greatest natural wonder.

The Japanese were the only race in the world dedicated enough to brave March in Niagara. By the Falls a frosted thermometer said it was minus ten degrees.

Several seagulls were frozen to the railings. Warnings had been issued to keep old people and small children inside. Further north, snowplough shovels were splitting in the cold and icebergs were moving up the St Lawrence River. Eight Japanese newlyweds in matching maple-leaf sweaters watched us, looking like small cheerleaders for a rural ice hockey team.

4

The roar from the Falls was magnificent: 34 million gallons of water vomiting down 100 feet of rock. The spray froze into speckled crystals which showered us in clouds of diamonds. It should have been perfect.

'I'm sorry, Jim,' she said.

My tears began to freeze. They collected at the point of my chin and formed a billy-goat beard that I remember thinking would have made a funny picture. The eight Japanese newlyweds watched me, but none of them pulled out a camera to record the moment, destroying one of my most cherished national stereotypes.

I should really, like Sundance and Butch facing the guns of the Bolivian army, have seen it coming. It was perhaps the finest chapter in a long and varied list of fuck-ups with women. My problem is I tend to be hopeful and enjoy buying flowers, a fatal combination. I always want to take them home to tea with my family; they just want to go to movies and have occasional sex. The cool girls ran a mile, into the arms of men who liked Kurosawa, or cocaine, or both.

So I ended up with women I never really liked, who didn't like me very much. We'd stay together a few months because it felt like we had to.

'We're young, mildly attractive and full of hormones, we should be together,' we thought, silently, trying to convince ourselves.

Eventually the clock would chime, we'd realise we lived in the free world rather than under some oppressive regime that makes unloving couples stay together for life, and we'd split up.

It always ended in tears, insults and my decision to become an alcoholic, which lasted until the first time I drank too much and threw up – usually the next day.

But with Angie it was different. I was hopeful, I bought flowers. But something scared me. By the time I figured out that what scared me was the fact that, finally, here was the woman I wanted to spend the rest of my life with, a woman whom I didn't just care about in a I'll-make-the-bed-after-we-have-sex sort of way, but in a you-get-hit-by-a-car-and-never-walk-again-I'll-stand-by-you-forever sort of way, it was much too late.

Angie believed a relationship must be perfect.

'You get what you settle for,' she always said, and she followed the courage of those words. She didn't settle for my imperfect, half-assed, wait-and-see sort of love.

I tried telling her I'd change. People change. Look at Muhammad Ali (okay, perhaps this was not the best example). But she did not see it. I tried outlining my faults, many of which she had helped me recognise, and how I would change them:

'I will be more joyful, more spontaneous. I will follow my emotions, not my head. I will put love first, before ambition, before creative desire. Because I love you.'

'People don't change,' she said.

'I will change. Because I love you.'

'I . . . don't believe it.'

I took it well, I think. She only asked me five times to leave. When I didn't she did, hailing a cab. I ran after her, falling over on the ice, probably in the hope she would turn back, take me in her arms and tell me how she didn't mean it and, by the way, could we have children, right now?

The cab drove away, past Ripley's Believe it Or Not on Clifton Hill. I watched it go, clouds of diesel fumes billowing behind like a ghostly wedding train.

I somehow reached the rental car and drove back along the Niagara escarpment, once described by Winston Churchill as 'the prettiest Sunday afternoon drive in the world'. But it was Tuesday and the ice-draped trees looked like a scene from *War and Peace*, without the dead soldiers.

Halfway along I stopped to figure out the defroster and cry for an hour or so.

If you've ever been disembowelled with a grapefruit knife you'll know the feeling. If not, try it. It hurts.

Above me General Brock surveyed the Niagara River with

a haughtiness that comes from being one of the few non-Vietnamese generals to have defeated an American army (in the 1812 war, when the Americans tried to take Niagara after they'd realised the amount of money to be made from hot-dog stands by waterfalls).

I wondered if Brock ever had his heart broken. Probably not. After all, he was made of lead.

It was dark by the time I pulled into the Holiday Inn. Nobody there was on holiday. Heaters buzzed, overweight businessmen coughed gently to each other in the purple bar. I went to my room and drank half the bottle of champagne I'd bought in the vain hope of being engaged by nightfall. Crying, I'd discovered, is as exhausting as running. If bawling your eyes out was an Olympic event, I'd have been tested for steroids. I fell asleep in my clothes to the sound of two marine mammals having sex in the next room.

I didn't give up. I tried calling, knocking on her mum's door. She didn't reply and after a while I grew scared the Mounties would slap a restraining order on me and start asking why I'd visited Canada seven times in one year without any discernible forms of financial support.

I had a feeling lovesickness would prove much less plausible to them than the smuggling of class A narcotics.

I posted a note through her mum's letterbox that said I'd stick around, just to see if she felt differently, say in spring. Or summer. Or maybe autumn. I could wait until Christmas if she wanted. The year 2010.

For a few days I stumbled around Niagara Falls, the saddest of the 14 million visitors this strange town gets every year.

Everywhere I wandered, I encountered Japanese couples who viewed me with the uneasy curiosity often seen in doctors examining sex offenders, this unshaven shuffling maniac with tearful eyes and a streaming cold. No one sat near me in doughnut shops.

It's not easy being around newlyweds when you've just been dumped. Their wedding rings glint mercilessly. They kiss a lot, giggle a lot and spend money on merchandise not even a six-year-old would be stupid enough to buy, like Niagara Falls tea cosies and waterfall wastepaper baskets.

I so desperately wanted to be one of them.

Newlyweds are difficult to avoid in Niagara Falls. Each year 500,000 freshly hitched sweethearts book into one of the fifty-five motels offering heart-shaped jacuzzis, tiger rugs and mirrored ceilings. That's 700 couples a day. No one is quite sure how this honeymoon craze began, but it seems that back in the 1830s rich aristocrats 'discovered' the Falls on their excursions northwards to escape the oppressive southern summer heat. Soon Niagara was an integral part of the American Grand Tour, like Florence and Venice in Europe. Charles Dickens turned up, without Mrs Dickens, and declared it 'an enchanted ground, an Image of Beauty'. By the mid-1850s every young bride south of Buffalo dreamed of surrendering her maidenhood to the accompaniment of the gushing falls. It was said many Mississippi brides clung to their virginity until they reached the raging waters of Niagara, a fact that dramatically speeded up the rail service between Biloxi and the Canadian border.

When Oscar Wilde visited in 1896, 'Honeylunacy', as the press dubbed it, was in full swing. To entertain visitors numerous tacky shops opened, selling everything from beaver fat (a well-known Canadian aphrodisiac) to moonshine liquor (a well-known American aphrodisiac), and shucksters from all around the world gathered to fleece the masses. A craze for crossing the falls on tightropes began, with the great Blondin traversing six times in one afternoon, then stopping midway to fry two omelettes that he lowered below to his adoring fans in the *Maid of the Mist*. The barrels came out, Houdini turned up for a day, and someone tried to fly off the Rainbow Bridge, to little popular acclaim.

Oscar Wilde saw Niagara as nothing short of a circus, stating that the Falls 'must be the second biggest disappointment of American married life'. Marilyn Monroe, who filmed *Niagara* here in 1951, disagreed, carefully explaining that, 'The Falls produce a lot of electricity but the honeymooners don't use much of it at night.'

Marilyn didn't use much of it either, conducting two simultaneous affairs in Niagara, one with producer Bob Slatzer and the other with Joe DiMaggio. A day after filming she married Slatzer in Mexico, divorced him four days later and subsequently married DiMaggio. Which, in some twisted way, gave me hope in my hour of need.

For forty-eight hours, I spent more time than psychologists recommend staring into the thundering water, especially at night, when – contrary to American popular opinion – the Falls are *not* turned off. I wandered the banks of the Niagara River in the snow, imagining a thousand different futures, each involving Angie's capitulation and a sex-filled, sun-drenched, margarita-guzzling life together.

At other times I read books about her home town, as if the histories they contained might in some way impart a secret that I could use to convince her. My favourite was a local Iroquois legend describing an ancient marriage ceremony in which the most beautiful woman in the tribe was 'wed' to the Spirit of the Water and ceremoniously chucked into the Falls. This, so the Iroquois maintained whenever they were up in front of the magistrates for aggravated assault with intent to drown, calmed the mighty Niagara River and dissuaded it from taking the lives of other young Iroquois women as they washed their bearskin knickers. In my darkest hours I took solace from a vision of Angie tumbling in slow motion into the mouth of the Falls, which made me hate myself even more.

Elsewhere I read that scientists claim the negative ions created by the Falls are a stimulant for sexual activity, which would explain the honeymoon syndrome (and Marilyn Monroe's stamina) but did very little to alleviate my malaise. On some days I could not eat but stayed in my room watching daytime soaps, all of which seemed to be full of couples splitting up or shooting each other.

Other times I ventured to Eagles Landing bar on Ferry Street, where I talked to no one, except one cold grey afternoon, a single young man, whom I thought might be a fellow suicide candidate (I was looking forward to a discussion of the relative merits of pills versus razor blades). He turned out to be a wedding organiser who runs sixty nuptials a year in Niagara Falls.

'It happens. They go to the Falls, they look at each other, get a little giggly and the next thing you know they're down at the park getting hitched.'

He'd just finished preparing a wedding for a Montreal couple who'd called him on the spur of the moment the day before.

'I don't know what it is. A psychology major I used to date said it's something about looking down, feeling the fear, your whole life flashing by, making you hold your partner closer. It's hard for me to realise it – I drive past the Falls every day.'

I kept quiet and drinking. By the time he'd explained his idea of a perfect Niagara Falls wedding – service above the Falls, pictures at the Waterworks, dinner at the Prince Edward Hotel in Niagara-on-the-Lake – I was having difficulty with the vertical bit of standing up.

'You come and see me if you ever find the right girl. I'll give you a special price.'

I thanked him.

After a week I began to regain a certain optimism. I started looking in florists again. Then I bought a bouquet at vast price (this was after all the frozen north, a thousand miles from the nearest living flower) and went to her mother's house, a neat little condominium on the outskirts of town.

It was minus eleven. I was wearing all my sweatshirts and a coat Angie had bought me a year previously. I thought the coat might swing things, by sparking a rush of nostalgia. In one begloved hand I held the near frozen flowers, in the other the ring. I stood for a minute, nose tingling, unable to ring the doorbell.

I wanted to be married to Angie. Why?

I was thirty. That had something to do with it. But it had more to do with her. With Angie. And the fact that she was the first woman in my life I knew that I loved.

How did I know? No one else had ever made me vomit from the fear of losing her.

I rang the bell.

Nothing, except my breathing. Darth Vader's wheezier younger brother.

Then footsteps. A form, a shape, a figure behind frosted glass. My future, stepping slowly towards me.

It was her mum.

'Sandra, please, I have to see her. Please . . .'

'She doesn't want to see you, James.'

'Please, Sandra, I have to. This is life and death, this is my future, her future, this is everything.'

Sandra looked at me. I knew she liked me. A flicker of a smile. There was hope. Was there?

'I'll see . . .'

Footsteps disappearing, my emissary retreating to plead for clemency.

I could hear the clock in the kitchen ticking. This house, where I'd spent so much time. It had seemed so easy entering in, crossing the threshold on which I now stood, unable to proceed. I'd taken it so much for granted, even feeling it was a chore at times, to see her mum, hang out with her family.

Footsteps. Lighter. A slender form, a shadow at first, coming down the stairs.

'ANGIE!'

She walked towards me, then stopped, six feet away. A barrier, impenetrable as rock.

I held out the flowers. Then the ring. Silence. I fell to my knees, quite gracefully, I think. 'Marry me, Angie.'

She looked at me. Breathed in, breathed out, her small beautiful breasts rising, then falling. I wanted her like never before.

'I can't see you anymore. It's over. You have to realise that.'

On my knees, tears in her eyes, no air in my lungs. 'But Angie, I want to marry you, live with you forever, have children . . .'

'Jim!'

I stood, quickly. She looked at me, deep, dark, brown eyes like deep space in which I saw myself drowning.

'I don't love you anymore, Jim. You have to go.'

And because I still loved her, I did.

Everyone's been dumped. It's part of growing up, something that toughens you, like fluoride tablets and reruns of *Knots Landing*.

But this was different. This wasn't dumping, this was being pushed out of Concorde at 60,000 feet with a grand piano tied to my testicles.

Back in Toronto, friends were sympathetic. They took me drinking, cooked me meals, called her bad names. But I needed to get out of the city, which was a place I loved for its cultural diversity, amazingly good food, funky architecture, subversive anarchic nightlife, wonderful interesting people – and mainly because Angie lived there.

Tips for those spurned when asking for a woman's hand in marriage . . .

1. Don't open the box and look at the ring until a good length of time has passed. Say about three years.

2. Don't look at any pictures you may have of her. It is better to tear them into bite-sized pieces, smother them in ketchup and feed them to stray dogs.

3. Avoid listening to any radio station for at least six months. Every song will be about losing the one true love of your life.

4. Don't go to the cinema. It will remind you of snogging and every film will star Meg Ryan or Julia Roberts getting over a dud boyfriend who asked them to marry him, and then meeting someone far more handsome/funny/witty/rich/well hung.

5. Every film, that is, except ones that star Meg Ryan *and* Julia Roberts. Those, believe me, are the worst.

6. Don't go to a travel agent and book a one-way ticket to the first and cheapest place she finds on her computer.

7. Especially if that city is Las Vegas.

2

Aki – The Vegas Showgirl

Single or return? the travel agent asked.

'Single,' I said, and we both knew it was true.

America seemed like a good enough destination. After all it was south, following my self-esteem. And it is, so the history books say, a traditional destination for the poor, destitute and desperate of the world, a nation founded on broken-hearted, disabused peoples arriving to reforge a dream in the image of the Founding Fathers.

'Reasons for your visit?' the US immigration official asked me at Toronto airport.

'The desire to forget the past and build a new and happier future for myself in the Land of the Free,' I replied.

'That's marvellous, sir,' he said, stamping my passport, tears of pity and joy welling in his eyes. 'Our nation welcomes you.'

Actually he asked me if I'd ever been a terrorist, a child abuser, a Nazi or eaten Iraqi food. I hadn't, which seemed to be the answer he was looking for.

I arrived in San Francisco after a tearful flight during which the staff at United Airlines generously replaced my blood with tomato juice and vodka. As the plane chewed up the air between me and my broken heart, lying like diced tripe in the ice of Niagara Falls, I tried to convince myself that at least heading to America was one sure way to avenge yourself on a Canadian. Canadians hate America in the same way everyone hates merchant bankers. In

14

the long run Canadians know they're better off, but in terms of the here-and-now, the instant six-figure bonus, they'd much rather be south of the 49th Parallel.

At San Francisco airport everyone was in love. Many were kissing. Some were pregnant and kissing. Some were cradling babies and kissing. One couple was sharing a pizza as if it was their last food together on earth, cheese stretching between salivating lips like an umbilical cord.

As I sat waiting for my connecting flight to Las Vegas I watched men being greeted by pretty young women with bunches of flowers. And, this being America, they were doing it really, really loudly.

'I MISSED YOU LOVE-BUCKET!'
'I MISSED YOU BIG BALLS!'
'I LOVE YOU TITTY-BUNS!'
'I LOVE YOU DANGLE-DICK!'

All the women were attractive, all the men were nerds. Geeks, all bytes and no bark, computer Jacks with soft wares. Each one wore khaki shorts, with a brown belt and striped polo shirt. Picture that. Then add white socks.

What disturbed me most was that they all seemed so sure of their love. There was no uncertainty. They went away on business trips to Taiwan and Vancouver and came back without doubting that their women would be there, sitting at the United Airlines gate, dewy-eyed and softly amorous. It seemed so ignorant. Didn't they realise at any moment their woman might turn round and say, 'Sorry Rick, I have to confess I've always hated you and I've finally got the courage to leave.'

Another couple threw tentacles around each other.

'I LOVE YOU FLAPPY LIPS!'
'I LOVE YOU SWEATY NIPS!'

Looking back on it, I suppose I was in a state of physical shock. In the past I'd not believed much in the physical impact of emotions. Now, however, I felt physically ill. Breathing was hard work.

I almost missed my connection to Vegas. For some reason

I could not read the departure information; I was finding it difficult to see anything clearly. The world, along with the future and past, was blurred. I hadn't felt this dizzy since skiing into a tree.

Announcements came and went, words like a foreign and abusive language.

'Waw waw waw wuahh . . .' said the loudspeaker.

'Musala mussumu mumumu . . .' said the woman behind the United Airlines desk.

The only voice I heard clearly was Angie's. 'I love you Jim,' she had said, many years before. Now I heard it as if for the first time.

'Are you all right?' Considering I was humming to myself whilst staring hard at a plastic spoon held between forefinger and thumb in the middle of a busy airport terminal, this was probably a rhetorical question, but I appreciated the gesture of the kindly old lady who touched my shoulder and smiled and pointed out that if I didn't get to gate 77A in the next minute and a half I'd miss the last flight to Vegas that night.

So I was finally going to Vegas. To be honest (or at least as honest as you can be when pouring out your heart to strangers), I'd never really wanted to go. Angie had wanted to visit once, for a long weekend. She liked to gamble. I didn't like anything I didn't understand.

But secretly I'd always fantasised about seeing a Vegas show, and more specifically a Vegas showgirl. But that is not something you should admit to your girlfriend. Even I knew that.

On the plane, half the passengers were reading the *National Enquirer* and the other half were asleep. I stared out of the window, seeking solace in the empty darkness, the vast endless hole of the American night, strangely primeval, not a light to be seen. Until Vegas.

I first glimpsed it from 33,000 feet. From the black heart of the American night comes the shining. The dazzle. Electric snakes of neon in a dark pit of desert. Or a bed of jewels shimmering and supplicant, waiting to be plucked.

What, I asked myself suddenly, were the odds on feeling better in Vegas?

To its vast credit, the city lived down to my expectations of tackiness, kitsch and chromatic armaggedon immediately. And that was just the airport.

In the arrivals hall huge video screens portrayed buxom women imploring me to come and try my luck at their casino. On the vast screens their breasts were as big as hippos.

Two cowboys in Stetsons carrying matching leather attaché cases (full of money or amphetamines) strutted down the escalator as if it was the most natural thing in the world to be dressed like Gary Cooper in *High Noon*, which in Vegas, apparently, it was.

There were slot machines jangling as soon as we stepped off the plane. I think they would have tried to bring one on to the plane so we could begin playing as we collected our hand luggage from the overhead lockers, but it's against Federal Aviation Authority regulations.

Never mind. There's plenty of them as soon as you step on to land. In the arrivals hall, in the car rental area, in the toilets and by the exit they stand, serried ranks of slots, all snarling like a race of half-starved coyotes. And people were actually playing them. Whether these were just folk waiting for passengers or flights, or whether this was their preferred gambling venue was unclear. Certainly the old man in the *Jurassic Park* T-shirt seemed to be enjoying the sight of ten-foot high breasts on the video screen as he absent-mindedly dabbed coins into the hungry machine.

I felt suddenly brave. I paused, put in twenty-five cents and thumped the button with disdain. The three lines whirred and for a second I could see my reflection in the neon glass – tired, red-eyed and homicidal.

Two bars, but a blank space between them.

No win.

No shit.

I headed outside. This was a mistake, since it was eighty degrees at 10 p.m. Vegas heat is dry heat, but that didn't stop me from sweating. After ten seconds, I looked as if I'd swum to Nevada.

I bought a ticket from a man who seemed to consider deodorant a deadly sin and found my taxi, a dark Ford van that looked like something O.J. Simpson might keep knives in. Inside three couples stared at me, arms around respective partners in sultry lust. I smiled faintly, feeling as damp and attractive as a flounder.

'Evening,' I said, soggily.

The couples ignored me and embarked on a kissing competition, one pair after another, a mini Mexican wave of mouth-sucking.

There are two attitudes to Vegas. There are those, like Angie, who think it would be a barrel of laughs, a fervent celebration of human tackiness. And there are those, like me, who think it would be hell on earth. The interesting thing is, as I was proving, the people who think Vegas will be hell on earth are still attracted by the place. All that neon has a mysterious, magnetic lure, like a full moon or car crashes.

1-888 RU MY DAD? read the advert on top of the O.J. Simpson taxi. I didn't think so – its driver looked nothing like me, being fifty-five, overweight and from Uzbekistan. But it sent me into reverie. What if Angie was pregnant? What if I was a dad and didn't know it? Maybe she'd keep the baby, realise she wanted me to be the father, we'd be reunited in soft-focus cinemascope serenaded by the Bee Gees singing 'How Deep Is Your Love?' I was so far lost in visions of happy families that I almost missed my hotel, which was quite a feat considering it was a 300-foot-high glass pyramid.

The Luxor Hotel is one of the four largest hotels in the world. It has 4,427 rooms. The largest, the Venetian, has 6,000 rooms, and it's just down the street; in total, nineteen of the world's twenty biggest hotels are found along the Strip. The hoteliers of Vegas are confident people.

But few are more confident than those at the Luxor. After

all, it's a pyramid the size of the Pyramids. Outside, amongst swathes of palm trees a fifty-foot-high Sphinx gazes down over the gambling public as the ancient Sphinx must have gazed down over the Israelite slaves. A more modern touch is added by the laser beam ejaculating into the night sky from the pyramid's peak, which rivals the Hassan II Mosque in Casablanca for the title of 'Biggest Beam on Earth'. It's all very impressive, if you haven't been to Egypt.

I'd booked into the Luxor because the travel agent in Toronto had said it would be worth the 'little extra cost'. What that was, I didn't know. I had no idea how much any of this was costing and cared even less. I'd saved up money to start a new (married) life in Canada, and since that new life had been aborted in a way even Pro-Choice campaigners would find brutal, I was more than happy to invest it in a headfirst plunge into an older, more primeval way of doing things.

For as Dr Johnson once wrote, as quoted by Hunter S. Thompson at the beginning of *Fear and Loathing in Las Vegas*: 'He that makes a beast of himself gets rid of the pain of being a man.'

This is what I needed, I decided. To rid myself of my pain by being more bestial. Get down, dirty and more than a little crazy in the craziest town on earth. Hell, I was halfway to Loonville already.

'This is not a good town for psychedelic drugs. Reality itself is too twisted,' said the man at the tourist desk as he handed me Hunter S. Thompson's tome, quoting directly from the Doctor of Gonzo Journalism. How strange, I thought, and how predictable, that the one-time scourge of Vegas, the abhorred and desecrated Dr Thompson, should now be used as publicity for the city he disdained.

Of course, I realised later, I'd imagined the whole thing. I'd bought the book at W.H. Smith in San Francisco airport. It was without doubt time to try and reel in some sleep.

I eventually found my room after traipsing past three pharaohs, King Tut's chariot and a pair of talking camels bitching about the price of Martinis.

* * *

It's 2 a.m. I can't sleep. I'm starving and have to eat. I dine alone. There are few things sadder than a grown man sitting alone at 2 a.m. in a Las Vegas all-you-can-eat buffet. Well, maybe world famine, war or Aids are sadder, but only just.

Chewing my third plate of rubber chicken enchilada, serenaded by the jingle bells of a million slot machines, I decide to wrap myself in aluminium foil the next morning, walk out into the desert and see how long it takes for my brains to boil.

Or purchase a sledgehammer and attempt to destroy twenty-eight video poker machines before the Luxor casino security men shoot me to death with their Uzis, one slot machine for every year Angie has graced this world with her slender, beatific presence.

It is, I realise, going to be a very long night.

It was. The next day I couldn't get out of bed. Partly because the duvet they'd given me seemed to be constructed from lunar rock, and mainly because I hadn't slept.

I tried not to look at the one picture of Angie I'd sneaked past my self-control, without much success. I passed several hours trying to decide whether I was tawdry enough to sign up for twenty-four hours of porn on the pay-per-view television: *Jennifer and the Seven Dwarfs, Asian Steam* and the one that really intrigued me – *Lolita's Farm*, involving some schoolgirls and a large pig.

'No Jim,' I heard a talking camel say sometime around five in the morning. 'You have morals.' And I'm not one to argue with a talking camel.

Outside the sun beat against my double-glazed window like a salesman. The Channel 7 local news announced it was going to be the first triple-digit day of the year (temperature, not fingers). Flicking through the channels I watched a discussion show about JFK's mistresses, followed by a study on colon cancer. Which got me out of bed.

Down in the casino, the herds had arrived early to the water-hole: the casino floor was heavy with punters dressed in shorts and fanny packs. So far Vegas seemed to confirm and even celebrate America's status as the worst dressed nation in the world. Those flocking around the poker tables made even the Germans look chic. American industry was well represented in the various T-shirts, sweat pants, baseball caps and children's bibs – Antoine's Natural Gas, Dwayne's Shagpile Carpets, Bubba's Big Wrenches, Nadia's Fine Toilets.

The haircuts woke me up. They were startling: big hair, huge hair, and neolithic hair. Male buzz cuts ending inexplicably in foot long strands that stuck like pasta to the middle of sweaty backs. Every trainee hairdresser in the world should go to Vegas to see how not to do it.

A large pack of warthogs was trying to win a black Mercedes not unlike the one Princess Diana died in.

'We're way over in the money stakes. I don't know how much but we're way over,' stammered one distressed man, rubbing his slab of stomach as if a genie might appear from his navel to save him.

Despite the grazing hordes, I was tempted to spend all day in the casino, where there was no weather, no time, no geography, no world beyond. We could have been at the North Pole or on Mars. The Vegas casinos are a human triumph, showing man can overcome nature. Outside it's 150 degrees, inside a constant 70. If NASA really wants to build a community on the moon, they had better hire the designers of Vegas, who've done it already.

I peeked out of the window. Beyond the airport a shimmer of desert hills crackled with heat, a million sprinklers hushing precious water on to the parking lot grasslands, on to the clipped-crisp golf links and the fat green back yards of the fervent rich.

When, in 1829, young Rafael Rivera, a scout for Mexican traders and part-time Rumba champion, passed from the dusty ridges of Red Rock Canyon into a verdant valley nurtured by desert springs, he named his discovery Las Vegas – The Meadows. Thirty million visitors now come to mow each year.

Stepping out on to the Strip I realised how the street acquired its name. Because that's what you feel like doing. Not for any erotic or monetary purpose, but because it's hotter than a Sicilian blowtorch. I turned to Dr Thompson for advice: 'The only way to prepare for a trip like this was to dress up like human peacocks and get crazy. Never lose sight of the primary responsibility.'

Just down the strip, alongside the Fat-Cat Diner, the Bombay Smart Guy shop welcomed me. I chose a blue Hawaiian shirt. I looked ridiculous but rejection leads to self-loathing and this was a shirt to feel bad about yourself in.

I wondered, just for a moment, if I should continue in Hunter's shoes (size nine, alligator) and find some drugs. He took them all on his 1971 trip – coke, mescaline, amyl-nitrates, hot dogs. But I'm a coward. I've never been into Class A narcotics. Mine are more Class R (Côtes du Rhône) and the odd Flaming Zambuka (Class J).

Judging from Dr Thompson, though, we should all be scagging it by the tub full – he seems indestructible, at his age (no one knows) still shooting at lamp-posts and bears. In fact, when he does die, at the age of 146, his body will be so full of drugs that it will lie, preserved, for hundreds of years like nuclear waste. Like some latterday saint he'll be propped up for public view, probably in the main lobby of the MGM Grand, alongside Mike Tyson and Liberace, the Holy Trinity of Vegas.

I stood on a bridge over the Strip, at the intersection of the Excalibur, MGM and New York, New York hotels. A Disneyland castle, a giant golden lion and the Statue of Liberty looked over me, a trio of plastic angels.

As Tom Wolfe once pointed out, when they opened Monte Carlo in 1879 they asked Charles Garnier, the architect of the Paris Opera, to design an opera house for the Place du Casino, and Sarah Bernhardt read a symbolic poem. In 1947, when Bugsy Siegel opened the concrete Flamingo, he hired Abbott and Costello.

Everyone has an idea of the history of Vegas. It's none too long and goes something like this – dustbowl, gold, railroad, Bugsy Siegel, Flamingo, Sinatra, Bugsy loses the big one, the corporations move in, viva 'the entertainment capital of the world', Mike Tyson bites ear, Picasso comes to the brand new Bellagio. This is a place built on names, not ground. Buildings come and go (none of the casino buildings are in their original state since the Sahara was demolished in 1992). It's the names that make Vegas – Siegel, Sinatra, Elvis, Liberace, Tom Jones and now . . . Michael Flatley and his *Lord of the Dance*. As you can judge from that list, Vegas is a man's world, a place of big swinging dicks, and none swung bigger than Frank Sinatra. (Angie had given me his biography – I'd always suspected that deep down she'd wished I was a wop.)

'There are no innocent bystanders in Las Vegas. Nobody comes to Vegas to be innocent,' wrote the author Michael Ventura.

But I felt innocent. I'd loved and lost, and in this age, only the innocent do that.

It had gotten hotter, as they say in Nevada. Triple digits, quad-ruple digits, quintuple digits – and it was only lunchtime. The rest of the day stretched forth in terrifying emptiness, reaching out towards night, then the next day, the day after that, a year, a lifetime.

I suddenly felt dizzy. My knees had been turned into a soda-stream circa 1977. I'm no Frank Sinatra.

I wandered aimlessly into the Excalibur, where a wench in armour was welcoming the Society of Insurance Research. At Lance-a-Lotta Pasta queues of fat people were waiting for lunch. By the looks of them, these were people who took All-You-Can-Eat as a life philosophy. Hunter S. Thompson called the city of Las Vegas 'a gross physical salute to the fantastic possibilities in this country', but this is also true of most of its visitors. I began to see possibilities for a future freak show – 'Come and see the thin people of Vegas.'

Outside New York, New York the escalators had broken. A crowd stood at the bottom not knowing what to do. The lifts had a capacity of 2,500 pounds, but in this town that's two people. I walked up the stairs, but no one followed my example.

New York, New York has its own roller-coaster, the Manhattan Express, part of a trend amongst Vegas hotels to provide as much 'family-based entertainment' as gambling. Roller-coasters, you see, are part of the Big Change in Vegas. Since gambling has become ubiquitous, and there are casinos worldwide, Vegas needs a new image to become more mass market. And what does the mass market want?

Roller-coasters and shopping. Most of the big hotels now also boast shopping malls, in the case of Caesar's Palace Forum Mall one of the busiest in America, attracting 50,000 visitors a day. Most have thrill rides.

I paid my seven dollars and spent a minute and a half zipping up and down above the Strip, long enough to have some remarkably cogent thoughts about the city I was seeing upside down.

Vegas, it struck me, is the seventh wonder of the plastic world. A city whose skyline is made up of other cities' skylines – New York, Rio, Monte Carlo, Bellagio, Paris, San Remo, St Tropez, Luxor and Venice. There were rumours of new hotels, bigger, better, with more roller-coasters, the London with Big Ben and real kebab detritus on the sidewalk, the Titanic with an iceberg as the casino. I had a few ideas of my own – the West Belfast (knee-cappings optional), the Sarajevo (all you-can-eat sniper fire) and the family-favourite, the Chernobyl ('Just follow the glow to your room').

I don't necessarily think these atlas-theme hotels are a bad thing. In a country where 80 per cent of the population doesn't possess a passport, they at least allow Americans to glimpse a vision of a wider world. Who knows, maybe after visiting the Venetian, complete with scaled-down Doges Palace and 'real gondoliers', the odd visitor might be inspired to visit Italy. Or at least Canada.

But there was a sadness pervading the city. Old Vegas, as far as I – a first-time visitor – could tell, is vanishing like quarters into a three-armed bandit. Sinatra is dead. The old high rollers are dying off to be replaced by software barons whose idea of gambling is not using the automatic spellcheck when they write a business letter. Even poor Debbie Reynolds is gone – her eponymous hotel went bankrupt and was bought at auction by the World Wrestling Federation, Hulk Hogan and all.

Some are trying to create a more cultured image for the city; witness the Bellagio – 'With special guests Pablo Picasso and Henri Matisse', owned by Steve Wynn, the biggest magician on the strip, who turns Monet into money at his latest hotel, dripping with authentic art masterpieces that cost an estimated $300 million. But it's difficult to see how Vegas will ever be sophisticated. This is, after all, the place that still loves Engelbert Humperdinck.

The roller-coaster came to a halt, I ceased my musing and wiped the vomit from my shirt.

'Fun ride?' asked the employee who helped me stagger from the car. As with most people in Vegas, she wore a name-tag (as Dr Thompson says, this city is 'what it would have been like if the Nazis had won the war'). Her name was Rachel and she came from Phnom Penh, Cambodia, according to the badge, which I ventured was a long way to come to help people out of a roller-coaster.

'I was born there. But I'm American now.'

Just like that. Instant change. There was hope. Rachel smiled at me, and I was irrigated with the warmth of human kindness. Then she moved on to the next customer.

Outside it was early afternoon and a billion and one degrees. The cars that clogged the Strip tried to keep moving lest they burst into flames as if zapped by alien gunships. You could have fried steel on the bald head of the homeless man shaking a Dunkin' Donuts plastic cup for change. I gave him a quarter and suggested he should purchase some headwear.

'Fuck you.'

Which recarved the Pit in my stomach. A pattern was emerging. I would find myself feeling all right, even, as with Rachel from Phnom Penh, almost cheerful. Then the Pit would reopen, a chill sucking through me, reminding me that something bad had happened.

I tried to remember what it was. An insulting letter from the bank? A bad omelette? Southampton FC's performance every season for the last fifteen years? And then I remembered.

And I had to sit down and eat ice cream milkshakes.

I had a vanilla shake in the MGM Grand, where I shared the food court with a gaggle of conferencees in matching beige Media One shirts. One of them, Bert Madden, was wearing a badge (in addition to a badge that read 'Hi I'm Bert Madden') that read 'I'm a legend in my own mind'. Judging from Bert's inability to eat a burger without decorating his lap with pickles, the legends of his mind would not command sell-out crowds at the Hollywood Bowl.

But I felt a certain sympathy with him. He was trying to make conversation with a slightly pretty female Media One shirt who clearly felt Bert was several strata below her in the periodic table of attractiveness, while malicious pickles plopped intermittently into his lap.

She tried being polite, then ignored him completely, gazing eastwards towards a handsome bemuscled Media One shirt who was holding court to a wallow of overweight managers, no doubt outlining the finer points of his golf swing. Which further depressed me. Is this what human relationships are all about? A food chain of attraction, each one of us getting consumed by someone just one level more desirable than ourselves? Why can't people just like each other? Why can't they judge on inner talents rather than external bumps and curves?

I felt sorry for Bert. After all, the object of his affections wasn't that pretty.

The Pit had become an open-cast mine in my stomach. I sensed the numbing of my cheeks, which is the ringmaster announcing the onset of tears. I stood, wanting to get back to the hotel before I broke down. And then Rod Stewart started to sing over the tannoy.

Rod Stewart was Angie's favourite singer. I hated him, at least to begin with. But strange things happen to us when we creep into love. Things we once disdained, execrated, and abhorred slowly take on a new sheen when basking in the light radiated by our loved one. I still watch *Newsnight* (Sarah). I still eat olives

(Emily). I still cut my toe nails rather than rip them off and eat them (Josey).

I came to love Rod for his ballsy, brassy songs, which seemed to reflect my ballsy, brassy girlfriend Angie. There's probably a mathematical formula for this process that goes something like:

$$emotion + time = loss\ of\ musical\ judgement$$

I hoped they weren't going to play the whole album. But of course they did.

By early evening the temperature outside had fallen to that required to bake meringues. For the first time since arriving in Vegas I felt a chill. It was, I later realised, the beginning of a cold caused by the dramatic difference in climate between the ice of Niagara Falls and the desert air of Las Vegas. But at the time I found it reassuring – a sign that change was imminent, if only in the climatic sphere.

Inside the casinos, of course, nothing changes, except the accumulator on the slots and the size of the casino owners' bank balances. I sat in the main hall of the MGM and watched the crowds around the Win A Million slot pull machine.

Joanne from Michigan was pulling the handle while a small crowd went, 'Oooh, Oooh.' She reminded me of Angie's sister Tina. I wanted to put my arms around her, as if she were some emissary from my loved one.

In my own limited experience it's rare to like your partner's family. But after my own parents and grandmother, Angie's family were the closest older people to me in my life. I'd chatted for hours with her grandfather about his times in a northern Ontario gold mine, I'd made pizza with her sisters, I'd got drunk with her dad (the basis of our relationship, which was fine by both of us) and gone shopping with her mum – just me and Sandra, the two of us – for underwear for Angie (how weird is that?). They'd seen me drunk and vomiting, tired and tearful, ill shaven, as badly dressed as a tramp, and naked. This last revelation came one summer weekend when I attempted to get from a bedroom to the shower in front of an extended family gathering. A towel I'd thought was secure slipped suddenly, revealing all to the shocked multitude. At least, as Angie gleefully pointed out later, they saw nothing there that might have threatened her.

And now, along with her, I'd lost her family, in particular her sister Tina – a larger than life, big Italian lady with a gargantuan laugh and an ability to drink anyone in Niagara Falls under the table, which if you know Niagara Falls you'll realise is no mean accomplishment. And it was Tina who Joanne at the slot machine vaguely resembled.

The slot-machine compere – what a job – how does he explain that to his mum? – watched on as Joanne failed miserably: 'Oh no, another single bar. But you know about single bars, don't you Joanne?'

Joanne blushed, another loser in Crapsville, and I began to wonder if this was enough to sustain Middle America through its long cold frozen winters. The memory of a slot pull, a free beer, an all-you-can-eat shrimp buffet. From the smiling faces, the answer was clear.

I was tempted to go up to the compere, insert his microphone up his ample nose, turn to Joanne from Michigan and say, 'That's from Tina,' but the compere was bigger than me and looked as if he worked out. Tina herself would have done it. She was always more man than I was.

I was now as blue as paint. To prove that eating when you're down is far from a female proclivity, I headed for my fourth all-you-can-eat buffet in twenty-four hours.

The best all-you-can-eat buffet in Vegas (low cost and quantity – the twin pillars of the Vegas faith) is reputedly found at the Rio Suites Hotel.

I got to the Carnival Dining Room thirty minutes before it closed. There was Chinese food, Italian food, Mexican food and soon my plate displayed the culinary equivalent of the Vegas skyline – a bit of everything from around the world, chucked together in one bright, tantalising mix, which looks good until you poke your fork below the surface. I eschewed the unlimited shrimp. There are no circumstances under which that can be good for you.

I ate and ate and ate, and didn't feel any better, listening to Abba beneath multi-coloured carnival streamers. I could literally feel myself getting fatter. To most of those around me it had already happened.

On the wall was a clumsily painted mural, the sort of thing schoolchildren do to brighten up a derelict space that no one will ever see. It was a strange reflection of how America sees itself: there was the Space Shuttle, Marilyn Monroe, George Washington, a cactus and a Ford Truck. I considered inventing a short story involving all five that I would submit to the *Erotic Review*, but I was too engorged to think, all blood in my system having been summoned to cope with the D-Day landing in my stomach.

As Dr Thompson did on drugs, I did with the Rio Buffet. Szechuan pork to take me up, lasagne to take me higher, a nibble on a beef taco to send me spinning, and a salmon mousse to ease me down. Desserts, however, were a hit too far. I'm no addict.

I don't know why I went to the Voodoo Bar. It's located on the fifty-first floor of the Rio and is supposed to be the coolest place in Vegas. Maybe it was my continuing predilection for self-loathing. Certainly, those up on the outside patio 200 feet above Las Vegas who could be bothered to glance my way viewed me with the contempt gorgeous yet vacant people usually reserve for the visually less endowed.

But after a couple of lukewarm margaritas on the lofty patio, I began to enjoy their antipathy. As I stood by the silver rail, finely polished by a generation of surgically enhanced flesh, I surveyed the kingdom of Vegas – a million neon lights buzzing away into the dark embrace of the desert night – and felt for the first time since Niagara Falls that I was in control.

All around me conventioneers were discussing golf swings and the widths of telephone cable. Men with paunches chatted to slim young women with diamonds, large breasts and fingers itching for banknotes. Miller beer and white wine stood side by side, doing the dance of commerce before hasty and expensive/lucrative sex in a company-paid hotel room.

The businessmen spoke to the escort girls, but there was little communication.

'Do you like golf?'

'No. Do you like shopping?'

'No.'

After this they would lapse into silence. Then the two men (this strange waltz seemed to be conducted wholly in pairs – the businessmen, I supposed, for moral support; the women, I'm sure, because it was safer that way) would start chatting about mutual funds or the Cleveland Browns, and the two women would natter on about their everyday lives in Sin City. Which from the way they talked about it sounded even more dull than Southampton.

'Look Cindy, that's the new hotel.'

'Yeah. I'm going there on my birthday.'

'Cool.'

'Yeah. Isn't it?'

'Did you hear about Anne-Marie's new boyfriend? He's a pirate at the buccaneer show.'

'No? Cool.'

'Yeah. Isn't it?'

Las Vegas stretched its hot lights into the darkness, teasing, tempting. Up here the rest of the world did not exist. Up here there was a lot of gilt and not much guilt – just what you need on a conference expense account. The businessmen bought another round, even though the escorts had barely touched their white wine.

I looked at these melon-bosomed young women (believe me, I looked) and wondered if they'd ever been in love, if they'd ever wanted to be with someone for the rest of their lives, till death or silicon leakage did them part. Or if being with a different, overweight man each night left them dulled to passion, like a butcher to steaks or a Ghanaian to sunshine.

I wanted to ask them, but I couldn't afford it.

Suddenly my confidence bungee-jumped once more. Here I was, alone up a tall tower in the middle of the neon-lit American desert. No one knew where I was. No one around me cared who I was. Suddenly I wanted desperately to go home with someone, to have someone put their arms around me and hold me tight against them like spoons in a drawer.

Like she used to.

I went down to the lobby to watch the free midnight Masquerade show. From the ceiling came a woman on a dolphin, a golden gondolier, a ten-foot-high blue peacock, some dancing beekeepers and Venetian carnival figures doing rock and roll. A giant gold woman sang 'I'm In Love'. It was loud, bright and brash, and the only people more bored than the audience were the performers.

Two hours after eating I didn't feel any thinner. I closed my eyes and pictured a lettuce leaf. It was a strangely calming image.

I stayed in Vegas a further five days, which was probably five days too long. Defying meteorologists and physics, it got hotter. I ventured out along the Strip, where fat Midwesterners clung to each other in pools of shade like elephants, and the Mirage employed out-of-work actors to spray the buccaneer show crowds with Evian.

'Friends, Romans, Countrymen, who wants a squirt?'

The free show takes place every ninety minutes, and people queue up an hour beforehand to see the fake battle between the British Navy and Bluebeard's pirates. I wanted to go past screaming 'THE PIRATES WIN!' but I didn't. I'm no rebel.

Further north along the Strip things became tackier. At the Frontier they were offering ninety-nine-cent margaritas to 'Beat the Heat', but I knew that was one I couldn't win. Outside the Riviera old men were having their pictures taken fondling the brass bottoms of the Crazy Girls statue. I walked as far as the Stratosphere Tower, which is the tallest building between the Pacific and the Mississippi. This being New Vegas, it has a roller-coaster on top, a mile above the ground, and the Big Shot ride, a hydraulic lift that hoists you up a further 200 feet and then drops you like an anvil, introducing your bowels to your mouth.

Everywhere I looked there were cranes. Building seemed to have taken over from gambling as the new religion. Vegas is the fastest growing city in America with 6,000 new inhabitants a month – that's eight new people an hour. They change the telephone directories here twice a year, and schools have two sessions a day to cope with the number of children, split between morning kids and afternoon kids. To cope with the current number of pupils wanting places they'd need a new school opened every month for the next two years.

The reason, apart from the sunshine, golf courses and fast easy poker money, is the job market. Each new hotel room is said to create three new jobs and the city is looking to add a further 20,000 rooms in the next two years. If you reckon each job supports on average three people, that's 180,000 new people added through the hotel sector alone. And thanks to low business taxes and the second lowest property tax in America, new factories are also opening – Ocean Spray run a vast new bottling plant on the outskirts. As a waiter told me, 'It takes me four weeks to read the Sunday classified jobs section.'

Oh, and did I mention there's no state income tax?

BOOM.

That's the sound of Vegas growing.

Las Vegas also has the highest suicide rate per capita in the United States.

SPLAT.

That's the sound of Vegas dying.

I had to call home. It had struck me outside the Fashion Show Mall, which, I think, is where Nicolas Cage bought Elizabeth Shue clothes before drinking himself to death in *Leaving Las Vegas*. At the time I had hated the film, the alcoholic writer's selfishness in spurning the woman who loved him. Now I wished I had his courage. A bottle or two of meths and I could have joined the bums in the parking lot outside the Stardust Casino, where the baked concrete was thick with desiccated advertisements for 'Adult Services' torn from free magazines handed out by jobless Mexican fruit-pickers at the north end of town. I'd stay there all night sinking bottle after bottle until my liver told the rest of me to check in to the great casino in the sky.

Everyone in England thought I was still in Canada. Maybe they thought I was engaged by now. My parents had probably bought new shoes for the wedding.

I didn't want to call. I knew I wouldn't be able to do it coolly, dispassionately, which was how I'd have to be if my mum wasn't to freak out and send my dad on a plane to Vegas to come and get me home.

I had a brace of ninety-nine-cent margaritas to prepare myself then dialled the number that was once as familiar to me as my name. It rang.

And rang.

I left a message.

'Hi Mum, Dad, it's Jim, I'm fine. Angie's fine too, she's got a lot on at work at the moment, so I haven't felt it was right to ask her yet. But we're thinking of going away for a weekend before the end of the month. So I'll keep you posted.' There must be something about Vegas that inspires high-quality deception.

Strangely, I felt a huge sense of relief. I'd obviously been dreading telling my parents (and with them the rest of the Commonwealth, such is the length and breadth of the Keeble family grapevine). And with this came a small hiccup of hope. What if Angie really was so busy at work she'd been unable to digest the true joy of my proposal? What if right now she was mulling things over on a slow day at Sunnyside Photographic?

I should call her.

Tomorrow.

Or maybe the next day.

It was about this time I started my diary. I'd never written one before, but it was cheaper therapy than Jungian analysis (there are fifty-one psychologists in the Vegas Yellow Pages). I would put down my feelings in a bid to exorcise the more negative emotions (an idea Angie had suggested a long time ago, which I'd rejected with derision).

The diary cost $1.99 at the Dollar Store (I never figured that one out either), and each day there was a single page on which to define existence.

I was suddenly excited. In this way I could continue the great tradition of American travel literature – including two of my great literary heroes, Steinbeck with *Travels with Charley*, and Jack Kerouac with *On the Road*.

I began to write with zeal. For example:

April 17th

10.30 a.m. got up. Had $2.99 breakfast at Cyclone Coffee Shop. Went for walk on the Strip. 1.30 p.m. lunch at Cyclone Coffee Shop. Watched TV in room. Felt sad. 7.30 p.m. dinner at Cyclone Coffee Shop. Read book. 12.15 a.m. lights out.

April 18th, 104 degrees Fahrenheit

Felt hot. Drank much . . .

Rather than dissuade casino activity, the heat seemed to increase the numbers in the gaming warehouses, where the air-conditioning hums like Nordic wind gods and the drinks are still cold. I ducked in and out of the jangling palaces as a crash victim dips in and out of consciousness.

After a while, the bizarre became normal. The surprise comes when you walk into a place and there are no bells ringing, no pensioners hammering coins into slot machines like pills into a mouth, when you see someone and they're not sporting a dolphin tattoo.

As you drive around you get the feeling there are some really smart people behind Vegas. It takes smart people to make crap. Just look at Hollywood – the cream of the Ivy League employed to make *Home Alone V*. In Vegas you're being manipulated every step of the way, but the trick is to make you enjoy it. It's like some sex club where you crave domination. Every step you're coddled and caressed, fondled and kneaded into submission.

'Take my money. Take my pride. Take me! Take me!'

In every casino there were an impressive number of men and women in wheelchairs. One of these was Hal, a wizened octogenarian from Destin, Florida, who had a drinks-holder built into his chariot so he could sip Seven-Up through a straw without taking his hands from the Hit Me buttons. He came to Vegas for two weeks every year and played the slots for fifteen hours a day. He was wearing sunglasses at 11 a.m.

'The key, son,' he explained to me while change spewed into his bucket, 'is to immerse yourself in the excitement and to gamble within your limits. Use that money to have fun. If there's any place in the world to have fun, it's Vegas.'

I took Hal's advice. I finally went to see a Vegas show, which is by far the easiest way to destroy any longing to see a Vegas show. At Legends in Concert in the Imperial Palace Hotel, I was the youngest person by at least ten years.

A sign forbade us taking any photographs of the performers or each other. Instead Mandi would come over in her Bunny Girl tights and take our picture for ten dollars. I found this shocking considering the pensioners had each paid thirty dollars to see singers pretending to be other singers. What's next? A sign saying 'No Clothes' so you have to come in naked and then rent them for the show?

At least Mandi was cute. But she didn't dare return my stare – I couldn't blame her, after all, what sick bastard would be at a show like this at the age of thirty?

The Elvis impersonator sang 'Heartbreak Hotel', and the old women threw their water tablets at him. It was a crappy show, but the old dears loved it.

And who am I to judge? In 1954 an unknown performer did little to impress at a dinner show spectacular at the Last Frontier casino. His name?

Ronald Reagan.

From the Imperial Palace I headed to the MGM and David Cassidy in *EFX*, in which the fifty-year-old plays a young buck who goes on an all-singing, all-exploding journey through time in search of his lost love, Lara.

'Take me to a world where fantasy turns to reality,' sang David and, this being Vegas, they did. After some swordplay and consorting with aliens, David won back his Lara.

'What about my Angie?' I shouted at him. 'When do I get her back?' But David was too busy blowing kisses to the audience to answer. I got the distinct feeling he didn't really care.

I kept spending at prodigious levels – buffets morning, noon, and night, new clothes (nastier and nastier shirts) and taxis everywhere (any destination in Vegas is $6.40 as far as I could see, so take the scenic route).

This was how I met Bernie Summers, a displaced cabbie from Brooklyn. For three days he escorted me from casino to show to buffet to casino. He was none too impressed with his adopted town, apart from how much money there was to be made there.

'You know, Jim, there's two r's in over-rated. This town's like doing two shots of acid, then going to the circus with Mom and Dad. Top shows? Give me a break, these are autopsy acts. We keep them off welfare. Did you know thirty per cent of cab-drivers here are degenerate gamblers?'

Bernie's most extensive ire was reserved for two men he called Bumfiend and Boy, otherwise known as the venerable German illusionists Siegfried and Roy, who do a glorified magic show in which things disappear, then reappear, then get sawn in half. It's a souped-up children's party act, but it costs $30 million to stage in a specially built $25 million theatre and at ninety dollars is the most expensive ticket in town. In Vegas such numbers grant instant respect.

In my pursuit of 'fun' I bought a ticket (returns only, the show is sold out every night) and submitted to Bernie's derision. 'You will pay dearly for this in a future life.'

To be fair, both Bumfiend and Boy showed admirable energy for old fellas (they could well be in their fifties, although only their plastic surgeons can tell), producing a glittering show that was higher camp than Edmund Hillary got to on Everest.

I sat at a table with a lawyer and his wife from Connecticut, well dressed and well spoken. To my left was a Mafia hitman called Tony from New Jersey. Tony didn't actually admit to his profession, pretending he was in construction, but I could tell. His right-hand forefinger kept flexing involuntarily any time anyone passed the table. His wife was called Sonia and seemed most impressed that I was English. I wanted to tell her I couldn't really claim the credit for that, but I didn't want to upset Tony.

Bumfiend and Boy appeared, along with their German accents. Their costumes were quite Wagnerian, a sort of post-Nazi chic, all shoulder pads and silver foil. When Boy came up to Sonia and sang to her, Tony tensed noticeably. Afterwards he laughed and confided in me, 'I was going to take a bottle and smash it over his head.'

The highlight of the show, after a helicopter appears and an elephant parades around for a while, is the appearance of Bumfiend and Boy's famous white tigers, truly magnificent animals, transplanted into a smoke-filled, neon-lit Las Vegas auditorium.

'They're already extinct in the wild,' said Bumfiend with obvious delight.

Don't get me wrong. This is a noble thing, the saving of rare felines that have been rescued from the wilds of Africa and given a dark blue Rolls-Royce to drive round in (something the Worldwide Fund For Nature should perhaps consider), but when the Michael Jackson song – specially written for his two good friends – started, and Boy began to show a predilection for straddling tigers, I'd had enough.

The Michael Jackson song went, 'Siegfried, uh, Roy. Siegfried, uh, Roy.'

Boy disappeared in a puff of smoke, the audience gasping with astonishment, and Bumfiend started an ardent and messianic chant.

'Bring Him Back Hallelujah!'

As the audience chanted, 'Bring Him Back Hallelujah!' and their evangelical fervour escalated, Boy reappeared to leave us with a message that reminded me of the homily at the end of *The Jerry Springer Show*, only less sincere: 'Look for the magic in nature and let it enlighten your life.'

Tony's trigger finger was twitching like a sardine on a hook, but Sonia was loving it, tears flowing. I expected the German magicians were safe, at least for tonight.

Walking out into the hairdryer night of Vegas I felt the city reach a parched hand inside me and wrench at my soul. I sat for a while on a bench next to a man who stank of beer and cheap Mexican food. He was sipping relentlessly from a brown paper bag. I felt jealous.

His name, he slurred in greeting, was Dave McClelland and he originally came from Chicago.

'Lost a thousand dollars in my first hour in town,' he said almost proudly. He went on to explain that he'd had a $60,000 a year job in sales in Illinois, but his mother died and she had a place down here. 'I moved down thinking I'd sell in Vegas. But you've gotta be tough to sell more than you buy in this town. I mean real tough.'

He asked for money. I had no change. He fell silent. Then after a couple more swigs he continued, 'Most of the people in this town are pretty rude. It's the greed. When I first came here, my sister said, "Dave you're not going to have real friends, just acquaintances." She's right.'

'I'm sorry.'

Down the street, convenience stores proclaimed, 'We cash payroll cheques' and 'Cash for gold and silver.'

'Come on buddy, just a couple of bucks.'

I gave him five dollars and headed to a casino.

Bernie drove me downtown, where the older casinos exist thanks to the renovation of Fremont Street and a nightly light show along a glorified pedestrian precinct that draws large crowds from the glitzier Strip hotels.

'You know the best way to enjoy Vegas?' Bernie confided. 'Win money. Win lots of money.'

He recommended Binion's Horseshoe, one of the oldest and most traditional casinos, if by tradition you mean smoky tables, an ugly clientele and cheap drinks.

'Where millions are played and legends are made,' said the sign. I entered the cathedral, ready to take Holy Sacrament.

Binion's Horseshoe is a legend and rightly so. Its founder, Benny Binion, was as wild as they came. He arrived in Las Vegas in 1951 from Texas – having been chased out by the cops for bootlegging and numbers racketeering – bringing his wife Teddy Jean and two suitcases each containing $1 million. Realising Vegas's potential, Benny bought the old El Dorado Club on Fremont Street and renamed it the Horseshoe Club.

Benny is as much a demi-god of Vegas as Sinatra or Bugsy Siegel. As one writer put it, 'Benny often found it necessary to arbitrate business differences with a .45 automatic.'

Benny boasted he'd take any bet. This was tested, so the myth flows, when an unknown Englishman (I see Richard Harris, in straggly locks) wanted to place a $750,000 roulette bet. Benny agreed and brought out two bags that matched the Englishman's bags of money. The Englishman won, and Benny gave him the cash, bags and all. Sceptics doubted that 'The Bet', as it became known, was real, claiming it was a publicity stunt, but eventually 'the Englishman' was tracked down by a *Las Vegas Review-Journal* reporter. He was, so the myth rolls, the head of an investment firm he'd founded with $1.5 million dollars.

But times have changed. Benny died on Christmas Day 1989. His son Ted took over, in more ways than one – he was an avid heroin-user and liked to hang out with Chicago mobsters. Ted continued the legend, being kind enough to die mysteriously in September 1998. The autopsy showed a large amount of heroin in his stomach, but you don't eat heroin. He was also three feet from his favourite TV, even though he was long-sighted and usually sat ten feet away. The video surveillance in his house was dismantled, and someone had called the maid and told her to stay at home that day. Ted's girlfriend, Sandra Murphy, 'found' the body, but called a real-estate agent three hours before she called the police, sounding distressed then abruptly ending the call. And three men were found, ten hours later, digging up $4 million in silver out in the Nevada desert.

I felt sorry for Ted Binion. They played The Doors' song 'The End' at his funeral, and it struck me that maybe he'd been waiting all his life for his own death. Unable to live up to the huger-than-life image of his gun-toting father in more regulated and conservative times, he could do little except die in strange circumstances. I hoped he'd found Jim Morrison in the afterlife and they were sitting playing pinochle.

In Benny and Ted's casino you can still get your picture taken in front of $1 million in cash (100 $10,000 bills). It's free, so a lot of people do it. For some reason, nobody under twenty-one is allowed in the photo, although they are allowed to die for their country, have anal sex and in certain states marry their sibling. Evidently one of the last taboos left in America is posing in front of banknotes.

I joined the line of punters waiting to get their pictures taken. People were combing their hair, as if going for a job interview. The man in front of me was a local. 'I have my picture taken here periodically over the years. It's sort of a tradition.'

I had visions of his bedroom, a series of pictures taken in front of $1 million, from twenty-one to his present mid-forties, the money the only constant, which in many ways I suppose it is.

Binion's customers are as traditional as its decor. An old man in dark glasses wearing a single golf glove was pulling slots. A woman in a wedding dress was throwing dice and whelping loudly, her husband nowhere to be seen. Perhaps she'd dumped him at the altar and rushed here to spend her honeymoon cash. In my present mood I would have considered offering myself as a prospective life partner (she did, after all, have the dress) had she been any more attractive and less prone to sweating.

I decided there was only one game for a real man – blackjack. I swaggered over to the two-dollar table where I joined Karen and Betsy from Illinois and Doug from Wisconsin. Judging from their name tags, Karen and Betsy were attending a waste disposal conference, and they were a little drunk. Doug was older and taking great pleasure in trying to put his hand on Karen's knee. I played long enough to get a free beer. It was three in the morning. Betsy wanted to go home, perhaps mindful of the pleniary session on toxic urine the next morning.

'Just one more,' said Karen, 'just one more . . .'

I caught the bus back with pensioners from Boston.

'We've been trying to find this bus all night,' they chimed. In the corner two crack addicts stared blindly past us, spit running down their chins. 'We just couldn't find it. Everyone kept telling us "just over there, just over there."'

As I walked back to the Luxor, past 6 a.m. men still howling at craps tables, I thought that summed up Vegas. Everything's 'just over there'.

My lowest point in Vegas – and there were many – came at the wedding. I know, I shouldn't have gone. But I was invited. I bumped into Darryl and Sarah at the Luxor coffee bar. They came from Nottingham in England and were in Vegas to get hitched at a wedding chapel, with just Sarah's mum and dad to fill the pews.

'We were sort of hoping some mates would come out, but they couldn't afford it. Would you like to come?'

Most mental-health professionals will tell you that going to a wedding two weeks after being rejected in a proposal of marriage by the love of your life is probably not the best thing for you, but I felt happy to have been asked. I possessed an entirely manufactured sense of belonging. Darryl and Sarah wanted me there. Of course I'd go.

Vegas has fifty-four wedding chapels. Most of them are found towards the north end of the Strip, alongside the psychic readers, adult movie boutiques and Korean souvenir stores. What Athens is to ruins so Vegas is to weddings. Elvis married Priscilla here. You can't top that. Darryl and Sarah had chosen the Little White Chapel, the most famous of the city's hitch-shops, which has hosted Joan Collins, Judy Garland, Mickey Rooney (twice), Bruce Willis and Demi Moore, Michael Jordan and, most importantly, Jack and Vera Duckworth for a *Coronation Street* special.

Nevada has no waiting period to get married, no blood test to check who you are. There's no need for a divorce certificate if you've already been married. 'You just need to remember when and where.'

Darryl was smoking heavily outside. We went into the chapel. They were vacuuming petals from the last wedding as we entered. The chapel owner herself had agreed to marry them, an honour not unlike the Pope agreeing to hear your confession. Charolette Richards was a munchkin of a woman, her dyed blonde hair pulled tightly back as if stopping something from escaping. She was wearing a jacket as pink as her cheeks.

The main chapel was as big as my gran's front room. The carpet was purple, and there were glass chandeliers and white wooden pews. No Food, No Smoking, No Drinking Allowed, said the signs. The message was clear. This was a place with standards.

At 4.40 p.m. the bride appeared in a cream dress. Her mum was crying. 'Here Comes the Bride' played from somewhere behind Charolette's left ear. Darryl started to giggle.

'You have come from a land far away to be joined in love,' began Charolette. She was doing the video recording as well as reading the vows, and intermittently checked the camera on its tripod to verify the tape hadn't run out. 'Do you remember when you first fell in love and hoped you'd get married? Well here you are in Las Vegas, Nevada.'

I remembered.

'I love you for 100,000 reasons but mostly I love you because of you,' read Charolette.

Darryl and Sarah nodded solemnly.

Charolette pulled out a candle from nowhere and lit it with a red plastic lighter.

'When you see a candle let it be a reminder of the glow in your hearts. To remind you you will never be cold again because you have the warmth of each other.'

Angie curled up in bed, two pairs of socks, my arms around her.

'You are my best friend, you are my everything and I love you.'

Sarah was crying now, as was her mum. Darryl remained strong – he was a man from Nottingham after all – but I knew my eyes were damp.

'You may kiss the bride.' Which he did.

Actually it'd been an emotional wedding. I know Vegas was tacky and it was too easy to get married here, and the Little White Chapel was a bit like a Kwik-Fit car exhaust change centre, but the wedding ceremony itself was moving and tender, and Charolette seemed as if she meant every word she said. I've been to much worse weddings in fancy churches in England.

As the happy couple were having pictures taken outside, I had a coffee with Charolette. She seemed to consider silence an affront to personal liberty.

'I came here in '61 with three kids, looking for my husband. He wasn't here. It was like a little sleepy village, with tumbleweeds blowing down the street and sand everywhere. You wouldn't see anyone outside. There were no sidewalks. But God was with me. A guy came up to me said, "Are you okay?" He gave me a job in the wedding chapel, back when there were just five chapels. He was like a father to my kids. When he died eighteen years ago I inherited the chapel.'

She's hitched the rich and famous, including Frank Sinatra and Mia Farrow in 1966, when Frank was fifty and Mia was twenty (Dean Martin was quoted as quipping, 'I've got Scotch older than Mia Farrow,' but maybe he was just jealous).

'Mia Farrow was very young, very cute,' said Charolette. 'I kept thinking, "She's so young, how come she's got this great big ring?" I was arranging the gladioli. I was still a young woman back then. Sinatra came up behind me, gave me the shock of my life. He winked at me and said, "Let them fall as they will." I'll always remember that. "Let them fall as they will".'

Frank divorced Mia two years later.

Now Charolette is the Bill Gates of weddings. She was the first to introduce the drive-thru wedding. She has a website, and Internet bookings, sixteen limos, three chapels and a ranch. Eighty-six staff. On Valentine's Day they have seven ministers going round the clock. 'All our ministers are ordained. They give beautiful ceremony.' The Little White Chapel hosts 25,000 weddings a year, but Charolette is discriminating. 'Couples cannot be intoxicated and cannot be the same sex.'

Given the average wedding costs $50 this nets at least $1,250,000 a year. Then there are the added frills. Charolette rents wedding gowns ($200) and tuxedos ($90) out the back. They do up to a size 22 wedding dress. She can organise a wedding anywhere in Nevada. 'I took some English people to Red Rock Canyon the other week – it was so pretty, sunset and everything. I asked, "What are three beautiful words you want to say to your husband?" She answered, "I want money!" I thought, yeah, that's right, girl! I like people from England. They know what they want.'

Charolette's seen a few changes in her time. 'Back then people were more proper. Now they tattoo their wedding rings on. Now they get married in the car wearing blue jeans with a finger in the baby's mouth saying I do. This one couple . . . I heard a scream and I rushed in, she was on the floor. He'd smacked her. She screamed, "I don't ever want to see him again." The next day they came back and got married.'

I had half a mind to tell her about my woes. She looked like some kind of pink fairy godmother, and she'd seen enough heartjoy and heartache to have some insight into the mind of the female. But she had no time. Another family came in, like shoppers to Safeway. The bride-to-be proclaimed she'd just been sick. She wiped herself down and hurried into the chapel. I left with a White Chapel mug and T-shirt.

'Let them fall as they will,' Charolette shouted after me.

I stayed in the Luxor, trying to find a breath of contentment. Sometimes I wondered if the pain wasn't some parasite, a bacteria that had lain dormant seeking weakness, then when it found a fissure attacking, eating away at the heart and lungs, coursing through the blood to each and every limb. Because it was a physical pain. I could feel it like a disease.

I felt a loneliness I had not felt since childhood, those times alone in the dark contemplating a new school, a new house, the death of parents or pet gerbil.

I called Angie.

It was like a dream. I saw myself standing at the payphone at the Stardust.

The phone rang. And rang. Then she picked up the receiver.

'Hello?'

'It's me.'

A long pause.

'I can't talk to you Jim.'

'Please, I have things I have to say . . .'

'I just can't. Please don't call me.'

'I still love you. I'm sorry about everything. I was wrong. I can make it right. I've changed, I'm still changing. You've taught me so much, you can help me. I want to be with you more than anything, you're the most important thing in my life, I know that now. I love you Angie. I love you more than I love myself.'

Silence. I couldn't even hear her breathing.

45

'Jim, I'm sorry, I can't do this anymore. I've got to go.'

'No . . . please . . .'

The receiver laid down, a lid on a coffin. Dial tone. The sound of emptiness, like the single tone buzz of the ECG machine after death.

It was early evening. The time the tourists head out from their dens, washed, perfumed, pink raw flesh ripe for devouring by the many-toothed carnivores that live in this city.

I wanted to be sick, but I'd eaten nothing all afternoon. I went into the Stardust, past the Big Win slots, the carefree card tables judged by careful dealers, and bought a ticket to see Aki. I needed her. Aki would save me.

I'd seen Aki the day I arrived in Vegas. She's difficult to miss. High above the Strip she has her own billboard: 'AKI – A SHOWGIRL FOR THE 21st CENTURY'. There she lies, resplendent in silver body armour, red lips pouting forth a message of possibility and hope. This is the soft end of the adult circus of Las Vegas. Because where there's money there's sex. Aki is the most famous princess in the flesh palace – the Vegas billboard is the ultimate sign of success in the royal circle.

Aki is foreign, which in America means she's exotic even before she does the splits. She's also considered somewhat of an intellectual in Vegas terms. 'She speaks five languages,' someone told me in hushed tones.

Her show is called *Enter the Night*. I made the mistake of attending the earlier 7.30 p.m. showing, not reading the small print that said there is no toplessness until 10.30 p.m.

Expecting a crowd of large burly men with moustaches, I was met instead by a pile of blue-rinse pensioners and the Japanese. At my table a couple were celebrating their wedding anniversary with their nine-year-old daughter, who was drinking a strawberry daiquiri with her eyes open wide as fourteen semi-naked dancers gyrated in front of her. I felt uncomfortable, but her parents seemed to think it was perfectly normal for their prepubescent daughter to be ogling such suggestive loins.

David Lynch would have loved this. The Japanese men looked blissful. A bored singer appeared from amidst the writhing bodies. 'I've been looking at you forever, but I never saw you before,' she sang.

The anniversary couple held hands, the nine-year-old stared at the half-naked men. Then, the moment I and the Japanese men had been waiting for: Aki appeared, resplendent in thigh-length red boots and a sequined bikini. She strutted up and down, wiggled her bottom and pouted. She was the best pouter I'd ever seen. I started counting my cash to see if I could afford the later show.

Enter the Night lasted an hour and a half. Aki changed her costume three times, but the pout never changed. Looking carefully, I saw she was not that beautiful close up, but she managed to avoid being close up for most of the show. Then some strange Argentinean gauchos appeared with spinning *boleadoras*, and the spell was broken.

'I'm going to spin my balls at ninety miles an hour,' said the lead gaucho. 'Only the President is faster.' Which actually got a laugh.

After the show I loitered around. I knew I wanted to talk to Aki, the 21st-Century Showgirl. In my confused unbalanced mind I sensed she would have some message for me, some wisdom to impart. She spoke five languages after all.

I showed an out-of-date press card to an ageing usher, who ushered me to a back office.

'I'm from the *Times Gazette Telegraph News* in London,' I said. 'We'd like to do a quick interview with Aki.'

To my surprise I was ushered deeper into the theatre complex, backstage to a small dressing room. There, dabbing her face in the mirror, was a thin blonde woman who looked just the wrong side of thirty-two. She smiled. She was evidently used to strange men turning up at her door.

'Come in.'

Out of make-up and the thigh-length red boots, Aki seemed more than normal, the sort of woman who works as a tourist information official in Rotterdam. She's Dutch and worked at Crazy Horse in Paris, then married an American who lived in Vegas. They're now divorced.

'Yeah. I had a real marriage, with all the therapy when it went wrong.'

She was down to earth, and reminded me of European girls I met at university – delighted to use their English, and slightly too earnest.

'Hey, it's my personality out there, not me. It's fake. Call us showgirls, whatever. Whatever we call ourselves, we're disrespected. A lot of showgirls are extremely interesting, I'm a law student. When I've finished jumping around, I'm hanging up the g-string, going back to Amsterdam and practising law.'

Her eyes or contact lenses were blue. She looked at me. I looked at my lap.

'We're not female entertainers. We're performing artists. It's done with taste. Any honest person knows the distinction between being naked to arouse and being naked to make women proud to be women. It's about the beauty of women.'

I decided that close up she was not beautiful. Pretty, but not beautiful.

'This showgirl image, drugs, sex, rock and roll. I have no time to do drugs. I have to pass my exams. I go to the gym every day, I work out with my boyfriend.'

She sighed, gently, for effect. I was affected.

'It's difficult now. You have to be special. Unless you can fold your legs around your ears and tie them . . .'

I asked her if she liked America.

'It's hypocritical here. I wish they could drop it. They talk about how shocking Clinton was, but he's a product of them. Half of American men are cheating on their wives. There's this facade, but underneath it, this country is much more wild.'

Her hand touched my knee briefly.

'You understand. You're European.'

I liked her, I decided, but I knew she was manipulating me.

I waited for the word, for the wisdom, for the hope. It came at the end of our fifteen-minute talk.

'I never thought my life would be like this,' said Aki. 'But sometimes things work out for the best.'

She walked me across the stage, a graceful walk, and shook my hand. Her hand was small and limp. Then she disappeared back into the shadows once more.

In my hotel room I flicked through one of the grimy free 'adult services' magazines handed out by the grimy homeless Mexicans. I needed human warmth. I was tempted. And there was no talking camel. In the Vegas Yellow Pages there are thirty-five pages under 'Entertainers – Adult' (I counted them). Among the services on offer are Asian Party Dolls. Full-Service Blondes. College Hardbodies. She'll Touch Your Life – Jeni. Mature Women, 30, 40, 50 Plus.

It's one of the more bizarre features of the human condition, the relationship between sex and love. As comedian Billy Connolly once said, it's a union doomed to failure. Women, so he suggested, need to feel loved before they want to have sex. Men need to have sex in order to feel they love someone. It's a miracle of life that the two ever meet.

I stepped out for the last time into the Vegas night. Night is Vegas's domain. The neon buzzes and burns. At night you can see the city from the Space Shuttle.

I took a bus to Fremont Street in the company of one complete (and very large) nutter, some tourists and sixteen schoolkids singing, 'Barney is a Dinosaur.' I knew where I was going, but I still hadn't admitted it to myself.

Vegas offers numerous temptations for the lonely single male. Of these the least scary (I'm no Gonzo journalist) are the lap-dancing establishments around Fremont Street, dives where you can sip beer while women take off their bikinis and writhe around poles. Such venues, I'm reliably informed, are found in most cities in the world, it's just in Vegas that they seem normal.

A Vegas by-law dictates that within city limits you can get total nudity or alcohol, but not both. I went for the beer. I walked into Glitter Gulch and sat down on a stool in front of the 'catwalk'. I got a beer for $15.50. Two women were on stage, their shins at my nose level. One was topless, the other imminently so. They were young, ish, and pretty, ish. When they bumped and ground to Bruce Springsteen, their breasts didn't move.

Two other women came up to me and started a conversation. The idea, I assumed from other johns around me, was that I paid them to take me to a booth where one or other or both took off their tops and danced in front of me for cash. A hand warm on my thigh.

I declined. They walked on immediately, no farewells, no disconnecting, just moved on as swiftly as a shopper moving down the supermarket aisle. It was at this moment that I wondered who was using who.

The bar had begun to feel industrial. This was a production line, a feeling enhanced by the blue-collar appearance of my fellow breast-oglers. Almost every man seated disconsolately at the rail sported a moustache, a baseball cap and outerware advertising some manufacturing company. Whether this was a disguise or not I couldn't fathom, but boasting neither I began to feel out of place and out of sorts.

'You want it don't argue let's go,' said Sasha, the latest woman to try and persuade me into one of the booths. I blushed like a teenager.

'Thanks, but I think I'm going soon.'

She moved on, instantly.

In front of my mouth a short woman was cupping her breasts together as if trying to get them to produce ice cream. Moustaches were stuffing dollar bills into her pants. Rod Stewart started to sing.

Glitter Gulch – I should have known from the name that it wasn't going to be pretty. The girls weren't ugly, just the atmosphere, which wasn't violent, just wholeheartedly unattractive.

I left the moustaches shifting grimy dollar bills into the girls' knickers. It proved to be an abiding image of Vegas.

As I sat in my pyramid room, high above the city, a train whistled long into the night, taking the spirit of Las Vegas to the four corners of the world. I recalled the words of Wendy, waitress at the Cyclone Coffee Shop. 'You need to be very strong to live here. It's not a friendly town to raise a family. A lot of gangs are coming in from LA. There's metal detectors in schools now, seven-, eight-year-olds bringing in guns. It's too fast, the life here, I don't want that for my kids. It takes away from your childhood. Las Vegas is an evil place.' She was moving to Ohio.

On TV the local *Eyewitness News* was covering a shooting at a grocery store on Sahara Avenue in which four people had been blasted to death with a shotgun. The national news channels weren't even covering it. It was just another multiple homicide.

Bernie took me to the airport the next day. The sun was already hot, although it was only 8.30 a.m. In the casinos the slot machines kept jangling, the old folks hammering coins into the ravenous mouths.

I told Bernie about Angie. He listened. Cab-drivers are used to listening.

'So, where are you going?' he asked finally.

'Los Angeles.'

'Why are you going there?'

'It's cheap.' Forty dollars one-way. 'And I always wanted to see Hollywood.'

'Listen Jim, promise me one thing.'

'What?'

'Try and get laid. It'll be good for you. LA girls are easier than your two-times table.' And with that he was gone, the cab easing away from McCurren International Airport back into the land of $1 million slots and $1.99 all-you-can-eat buffets.

As I waited for my plane, I read the *Las Vegas Review-Journal*. A report informed me that nuclear testing has been taking place near Las Vegas since the 1950s. There was a picture of Benny Binion and his gambling crowd atop Mount Charleston watching a mushroom cloud through dark glasses. Today, continued the report, at Yucca Mountain, 100 miles from the Strip, they're digging a tunnel 1,500 feet underground to bury all radioactive waste from the US Weapons program. It takes 250,000 years for uranium to decompose.

Something tells me Vegas will still be around.

3

Mary – A Californian Girl

I made the mistake of taking the bus. It crossed Los Angeles from Union Station to Beverly Hills, passing close to the hotel I'd booked at the airport using a machine that was so advanced it probably earned more than I ever would and read Baudelaire in its spare time. The thing about buses in LA is that only poor people, deranged mental patients and escaped convicts use them. Since, unlike the tall white-haired man at the front of the bus I wasn't shouting, 'Fuck Madonna's Dog,' at the top of my voice, everyone assumed I was on the run from jail and left me alone.

My first impressions of Los Angeles were that it is very poorly named. There are not and never have been any angels here. Instead there are a lot of very poor people of Latin descent, some mean-looking policemen, and lots of cars. I was unnerved by so many cars. If some alien life form came to LA – and plenty of its inhabitants are ready to swear that this has already happened – they would be forced to conclude that it is a city designed, built and lived in by cars. Humans are merely there to facilitate the automobile in its daily tasks.

'Fuck Cher's fish,' shouted the man at the front. I got out on Wilshire Boulevard, humping my bags a mile down Beverly Drive to the Holiday Inn.

The first thing I had to do was to rent a car, which is easy in a town run by cars. The local branch of Rent-A-Wreck found me a Japanese number that didn't quite live up to the diffident company name and was endearingly cheap.

'Any advice for LA driving?' I asked the small Mexican at the counter.

'Don't,' he grinned, showing an admirable lack of front teeth.

Yet LA's huge traffic problem is a good example of that great American pastime – hype. Compared to London or even my home town, Cambridge, driving around Los Angeles is a piece of toast. Freeways, boulevards, avenues, all are designed to get you THERE without having to look at a map. And even if you do get lost you go right, right, right and you're back where you started. In London you'd be in Hainault.

Yet such geo-auto ease helps to rank Angelinos among the most boring people on earth. Because of the myriad options available to them to get from health club to office to health club, the main topic of conversation seems to be 'the best commuter route ever'. A typical exchange at a dinner party goes something like this:

'No, no, no, you take La Cienaga to Clifton, right on Elm, left on Dayton . . .'

'Sure if you want to take an extra six minutes. Otherwise take Cadillac north, which becomes Hillsboro by the Seven-Eleven, then Beverly Drive to Brighton . . .'

'Are you crazy? At that time of day? You've gotta take Motor Avenue through Hillcrest to Avenue of the Stars, right on Santa Monica, then Rodeo, left on Wilshire and if there's no cop there, back on to Rexford to Foothill.'

In London you just say, 'Take the North Circular.' Because that's your only choice.

For the first couple of hours I drove down Wilshire Boulevard and up Sunset Strip. The purple Nissan was by the far the least impressive car on the road, but I didn't care. At least I wasn't on the bus with Mad Marvin.

Wherever you drive in LA you feel cool, because the whole city looks like a movie set, mainly because it is a movie set. Reality, you quickly realise, is not one of LA's specialities. On an average day there are between thirty and forty films shooting across the city, and everywhere is eerily recognisable. From *Sunset Boulevard* to *LA Confidential*, these streets, palm trees, even the rubbish bins are familiar, because in some ways we've all grown up with this city through the movies. Which, at least for me, made driving in LA such a pleasure.

My spirits lifted. LA, I thought, was going to be good for me. A place that specialises in reinvention, in superficiality, was exactly what I needed – to reinvent myself in a superficial way. To get out, have fun and forget. And drive up and down a lot.

I zipped along Wilshire Boulevard by MacArthur Park in the shade of countless palm trees, as tall and willowy as the numerous young women I passed.

None of the beautiful women returned my stare, which obviously must have had much to do with the purple Nissan and nothing to do with my pale and disturbed appearance, but like a rodent-catcher staring at a field of molehills, I was simply glad to know they were out there. After Vegas the pretty bits of LA are really pretty.

As dusk eased itself on to the city like a silk shirt, I realised I felt exhilaration. Here I was in the home of the movies and I was going to meet a film producer for dinner. Sebastian Moss was a friend of a friend whom I'd met once in London. In that ebullient American way he'd handed me a business card and said, in all apparent sincerity, 'Call me if you're ever in LA.' I'd written the number down, in case Angie and I ever visited, and I needed to impress her. Now, more than ever, I needed to impress myself.

Sebastian had sounded surprisingly pleased to hear from me when I called from Vegas. 'Of course I remember. Let's do dinner. I'll meet you at the Mondrian. Be sure to mention my name at the door.'

The Mondrian Hotel is a Hollywood power-hole where the beasts come to water. Redesigned in 1995 by Philippe Starck, it is as near to stepping into the afterlife as it gets without stepping into the afterlife. Everything is white. All the staff are unfeasibly beautiful, dressed in immaculate white suits. For a moment I believed in angels in Los Angeles.

I barely made it through the Pearly Gates. Archangel Gabriel looked down at my black Top Shop trousers, my hastily buffed Hush Puppies and my jacket, which I admit was fraying a little at one elbow.

'Sorry sir, it's a private party tonight.'

'But I'm to meet someone. Sebastian Moss.'

'I see. You have an appointment with Mr Moss?'

'We're having a drink, yes.'

'Just a moment.'

With a flutter of wings, Gabriel disappeared inside, then returned with Saint Peter.

'Follow me, sir.'

Since many of the movers and shakers in Hollywood are descended from people who suffered greatly under the Nazis it seems a little strange that Los Angeles is such a Nietzschean city in which the wealthy and beautiful rule over those of us in Hush Puppies.

'*Kommen Sie hier.*'

Saint Peter marched me past High Command into the garden bar. Here, in a ridiculously plush setting of marble and tropical plants, was a bustle of beautiful young things lounging on mattresses, like Romans dressed by Armani, around a swimming pool that I'm prepared to bet my first born is never swum in.

Saint Peter handed me over to a young woman also dressed in white whose beauty made me want to cry.

'Sebastian Moss,' I stammered.

'Right this way.'

Sebastian was sitting at the bar reading *Variety* next to two men who looked familiar, until I realised they were TV stars. I tried to walk nonchalantly, as if seeing superstars or even the cast of *Friends* was as common to me as eating apples.

'Jim, how nice to see you,' said Sebastian, taking off his sunglasses for a moment before returning them to the bridge of his nose. We shook hands, and I brushed against a TV star.

'Sorry,' I blubbered, but the TV star had not even noticed, being engrossed in the vast chest of the woman to his right.

Sebastian was charming and talkative and evidently aware it was my first time in LA. He outlined places to visit, then gave me a couple of restaurant recommendations and a warning: 'Sometimes this city is a little like a nightclub with the lights on. Oh, and don't believe any compliment. LA is the only place in the world where you can die of encouragement.'

We chatted about mutual friends, and he mentioned that he was meeting a couple of German models, and maybe we could go with 'the *Frauleins*' to a party in the hills. Of course, usually I'm not in the slightest bit interested in going to a party in the Hollywood Hills with two German models, but my ego was small and my excitement levels high.

I nodded, a little too vigorously.

After a couple of vodkas Sebastian whipped out his mobile phone and dialled furiously. He talked for a matter of seconds, then turned to me and grinned. 'They're on their way.'

An hour later we were joined by two tall German women.

'This is Helga and this is Gretchen.'

Helga was blonde and beautiful. Gretchen was brunette and beautiful. I grinned inanely at the TV star, but he had gone.

The models departed shortly afterwards to the party. We would meet them later, Sebastian insisted, because right now Julia Roberts was about to arrive. I held out my vodka glass in anticipation.

While we waited, several tanned young men came up to Sebastian, shook his hand and chatted for a minute or two. I understood various words, like 'Spielberg', 'asshole' and 'percentage of gross' but most of it was movie-insider speak, a code of mystification. When one black-suited Aryan had departed I asked what he did for a living.

'A development executive at Tristar.'

'Wow.'

'You have to understand, Jim. In LA, executive is just another word for employee.'

Julia Roberts, it turned out, was about to arrive all evening. Eventually we caught a cab up to the party in the canyons, a hair-raising, white-knuckle ride into the hills north of LA with a Salvadorean taxi-driver whose two words of English seemed to be 'no' and 'problem'. We arrived to find Helga and Gretchen had just departed. Sebastian dialled furiously, talked for a matter of seconds, then turned to me and grinned.

'They're in town. At Arena.'

Back in town we hit Arena, a loud smoky neon-bright ex-ice-making factory, but once again the models had just left. By now I was as drunk as an England centre-forward, and in desperate need of food.

Sebastian was on the phone. 'They're at the Coach and Horses.'

Except they weren't. The Coach and Horses was a pretend English pub with dartboard, snooker table and landlady who made the British Bulldog figurine on the bar look pretty. She had an attitude to match. 'Can't you read? No food after ten,' she bellowed in an Essex accent.

In the back a couple of shaven-headed men who may or may not have been builders from Basildon started fighting. It did, I admit, feel like home.

Outside, Sebastian tried the models one more time, whilst pointing to a yellow fire hydrant on the other side of the street. Apparently it was where Hugh Grant was caught in *fellatio delicto* with prostitute Divine Brown.

'You know why the cops came to check out Hugh's car?' inquired Sebastian. I shook my head.

''Cause the brake light kept going on and off. Hugh had his foot on the pedal while Divine sucked his . . .'

'I get the picture.'

Finally Sebastian conceded that the German models were prob-ably tucked up in bed with a Horlicks or a major movie star. We ended up at 3 a.m. on the floor of a Thai restaurant while Sebastian pleaded with the shrunken Thai manageress for beer.

'But I come here all the time and you always serve me beer.'

This expert tactic failed to move the tiny woman, so we settled for milkshakes (my recently discovered anti-depressant of choice) and Pad Thai, a strangely satisfying combination.

'Want to hear an LA joke?'

I nodded, being too busy ingesting to talk.

'This actor comes home to find his wife on the floor, naked and bleeding. "Baby what happened?" he asks. "This guy broke in, made me perform perverted sexual acts and raped me," she replies, in tears. "The bastard, I'll kill him, I'll rip him limb from limb," says the actor. "Who was it?!" "Your agent," weeps the wife. "Oh," says the actor. "Did he leave any messages?"'

I laughed politely into my spring roll.

Suddenly Sebastian took my hand, fork and all. 'Jim, I'm lonely. I like you a lot. I've liked you since that time we met in London. Will you come home with me tonight?'

I looked at him trying to figure out if my hearing had been affected by the hot sauce. Sebastian looked into my eyes. 'I've got a pool and a hot tub.'

He released my hand, I put down the fork, and told him about Angie. About the ring still in my suitcase, about my love that had turned evil and was now eating away at my inner organs like a many-toothed worm. I talked for ten minutes, non-stop, without tears, without much emotion. Thinking back on it, I must have sounded like I was reading the news.

'And on the 21st she said she never wanted to see me again. This was followed by two days of intensive telephone exchanges . . .'

By the end I felt surprisingly sober. Sebastian sipped his milkshake. 'Which is exactly why you should stick to men. Much less devious.' He smiled.

I yawned, purposefully. 'I think I need to go back to the hotel and sleep.'

'Of course my dear. I'm sorry for the crude proposition. It must have been the shrimp.'

The following day the sun grinned down like an investor in *Titanic*. I woke with a head like an old teabag, and the Pit freshly redug in my stomach. Is this what the future held, I mused over a bagel and watery coffee? Being propositioned by male Californian film producers on the floor of seedy Thai restaurants? Maybe it would be so much easier if I were gay?

The only problem was that I didn't fancy men.

It was evidently time to go to Hollywood. I parked the purple Nissan on Sycamore Avenue behind Mann's Chinese Theatre. I joined the population of Japan tracing the foot- and hand-prints of stars embalmed in concrete outside and to my delight discovered I have the same size feet as Jack Nicholson. Marilyn Monroe's feet are the most caressed, worn smooth by adoring fans. Paul Newman's are untouched, which says something about movie fans. I gave them a little stroke, for *Cool Hand Luke*.

Hollywood, say LA's tourism managers, is changing. Once a seedy mire of disappointment for tourists whisked through at high speed in armoured buses, this one-time paradise of plastic souvenir shops, drug dens and monochrome brothels is being transformed into a happy meadow of shining architecture. They're kicking out the pimps, junkies and penniless scriptwriters and building a new $400 million entertainment complex with a 3,300-seat theatre that will bring the Oscars back to Hollywood, and they've established a Hollywood farmers' market. You know – for all those Hollywood farmers.

I turned away from Mann's in time to glimpse Quentin Tarantino walking down the street followed by a giggle of Japanese schoolgirls. So unreal, so movie-like was the image that I pinched myself to check I wasn't daydreaming (although why I'd daydream Quentin Tarantino followed by giggling Japanese girls is something I'd rather not analyse).

The pinch hurt, and Quentin disappeared around the corner. To avoid a large tour of large Germans, I ducked into the new

Hollywood Entertainment Museum, and marvelled at an original Max Factor beauty calibrator, an ancient torture instrument comprising a 360-degree mask placed on the actress's head, which then had dozens of screws that tightened until its exact shape could be measured, the product quantified. I tried to imagine Gwyneth Paltrow putting up with such a device today, and realised why the beauty calibrator ended up in a museum.

There was Marilyn's dress from *Gentlemen Prefer Blondes*, and I swear it was smiling, the happiest dress in the world. And there was Tom Cruise on tape, talking about his love of collaboration, but I'm sure he was lying.

My fascination was held by a scale model of Hollywood in 1945, placed beneath the floor and covered with glass so you can stamp across Tinseltown like Godzilla. On the hills of the model the famous sign still read Hollywoodland, the original name of the district created by real-estate developers in 1911, until the l-a-n-d fell off, changing history and song titles. 'Hooray for Hollywoodland' just doesn't sound right.

I jumped up and down for a while, feeling huge and monstrous, which made me feel a little better.

The museum is funded by major industrial players in Hollywood – Kodak, Panavision, Rolloflex – and there was a tour designed to show what these companies do, which would, so the advertising promised, reveal 'the Hollywood magic and how it works to make us happy individuals'. The time was right, I thought, for me to be made a happy individual.

The tour, however, turned up no surprises. The costumes didn't look as real as they did on film (which is not very), and neither did the *Starship Enterprise* control room from, as the guide put it, 'that *Star Trek* film in which they all go down to the planet and only the famous ones get back'.

But there was an instructive highlight. I've always wondered how in films they get the sound so crisp, booming, epic and detached from what the actors are actually doing. The answer is, of course, they add it on later. It's called Foley, after Jack Foley, who was head of Universal Studio's sound department in the 1930s, a man revered amongst sound engineers for replicating the sound of Niagara Falls with a water hose and a tin advertising sign.

Well okay, but I didn't know, and the museum had a mini Foley studio, named after the process named after the man, where we clumsy atonal punters could try to add the sound to a three-minute film called *The Chicken Detectives* in which two off-duty cops locate a baddie, who then scares them and they run away (unlike real LAPD cops, who locate a baddie, who scares them, and then they shoot him dead with automatic weapons).

I was the footsteps guy, a responsibility that far from making me a happy individual filled me with a dreadful sense of responsibility. I had a block of concrete to walk on. As the chicken detective walked down some steps on screen, so I stepped on the concrete, filling in the sound, making the film sound right. The Foley guy.

As I stepped, I started to wonder. In the film of Angie and Jim's relationship, what if I'd had my own personal Foley guy, a little bearded, pot-bellied man perhaps, called Frank perhaps, who followed me around and filled in the gaps. Whenever I said something wrong, which I was beginning to think I'd done as frequently as I'd opened my mouth, Foley Frank would leap in and dub over it, making the right noise, saying the right words. When I said, 'I wish you were ambitious about your career,' Foley Frank would have dubbed in, 'What do you want from your life?' When Angie said, 'I love you,' for the first time, Foley Frank would have dubbed in a deep, joyful sigh and a corny but sincere, 'I love you too,' instead of a long and embarrassed silence.

I was terrible as a Foley guy. When the guide played back our attempt in time to the video, our added sounds were out of sync with everything. Especially the footsteps. Much like my relationship with Angie, I thought.

Los Angeles had turned grey, clouds rolling in from the Pacific. A dull weight seemed to hang over the city, mixing with the smog. I drove up Sunset Boulevard, past a large billboard of Elizabeth Hurley advertising Estée Lauder, looking virginal in a meadow of white flowers. Her smile seemed more of a sneer; her huge beatific presence over the road where Divine Brown plied her trade seemed to say, 'Fuck you, Hugh.'

The twin angels of LA: Liz and Divine.

I passed a middle-aged couple sitting at a coffee bar, shouting at each other. I passed a beautiful girl, a model maybe, and tried to catch her eye (quite a feat from a speeding car) but she walked tall, past the Chateau Marmont, with a haughtiness that comes from being beautiful in an ugly world.

Suddenly LA seemed a cruel place, a place of separations, the roads that had been so glamorous and vibrant now arteries of sludge and slime and sorrowful sex. Behind me a Lexus honked its horn, ahead gridlock, above a 747 spluttering fumes into the hazy sky.

And then I saw Eddie, his beautiful cheerful cross-dressing self on a Sunset Boulevard billboard: 8 p.m. Eddie Izzard. My favourite English comedian. Here in LA. A gift from God. Or at least the show's producer, actor Robin Williams.

I stopped the car and ran up to the ticket booth of the Tiffany Theatre. The goateed youth behind the perspex glass looked up, his eyes leaden and baggy from too many or too few mochas. 'Sold out. Sorry.'

It might have been my face, it might have been my whimper, but Goatee looked at me and spoke tenderly. 'Listen, come back at seven. Sometimes we get returns. You might be lucky. You never know.'

You never know.

I reached the Tiffany Theatre at 6.45 p.m. Already some people were milling around in an LA sort of a way – air-kissing, checking themselves out in any available piece of glass and not looking at anyone they were talking to.

I bounded up to the kiosk. Goatee looked up. I looked expectantly. His eyes furrowed, grasping for recognition.

'I was here earlier. You said come back. In case of returns. You said you never know.'

'Oh yeah. There's a woman, her date's not shown. She says if he's not here by 7.15 she'll sell the ticket. Come through, you can wait in the lobby.'

I could have kissed his scrubby beard.

People dressed in black busied into the tiny auditorium – a hundred seats at most. In England Eddie sells out the Royal Albert Hall.

A woman came into the lobby, petite, blonde, pretty in a Meg Ryan sort of a way, which is a good way in my opinion. She walked up to me and said, 'Hi. You the English guy? You want a ticket?'

I nodded, momentarily devoid of language.

'My date didn't show.'

Her eyes were ice blue. Mid-thirties maybe. Cute, in that way only American women can truly fill the adjective.

'Forty bucks,' she said. 'Face value.'

She sounded pissed off.

'That's great,' I said, overexuberantly. 'I'm a big fan of Eddie and I've been having a shitty time – this is the first bit of good luck in a while.' A bit too personal? Who cares, this is America.

She smiled, maybe. I handed her two twenties and we walked into the auditorium.

'It's numbered seating, I'm afraid you have to sit next to me,' she said, and I hoped it was flirtation in her voice. (As if I could remember what flirtation sounded like.) 'My name's Mary.'

Mary, Mary Quite Contrary. Something About Mary. Mary, Queen of Scots. Mary Poppins. The Virgin Mary. Mary. Sounds a little like marry.

What the hell was I thinking? I diverted such desperate thoughts into a memory from childhood. When I was little and my sister even littler, I'd play Robin Hood with my friends. My sister came up one day and asked if she could be Mary.

'There's no Mary in Robin Hood,' I said with all the contempt a ten-year-old can muster.

'Yes, there is,' she insisted. 'Robin Hood and his Mary men.'

So we tied her to a tree and threw mud at her.

Which demonstrates two things:

1. Mary is a name that sounds old, dependable, medieval. Biblical, even.

2. I was a cruel little bastard.

I didn't realise anyone still named their daughter Mary. It seemed so old-fashioned. Except this was America, where a president's daughter is named after an English soccer team, the CNN weather forecaster is called Flip Spiceland, its White House correspondent is Mr Wolf Blitzer, and some poor souls go round all their lives with the name Randy Duck (it's true, I've met him).

Eddie was fantastic. At least I thought so. He had a cold, poor love, and sniffled a little, but he was still absurdly fantastic. I laughed and clapped and the LA audience looked on in complete bafflement.

He did jokes about Nazis and Catholicism and transvestites in the military. The audience coughed politely, and Eddie did his best to draw them in. He asked them what Los Angeles meant, and I could see where he was going with it, and I hoped, I prayed he would go there because I had the answer, bottled up, wrapped in gold paper, ready and tongue-tippingly pert.

'The Angels,' shouted the crowd, wondering how this English guy wearing lipstick could not have known that.

'Ah-ha, yes, of course,' says Eddie and now I know it's coming, I'm damp with excitement.

'But what does Las Vegas mean?'

Silence.

Except for a small voice from the back trying to sound as English as it could. 'The Meadows.'

Eddie looked up at me. 'The what?'

'Las Vegas. It means The Meadows,' I said.

'Oh,' said Eddie, and started another gag about Hitler.

So near, so not near. I'd envisioned a whole future, a sequence of sweet interactions with Eddie following my linguistic revelation – he'd ask me where I was from, make some jokes at my expense, and somehow I'd tell him about Angie and he'd grow suddenly tender in that pensive way he has, and offer me consolation and advice and next to me Mary would take pity and invite me over to her place for rampant consolatory Meg Ryan sex.

But he talked about Hitler and war rationing and was still fantastic and the LA crowd still didn't get it.

At the interval, Mary and I chatted. She said she liked Eddie, and I allowed myself the feeling that maybe she said it not just because she did like Eddie but because she also liked me. A little. I bought us wine, and she said she worked in advertising, organising promotional events for big companies, and I asked her about her date and she said, 'I didn't really like him anyhow,' with a bit of a drawl.

She looked a lot like Meg Ryan.

Eddie's cold worsened in the second half. Some of the audience had gone, empty seats insulting the performance, gone to another show, another party, the social round that seemed from Sebastian's descriptions harder work than work.

Eddie finished. Did one encore. Left.

Mary and I filtered out on to Sunset Boulevard and I wanted to ask her if she'd like a drink, which she probably didn't and anyway it was 11.00 p.m., which is late in this city, at least according to Sebastian.

As we stood on Sunset, Liz Hurley sneering down, I thought that I had no idea how to ask her, even though I really wanted to. Seven years of not asking leaves you rusty. Or rusted. Shut up, locked, like the Tin Man before Dorothy lubricates his joints, oh yes.

'So, did you eat?' she asked.

'No,' I replied, which I thought was a good answer.

'I wanted to check out this new place on La Cienaga. I was going to go with my girlfriend last weekend, but she had boyfriend trouble. Men, huh? Wanna go?'

Americans do really say 'wanna'.

'Whoops,' said Mary quietly as we walked in.

Everyone else in the restaurant was black.

Not that they stared at us, no. They ignored us, which was more disconcerting, this being a city in which everyone eyeballs everyone. For a moment I had a glimpse of what it must be like to be black in a white-dominated world.

The Shark Bar was very chic, the men in suits so sharp the waiters wore protective clothing, women so tall, so athletically elegant that Mary and I squirmed deeper into the crimson leather sofa in a bid to escape their superiority. No one, I noticed, had a mobile phone. Which in LA seemed to denote special power. They had people hidden somewhere to answer their phones for them.

We left the Shark Bar at 1.00 a.m. and stood on the pavement while valets the size of cars brought our cars. Mary dug in the pocket of her black Levis and handed me a business card.

'If you're around for a while, give me a call. Maybe we could do lunch.'

'I really enjoyed tonight,' I said, suddenly a little emotional. 'Thanks for the ticket.'

But she was gone; the car had decided, speeding away into Autoland.

I stood looking at the business card. Despite its embossed gold lettering, it did seem a little impersonal, but in these times of stalkers, rapists and the fine work Hugh Grant did to soil the reputation of the English male in Los Angeles, it was hardly surprising that Mary didn't want to give me her home number just yet. Even in my slightly inebriated state, I realised she might never want to see me again.

Eventually the purple Nissan decided it was time to appear, just as a shiny grand huge Lexus pulled up, out of which stooped two shiny grand huge men, gold clinking, a small tornado breezing my face as their combined bulk strode forth into the restaurant.

Okay. I didn't understand it either. The simple facts were that I loved Angie. To distraction. But Mary was, well, cute, and for the first time in many months, if not a year, I was, however momentarily, made to feel good about myself by a woman. YOU SHOULD FEEL GOOD ABOUT YOURSELF BECAUSE OF YOU! I could hear Oprah holler.

But the truth is, women, that men need you to make them feel good about themselves. We're that simple.

In this confused state I called Sebastian, who gave me a list of 'offbeat things to do in LA' to take my mind off things. These, in order of offbeatness (least to most) went like this:

1. Canoeing around Venice Beach.

2. Grave Line Tours – a tour around celebrity death spots.

3. LA pet cemetery.

I mentioned I'd met a woman called Mary.
'Something about her?'
'Ha, ha.'
'Is she?'
'What?'
'A virgin.'
'Ha, ha.'
'No, that's great, you going out on a real date?'
'Maybe.'
'You haven't called her?'
It had been two days. 'Not yet.'
'Jesus, Jim, this is America. Remember? Instant mash potato, wham-bam, no wait in checkout lines, loan over the phone, now is here here is now America. Call her. Tell her you got two tickets to the House of Blues.'
'I do?'
'Yeah. Because someone gave them to me and I don't want them.'

'Thanks,' I said, not knowing where or who or what the House of Blues was.

'And if it doesn't work out, call me. I'll console you.'

'Pool and a hot tub, right?'

'You tease.'

I called Mary from a phone box on Santa Monica Boulevard. It was definitely a scene from a movie. In fact, everything at this time seemed a little unreal, as if I was observing myself, detached yet involved. Lack of sleep and too many decaff lattes can do that to a man.

She sounded pleased to hear from me. 'Where have you been?'

'Oh, you know, round and about.' In my room mainly. Too scared or guilty or confused to call.

'I had fun the other night.'

'Me too.'

Evidently Sebastian had misjudged American Mary. Two days without calling seemed to have done me no harm at all. The European way, the old way, wait be slow there are rules, take time, get there in the end.

I mentioned the House of Blues, which I'd discovered was, well, a House of Blues, a blues restaurant part owned by Dan Ackroyd, next door to the Mondrian on Sunset Boulevard.

'That'd be fun. I haven't been there in years. Who's playing?'

I had no idea. I'd get back to her.

I put the phone down and felt a shudder of thrill, like I was sixteen again, before Angie, before commitment, before true love and truer heartbreak. Then I remembered the engagement ring in the safe at the Holiday Inn. The Nissan drove me back to Beverly Drive and I went to the safe and took it out. My grandmother's ring. She was dead now. It was a thin gold band, one diamond, two sapphires, that my grandfather had given to her in 1932.

At the Holiday Inn bar I tried to put the ring on my own finger. It didn't fit.

Sebastian worked out of an office on the Disney lot in Burbank.

The clouds persisted, flatly limp over 13 million people, the air so heavy you had to peel it like a banana as you walked. Except nobody walked. The cars made sure of that. The Nissan cut through the smog like a brick through butter.

I'd driven 300 miles around the city in four days, up and down, across and back, because I couldn't help it. That's what the car wanted to do. To join its brethren, its kind, the master race, cruising, patrolling their city.

It took me an hour to get to Burbank as the cars were tired and irritated, their tail-lights blinking angrily. The Disney lot was easy to find: the tall dark-green hedges were clipped in the shape of Mickey Mouse's ears. The guard in the sentry box looked mean in a peaked cap and uniform. 'Name and reason for visit?'

I was humble and polite, just as I'd been many years before, entering East Germany. It doesn't do to mess with empires.

Sebastian's office was away from the main building, which was a good thing because I wouldn't have been able to control my giggling. Its vast neo-classical entranceway was crowned by ten-foot-high representations of the Seven Dwarfs.

Sebastian was on the phone. His secretary, a tall tanned man who said his name was Duke or Puke or Nuke or something made me an espresso. With a twist of lemon. Of course.

I looked around the room at various movie posters – *Rainman*, *Mighty Joe Young*, *Simon Birch*. But Sebastian's name wasn't on any of them.

Outside, men in chinos and polo shirts and women in trouser suits dashed this way and that clasping bundles of papers to their breasts while talking on mobile phones. Sprinklers hushed and small stooped Mexican men pruned rose bushes. *Die Maus über alles.*

Sebastian was still on the phone. When Juke showed me in, he waved, I sat, he talked, I understood words like 'finance', 'Colombian' and 'against Federal law'. I stared around the small office, piles of scripts, a poster of a film I'd never heard of called *Happy Nights* on which Sebastian's name appeared as 'Executive

Producer', a yucca plant and an old-fashioned sixties TV with a brand-new video-player.

After ten minutes Sebastian cupped the phone, and said, 'Sorry Jim, I won't be long.'

After twenty minutes he reached into a drawer, still talking on the phone, occasionally in Spanish, handed over an envelope containing two tickets, cupped the phone and hissed, 'Sorry, it's going to be a long one – can I call you at the hotel?'

In the Disney Studio shop, which was full of kids being fitted for their Mickey Youth uniforms, I bought some black clip-on mouse ears, just in case.

I spent the afternoon at Venice Beach. I liked it immediately. It was unlike so many places, as it should be, and was populated by cartoon characters – lanky hard-swearing basketball players, chubby old men singing the blues, bodybuilders who'd make the Incredible Hulk think about taking steroids, bikini girls with new breasts and baffled European tourists taking pictures of fire hydrants. I strolled up and down Ocean Front Walk and it struck me that what makes the Venice Beach promenade so special in LA, what gives it that vibrancy, that jive, that hoopla, is that it's a place where all humankind and creed can mix freely without fear of oppression for the simple reason that there are no cars there.

Look at their faces. Beaming, happy, joyful. Because in this small sanctuary at least, they're free.

The other place to escape the cars is the canals. These were a revelation to me. It's called Venice Beach, but did you ever wonder how it got its name? Because on the face of it this part of LA is as far from its beautiful Italian namesake as Madonna is from a nunnery.

A brochure told me the area was christened in 1913, when a real-estate developer named Abbot-Kinney bought some land that encompassed Santa Monica and the marshland to the south. He and his partner split the land in half and Abbot-Kinney chose the marshland, much to his partner's ridicule. An eccentric, Abbot-Kinney wanted to recreate his favourite city, Venice, and drained the mosquito-infested bogs, constructing a series of canals and promenades, which in the 1920s became the most fashionable district of Los Angeles, leaving Abbot-Kinney laughing last.

Unfortunately his vision was a little too European for most Angelinos, and more importantly for their cars. As in its namesake, road access was minimal and in post-war America, where the drive-in cinema caused the baby boom (an as yet unwritten thesis of mine), anywhere not accessible for the mighty car was shunned.

During the fifties the district fell into disrepair. By the sixties and seventies it was a virtual no-go area, where gangs of Hell's Angels lived in shacks, stabbing, shooting and drowning each other, and the once beautiful canals filled with beer bottles, syringes and old copies of *Horsepower Weekly*.

It wasn't until the late eighties that the LAPD cracked down on the motorbike gangs and the Venice Beach Canal Association was formed to refurbish the canals, declaring them a National Historic Monument. Today the district contains some of the most beautiful houses in the city, inhabited by actors, singers, movie producers, and people too cool to have job titles.

So like the other Venice there are canals, but unlike the other Venice there are canoes. You rent them from the Dine N'Dash hamburger joint on the corner of North Venice and Pacific Boulevards, slogan – 'Have a burger, rent a canoe'.

The rental business was started at the beginning of 1997 by Mark Suminski, a local Venetian who wanted to 'bring back the golden age of the canals'. He also does a mean cheeseburger. When I entered the cafe he was counting out salt shakers, 'See these? Lost ten in the last two weeks. There's that many ducks now on the canals, the homeless guys collect their eggs and cook 'em up to eat. I guess they like a little salt and pepper.'

I rented Mark's top-of-the-range canoe and, as the sun finally appeared, listened to the safety instructions. 'The canals are only three feet deep, so don't worry if you tip over, you can always get out and walk.'

So it was that I set out to canoe around Los Angeles.

Slipping under the first bridge, I emerged on to a river where willows wept and palm trees sighed. It was intensely calm. All was silent, except for the ducks jabbering like film critics. As you'd expect, even ducks in LA have attitude.

Alongside the canals were pathways where couples ambled hand in hand in the freshly polished afternoon sun. Hugging the water sat enticing homes – Mediterranean-style haciendas shaded by palms, wooden Northwestern cabins bedecked with bougainvillaea. Bird-of-paradise flowers nodded sagely, jazz drifted across the water, fish darted amongst the reeds.

'Watch out for crocodiles,' a fat man bellowed from the banks. I waved back, beginning to feel adventurous, a nineteenth-century explorer heading into uncharted waters. Which I was, in some respects. Most Angelinos I talked to knew nothing of the Venice canals, and if they did, they still thought of them as the Hells Angel's wasteland, a place you'd not be seen dead in, unless you were dead.

Sebastian had only discovered them, so he claimed, when he met one of the producers of *The Simpsons* there to talk about a live-action, live-actors version of the cartoon (a concept that goes a long way towards summing up Hollywood for me).

Two main canals run north–south, intersected by three smaller canals. The water is cleaner than the stuff in London taps and is tidal, being fed by the Pacific through the Marina Del Rey harbour. I rounded the corner and headed north again along Sherland Canal, narrowly missing an inflatable dinghy where an immaculately coiffured man and blonde woman lay sleeping in the sun. They were Joe Pesci and Farrah Fawcett-Majors, I was convinced, just as I believe I regularly see Robert De Niro at my local library (a Dick Francis fan in case you're wondering).

As I handed back my paddle, Mike Suminski beamed with

pride. 'You know, I reckon those Italians better watch out. Pretty soon this Venice'll be the one everyone wants to see.'

By 6 p.m. I was nervous. A date. I didn't want to go on a date, the word, a single syllable, suggesting organisation, detachment, finity.

I hadn't been on a date in eight years. I never really went on one with Angie; we met and just drifted closer to each other, like icebergs or plastic bags left in a canal. I didn't want to go on a date. I wanted to be with Angie. In her arms, that warm, tight familiarity where it didn't matter if I was witty or charming or sexy or funny, because it was understood that we loved each other and nothing would change that, not even a bad joke about Italian transvestites.

And if you go on a date, any number of things can happen to you. You get stood up. You get laughed at. You get dumped after thirty-five minutes for someone in a Freddie Mercury T-shirt (back in the days before any of us had figured out he was gay, despite the name of the band and his penchant for sequins).

In an unstrung and shaky state I walked into a bookshop on Sunset Boulevard.

American bookshops are nothing like British bookshops. For a start the books are not there to be bought, or even really read that much, but act merely as decor, a backdrop to the more serious business of selling hot beverages and cakes, because American bookshops are really coffee shops with books. And as such are places to sit for hours, secretly fancying the pert young mum with her two-year-old to your left.

I found myself inextricably drawn to the book aisle marked 'Self-Improvement'. Not 'Self-Help'. That would suggest there was a possibility of failure, one of the things banned by the US Constitution, along with poverty and losing in tennis finals. The aisle was half a mile long. There must have been a thousand or more books in the section marked 'relationships' alone. Round the corner was 'death' alongside 'making more money' and 'bonding with your rabbit'. I pulled out a big orange book: *Dating For Dummies – The Down-To-Earth Guide To Dating Success!*

There are two things these self-help books really like! One is exclamation marks! And don't you think that the other thing is the rhetorical question?!

I took *Dating For Dummies* to the cafe (buying books in these places seems bad form, rather like trying on armour in the British Museum), ordered a nettle and turnip tea and settled into the faux-leather armchair to read.

The chapter headings were promising, bouncy, full of encouraging present participles such as 'Polishing Your Social Self' and 'Getting Your Outside Ready' (followed by 'Getting Your Inside Ready' – I had visions of renting a home X-ray machine). The most encouraging chapter heading was 'Having A Way Cool Time', which sounded like a preferable option.

Then it became less encouraging. There was one chapter entitled 'Your Date Hates You!'. And another called 'You Hate Your Date!'. And a third that began 'You Hate Each Other!'.

Then came the advice, which was concise and enthusiastically patronising:

'Remember sulking is not sexy and it's not productive!'

'Beware of using the same criteria for adult friends that you used when you were twelve!'

'Look at your shoes. Do they match?'

'I'm not against plastic surgery, but not before your first date, please.'

The author was evidently a frustrated poet. 'Charm,' she wrote, '*must* include eye contact . . .' In short it's 'a butterfly's touch on a flower petal, the breeze of a humming bird's wing'.

Some of the advice made me wonder if the writer had decided love might well have rendered her readers stupid, or whether she was simply writing for a strata of the American populace who had been lobotomised at birth. 'You don't have to spend gobs of money getting your colours done. Go to a large department store with good lighting (not fluorescent), pick up the same shirt in a bunch of different colours and see which colour looks the best with your skin and eyes. Then decide which colour looks worst. Avoid the latter and focus on the former.'

Much of the advice made me want to weep, and not just with mirth. If there was just one poor soul out there who needed such advice, the world was without doubt a cruel and ghastly place. 'To help with shyness: Meander around a busy public place for an hour or two so you get used to being around people. Practice smiling and making eye contact. Calm yourself by telling yourself over and over again that you're safe and everything's going to be okay.'

There was a helpful list of good places to meet people, which ranged from grocery stores (if you want to meet a sixteen-stone trailer-park inhabitant with an addiction to caramel-coated tortilla chips) to bus stops (if you want to meet Mad Marvin, the celebrity pet fetishist) to laundromats (if you want to meet the 0.1 per cent of the American population who don't possess their own washer-dryer, which usually means the same people you meet at bus stops, i.e. nutters, serial killers and the really, really poor). The laundromat section included advice on how to pull whilst watching your knick-knacks spin. 'Always carry extra fabric softener and change (you never know who may need to borrow something) and *under no* circumstances mention underwear.'

The one place suggested for finding true love that came as a surprise to a secular Englishman was 'church'. I know my grandparents met in church, but that was back in the days when everyone still believed in the possibility of immaculate conception. How could you possibly meet anyone in church in this day and age? Do you sidle alongside them at the communion rail and murmur 'nice buns' just before they swallow their wafer?

Tragically, *Dating For Dummies* did not have the answer; all it pointed out was the drawbacks of church dating. 'The only problem with church is that you can't date lots and lots of folks at the same church or you'll get a rep. So either be selective or plan to change congregations should the need arise.'

Despite my growing hilarity, which many in the bookshop cafe were evidently interpreting as an overdose of nettle and turnip tea, some of the book's guidance made sense. Such as: 'For the wrong person there is no right time.' And one paragraph that struck home like a Brazilian free kick: 'There is a piece of folk wisdom that says if you've just been thrown from a horse the best cure is to get right back on. That may work well with horses, but don't even think about applying it to dating situations.'

Wasn't I about to hop into the saddle, Butch to his steed? Why? Why was I doing it? Why had I called Mary up and asked her to go out?

The answer, I suspected, when I'd calmed down with a cup of tangerine and broccoli tea, was simple. I wanted to feel better about myself, and how better to feel better than by going on a date with an American?

Ever since I was old enough to possess a house key, I'd wanted to go out with an American woman. Every British male has. Probably every European male. Because American women were it, everything English girls were not – sexy, sassy, long-legged, big-breasted and most importantly easy. They gave out on every occasion, like toasters, at least according to the movies. Hell, Drew Barrymore even snogged ET. At the age of five.

And what's more, Mary wasn't just an American girl – she was a Californian girl. This night I could step right into my own personal rock song.

I went back to the book, searching for ways to make the date go well. It seemed straightforward enough: 'Pick a place you know. You'll sound like Cary Grant if you lean over and say, "Try the duck, it's out of this world." Avoid arm wrestling on a first date. Do something that doesn't require new clothes. Never say, "My wife doesn't understand me."'

For those like me, who fall sprawling into the water pit at the first hurdle of conversation (I always win the race in the replay of my mind), there were sure-fire lines to get the chat zipping along. Such as:

'What did you do today?'

'What book is your favourite?'

'Are you a cat or a dog person?'

Topics to avoid on an American date included 'police brutality, immigration, women in the military'. Which just about knocked out my classic conversational gambit: 'What this country needs is women soldiers in the police force to show those spics the meaning of law and order.'

The book concluded with recommendations for rustling up sexual frissons between you and your datee: 'Don't be afraid to giggle and tease. Touch. Brush arms, bump knees beneath the table, tweak noses.'

TWEAK NOSES?

Apparently it's big in Alabama.

And finally, so the writer informed me, if I was lucky enough to get to the end of the evening without hating my date, her hating me, or either of us having recently had a sex change, and I wanted to gauge whether the woman in question wanted to kiss me, I should note the following key signs: 'She's facing you arms down, body relaxed. Her head is tilted up and her lips are parted.'

As they say in the sewage business, no shit.

Mary was late. I stood outside the House of Blues watching a group of twelve-year-olds in T-shirts that read 'Carnival of Carnage'. Their faces caked in white make-up, eyes shadowed black, they milled around like angry Pandas. I found them strangely disturbing, a glowering hormonal presence, tormented not by their disadvantages but by their advantages, the ease of middle-class suburban upbringings, Valley kids desperate for rebellion, fed on a diet of sugar-sodas, slasher movies and Marilyn Manson, the sort of high-school students who find nourishment in obscure Internet sites marked by swastikas.

Mary finally arrived just as a fleet of SUVs delivered yet more suburban kids dressed in horror film T-shirts, make-up and the sort of baggy trousers you could keep a family of ferrets in and still have room for a strawberry sundae.

'Hi.'

I was pleased to see she still looked cute.

'Who are we seeing?'

I looked at the tickets. 'The Insane Clown Posse.'

'Who are they?' she asked, glancing around worriedly at our fellow concert-goers.

'No idea,' I said, glancing around worriedly at our fellow concert-goers.

Thanks to Sebastian's free tickets we had a dinner reservation. We sat at our table as blues music pounded and a family devoured a plate of shrimps the size of a small boat. I looked around for the stage and the horror-film kids, but they were nowhere to be found.

'The bar's on a moveable platform,' explained Mary. 'When the gig starts it swings round to reveal the stage.'

We talked, or rather shouted over the rock music, and to my surprise I found myself telling her about Angie. Not just an overview in a 'Yeah, there was this girl but it's over now' sort of way, but in a 'My heart was broken and I don't know what I'm doing with my life' sort of way. Mary listened, nodded occasionally and devoured a bowl of gumbo before I'd lifted a spoon.

Guilt, it seems, is a wonderful laxative for the soul. For the first time I could understand how murderers confessed to crimes years after they'd buried the body under the patio. I poured out my heart to make myself feel less bad about being in a club with a blonde woman I'd only just met whilst keeping another woman's engagement ring in the safe at the Holiday Inn.

'So you're on the rebound,' she smiled when I'd finished.

'Er . . . maybe.'

'You think there's a chance you two will get back together?'

Asked, like that, coolly, calmly, dispassionately, the answer seemed equally clear. There was no way. Was there?

'Maybe,' I said, carefully watching a video over the bar showing Grace Jones topless.

The clock struck nine and, as Mary had said it would, the bar divided into two, swung to the side and a hole appeared below, revealing the stage. The view was perturbing. A throng of white teenagers, drinking beer, smoking, many of them in white make-up. But it was their T-shirts that I noticed most. Apart from the Carnival of Carnage slogans were others saying simply 'FUCK OFF' in big black letters. Some wore clown masks.

'Whatever happened to Simon and Garfunkel?' asked Mary.

The first band were called The Urge and came onstage to recorded screams, wearing ice hockey masks like Jason in *Friday the 13th*. The crowd surged forward, fists punching the air. Mary and I leaned on the rail gazing down like divinities bemused by mortal folly.

'Fuck motherfucker, fuck motherfucker, fuck,' sang The Urge, two men in hockey masks and baggy ferret trousers, hollering into mikes. The teenagers chanted along, a seething mass of sweat and limbs and barely broken voices;

'Die motherfucker, die motherfucker, die.'

In the pit below someone jumped up and started to bodysurf across the throng, his scrawny body passed through the air by grasping hands; he was thrown down, seemingly stamped upon, only to rise again, fist punching the air.

'Fuck you fuckhead, fuck you fuckhead, fuck.'

There were two other acts before the headline band, much in the same vein – young white kids in baggy trousers screaming profanities into the mikes. To our side stood a family, three young kids and their mother, all nodding their heads to the lyrics. The influences of each band were strikingly similar – blood, gore, obscenity, profanity. A subculture of the macabre, born in adolescent bedrooms and transported around the nether ether of cyberspace.

'South Bay is in the house,' shouted the black caped boys on stage, referring to the areas of Orange County around Long

Beach, some of the most politically conservative districts in America (the local airport is named after John Wayne).

Mary wanted to go. 'Listen Jim, I'm thirty-nine years old. As far as I'm concerned these guys live on a different planet.'

The main act appeared on stage. Circus music played, a fairground backdrop was wheeled on, and a drum roll brought three puny white boys, dressed in baggy gerbil shorts and army fatigues, as well as a tall skeletal figure dressed as a skeleton who did Michael Jackson robot impressions for the whole show.

Hailing from the arid desert of Phoenix, the Insane Clown Posse seemed to do nothing different from their predecessors to merit their headline status, except one. On to stage was wheeled a cart full of plastic root beer bottles. As soon as the music started – a deafening booming base, screeching guitar and the by now usual stream of 'Fucks' – the members of the band picked up bottle after bottle, shook them, unscrewed them slightly and threw them into the crowd, spraying the entire stalls section in brown, sticky root beer. I stopped counting after the hundredth bottle. Soon the pit of teenagers was drenched, as if in blood.

I turned to Mary for explanation, but she'd departed for the ladies' room minutes previously and had not returned. As dates go this was going about as well as a Spanish naval invasion. I decided to wait and see if Mary reappeared. To be honest, I was intrigued by the mayhem ensuing below.

As the teenagers stripped off their shirts, jumping, punching, kicking, spitting through their clown masks and the Posse shouted, 'What the fuck, what the fuck, what the fuck . . .' I came up with a pocket theory to explain the circus themes, the supernatural, the macabre. It was, I thought, akin to medieval carnival, in which the macabre was key, a usurping of everyday reality into a reverse world where peasants were kings, the dead were alive and clowns took the place of wise men. In the fourteenth century, carnival was a momentary escape from extreme hardship. At the House of Blues, the Insane Clown Posse provided an escape from extreme ease, from the monotony of wealth and home delivery. Like many Americans these white suburban kids from South Bay had it too easy. They craved mayhem because their strip-mall, solar-panelled, five-door-SUV, dial-a-pizza, doggy-bag, all-you-can-eat lifestyles had none of it.

Cut back on ease. Make things a little harder. Then see if kids love the thrill of slasher movies, occult websites, Hitler's birthday and gunning down their classmates in high school libraries. That was my theory.

'Let's go,' said Mary, returned from the toilets with fresh and unalluring lipstick.

'Okay.'

We went to the bar at the Chateau Marmont across the road. This gothic horror house mansion was originally an authentic mock Norman castle built in 1927 before becoming a highly expensive and therefore private hotel. Favourite with Greta Garbo, Howard Hughes (who rented the entire penthouse to ogle the starlets in the pool below), Jim Morrison (who enjoyed drug binges here before dying in Paris) and John Belushi (who enjoyed drug binges here before dying here), the Chateau is part of Hollywood folklore, a hideaway bolthole for those wishing to be found only by the best-known magazine writers.

We sat in the salon on a sofa next to a grand piano. It felt like an old person's living room. The drinks were really expensive, and every so often Northern Irish actor Stephen Rea would appear in the lobby to entertain us, shuffling around with a hang-dog expression of loneliness, as if almost daring us to recognise him. I could have sworn he was wearing a pair of bedroom slippers.

There was no one else around. Not even any staff. The hotel had the feel of a haunted motel, the sort of place where Anthony Perkins or Peter Cushing would be manager, with a freezer full of body parts in the basement.

We sat in silence, champagne fizzing in Mary's glass, a clock ticking somewhere.

'So . . .' said Mary. She looked like Meg Ryan.

'I'm sorry,' I said, because it seemed like a good start.

'For what?'

Which threw me slightly. 'I shouldn't have told you all that, about Angie . . .'

'Jim. We're just having a drink.'

'Yeah. We're just having a drink.'

Stephen Rea shuffled into view again. He looked like he was about to cry.

It was one of those times when you step outside yourself, look at the film of your life and say, How did they come up with this naff plot? None of it hangs together. I just don't believe it.

Here I was, sitting in a famous Hollywood hotel with a woman who vaguely resembled Meg Ryan whom I'd met at an Eddie Izzard show three days previously. Now some people might have found that inspiring – an example of how life can be unpredictable, fortuitous, charged with mind-blowing possibility. I, however, found it depressing. It told me that life is random, haphazard, disconnected and ultimately meaningless. I felt a million miles from anything I knew, or cared about, or loved. I felt a stranger, an outsider in a corrupt and crazed city where boys wore clown masks, women were older than they looked and semi-famous actors traipsed around hotel lobbies in bedroom slippers looking suicidal.

We drove to the Dresden, on Mary's recommendation, a 'lounge bar' just off Hollywood Boulevard that featured as the main venue in Doug Liman's film *Swingers* about a group of male friends doing the LA scene in search of true love (only one of them found it). Its sixties kitsch decor and low lighting seemed to ooze magazine-style hipness. The clientele was young, many of them laughably good-looking, dressed in fifties zoot suits and cocktail dresses – and that was just the men. We found a booth and listened to a tiny woman draped in gold singing Frank Sinatra numbers. I stared at the olive in my Martini.

It looked like an eye, staring back, ridiculing.

We sat for several minutes before Mary turned to me, brow furrowed in anger. 'Get over it Jim. You're not the first person in history to get dumped.'

'I'm not?'

'Jesus.' Which didn't refer to me.

'I'm sorry.'

'Don't be fucking sorry. Just lighten up.'

She was right, of course. This was America, where the present becomes the past and the past becomes dogfood quicker than a heartbeat.

But I was trapped. The Pit had returned, oozing from olive to Martini to stomach. We stayed for another quarter hour, until Mary had had enough, and she dropped me at my car.

'I'm sorry,' I said.

She kissed me briefly on the cheek, said nothing, and drove away into the eager hot night of Los Angeles.

So much for the rock song.

The following day seemed like a good day to feel miserable. As such I woke late, realised I hated the Holiday Inn and checked out. Self-loathing makes you reckless, and I decided to worry about accommodation later. I drove to Mann's Chinese Theatre, parked once again in my spot on Sycamore Avenue and after a brief and slightly restorative communion with Paul Newman's hands in the cement, I climbed into an old black hearse for a tour around the celebrity death spots of Los Angeles. Because there's only one person more famous than a Hollywood star and that's a dead Hollywood star.

The publicity for Grave Line Tours offered a trip around 'The Best of the Worst of Hollywood', an excursion beneath the shiny happy veneer of Movieland to the bizarre, sordid reality behind the razzle-dazzle.

To book you have to call a number in Kansas City, as the company's owner has moved back there from LA after he nearly got killed in a drive-by shooting. 'Hey, I didn't want to become a sight on my own tour,' he said with a bowling-alley chuckle.

I was in the mood to enjoy other people's misfortune. I wanted to embrace that warm snug feeling that comes from the knowledge that whilst the actors mentioned on the tour might once have been famous, rich and seductive, at least I was still alive.

My fellow death junkies were all men, which clearly delighted our driver, Stanley, an effete pygmy who made Liberace seem butch. My fellow passengers were both from New Jersey, and looked like colleagues of Tony from Las Vegas, with eyes that suggested they knew a thing or two about death from unnatural causes. I was pleased. Sitting in a hearse with two hitmen seemed like the most appropriate way to spend today.

As we pulled away, the stirring strains of a funeral march blasted from the tape-player and a melodramatic voice-over began, 'Dearly beloved, welcome to eighty fully documented deaths.'

You quickly realise there are sick minds at work on this tour.

Our first stop was the apartment building where singer Janis Joplin overdosed on heroin on 4 October 1970.

'Look to the second air-conditioner on the right,' whispered Stanley, so we did. A frisson went through the hearse as the apartment's lace curtains fluttered. Joplin's music played hauntingly on the tape-recorder, and we looked on in deep reverence. The innocuous block of flats had been transformed into a place of dreadful legend.

Stanley broke the mood. 'We had Peter Lorre's embalmer on the tour last year. Now that was cool.'

The tragedies came thick and fast. We passed by Plaza Suites apartments where 350-pound drag queen Divine expired in 1988 while filming the hit TV show *Married With Children*. I began to wonder how many Divines there were in Los Angeles, but then I suppose it is a City of Angels. At Divine's funeral there was a wreath with a touching card from the cast that read, 'If you didn't want to do the show you should have just said so.'

Nearby was the apartment block where twenty-eight-year-old Marilyn Monroe lived after splitting up with Joe DiMaggio, an unhorrific place, apart from the fact that Melanie Griffith once lived there too.

Back on Sunset we stopped at a red light by a cafe. Stanley pointed and people in the cafe looked jumpy. He turned and whispered with a giggle, 'Nothing happened here, but it's always fun to point as if something did.'

The gore continued shortly afterwards with the apartment where David Cassidy's father was burned to death ('LA gives discounted cremations to burn victims,' joked Stanley – the boys from New Jersey liked that one), and on up Sunset to the kingdom of John Belushi.

I've always been a big fan of Belushi. The manic comic actor who made his name in *Animal House* and *The Blues Brothers* died at the Chateau Marmont following a party with Robin Williams and Robert De Niro. Belushi used to roam Sunset Boulevard, causing chaos everywhere he went. We paused by Gil Turner's liquor store, where he threw a famous fit after having been barred for the umpteenth time. I imagined, without much difficulty, the scene – a bullish Belushi pounding his substantial fists against the glass door – and wondered, not for the first time, where the real film stars have gone.

From the liquor store we rubber-necked to take in the black awning of Johnny Depp's Viper Room, site of his friend River Phoenix's death from a drug overdose in 1994. Next door was the phone used by Phoenix's brother to make the 911 call for help. The sidewalk was empty, dirty, ordinary. It seemed a sad little place to die.

After an hour and six miles, I was beginning to feel less content. Rather than make me feel better, other people's tragedies were making my own case seem more tragic.

Yet the worst was still to come.

We headed on through Beverly Hills, past the dazzling Beverly Hills Hotel, last call for actor Peter Finch, who collapsed of a heart attack in the lobby before receiving a posthumous Oscar for Best Actor in *Network* in 1977, and on up Benedict Canyon.

Benedict Canyon is the most chilling place in LA, and perhaps therefore in America. It is a beautiful road, lapped by palm trees, the plush mansions gleaming angelic white in the hot Californian sun; the only sounds are water sprinklers dousing the bougainvillaea and the splash of bodies in swimming pools.

It was here on 8 August 1969 that a pregnant Sharon Tate and four others were stabbed to death by Charles Manson and his gang. This seemed to be Stanley's favourite story – on 8 August each year since, he said, he met with friends at the El Coyote restaurant where Sharon had her last meal. They'd dress up as their favourite murder victim and describe the killings in terrifying detail. Stanley, I was rapidly realising, was not someone I'd like to introduce to my parents.

Seeing the house, hearing the gruesome story, I was reminded of the gore-obsessed teenagers from the House of Blues. There is an undeniable underbelly to the American Dream, a rough, rancid, rabid streak that revels in violent mayhem. On this hot day, it made my neck hairs freeze.

By midway the group had fallen silent while Stanley continued his commentary in a singing alto that seemed at odds with the subject matter. He dropped us nuggets of Hollywood gossip – 'What do Liz Taylor and Alec Baldwin have in common? They both have hairy backs' – while expounding his love of Judy Garland.

Back in Beverly Hills the death rate increased: there was the house where Bugsy Siegel was machine-gunned to death . . . where actress Loopy Valez committed suicide . . . where the Menendez brothers blew away their parents . . . A police car zoomed past, sirens blazing.

'I do like the sound of sirens in the afternoon,' crooned Stanley. 'Someone, somewhere's having a tragedy.'

Our last stop in Beverly Hills was the small house where blonde bombshell Jean Harlow lay in agony before her death from uraemia, swollen and stinking of urine. It was getting too too sad. I almost asked to be let out then and there, but some twisted chromosome made me stay, as we hurtled onwards, to the Cedars-Sinai Hospital, 'the place to die if you're rich and famous'.

Finally we returned to Hollywood itself and the Knickerbocker Hotel, deathplace of D.W. Griffith, Harry Houdini and a costume designer whose body was found on top of the lobby awning four days after she leaped from the roof.

Hollywood, you feel, is not a happy place. Even Aunty Em, the kindly character from *The Wizard of Oz*, ended up committing suicide here – actress Clara Blandick took an overdose of sleeping pills then pulled a plastic bag over her head two months before her eighty-first birthday. What is it, I wondered, that makes LA such an emporium of suicides and murder?

'I don't know,' laughed Stanley. 'But it's so great, isn't it?'

I waved goodbye to the old black hearse and stood alone on Hollywood Boulevard, my life packed into the trunk of a purple Nissan.

If this had been a movie I would have seen my reflection in a drugstore window, realised I had to change things, got in my car and driven across country to New York City, meeting the new love of my life and several gangsters on the way.

In real life I drove to McDonald's.

'Don't say the word sorry.'

'I wasn't going to.'

'Good.'

'I'd like to see the beach. The real California.'

'You could try Hermosa Beach. It's not far from my work.'

'Great. Doing anything tonight?'

'Yeah.'

'Tomorrow night?'

A moment. 'Call me tomorrow.'

'Okay.'

'Bye.'

'Bye.'

I drove south to Hermosa Beach, ten miles beyond LAX airport. Hermosa is Spanish for beautiful said the brochure (in America there is always a brochure), and it was: a stretch of white sand, the odd palm tree, white-board wooden beach houses and tall blond surfers called Woody and their beautiful surfer-chick girlfriends. This was California as I'd imagined it at the age of ten watching Larry Wilcox and Erik Estrada in *CHiPs*.

I parked the car and walked down Pier Avenue, a pedestrianised precinct lined with palm trees and cafes. It felt almost Mediterranean, with people sitting outside sipping coffees as if they were in Sorrento. Except there was a skateboarding ramp and people calling each other 'dude'. This in itself was a revelation. I didn't think people actually called each other dude, but then I didn't think people actually dressed up as clowns and shouted, 'Die motherfucker, die.'

They also used the word 'like' a great deal. As far as I could tell it could be injected into any part of a sentence. As in: 'I like totally like know what I like. Dude.'

The rules for this laid-back beach community seemed few and simple. Don't wear socks. Or shoes. Bleach your hair blonde. Or shave it off completely. Tattoo yourself liberally, pierce yourself liberally and display your tanned flesh liberally. It was a pretty liberal kind of place.

I got a room at the Sea Sprite Motel for fifty dollars. It had a double bed with a large sag in the middle like someone had slept with their arms around a keg of beer or a small fat person. It was right on the beach. I could hear the surf pound and the gulls mewl. It was perfect.

As the afternoon shadows lengthened, I strolled along the boardwalk. LA felt a million miles away. As often in my life, a bit of sea, sun and sand had the ability to invigorate, dazzle and lift the soul, my drugs of choice.

The houses on the boardwalk were populated by bohemian types, or at least the sort of people who were at home sitting with a beer wearing few clothes at 4 p.m. on a Thursday. One guy was reading or writing a script. Others chatted as their dogs negotiated sexual congress at their feet.

The dogs, I noticed, were either very large or very small – a sure sign of wealthy owners. Only the wealthy can afford the food bills, kennel construction and walker fees that a huge dog demands. Only the wealthy are secure enough in their image to walk around with a rat on a lead.

People ran, jogged, walked, rollerbladed, skateboarded and cycled along the footpath, a race of fitness fascists, bedecked in the latest exertion gear, sweating just enough to seem strenuous without being unattractive. The men were muscled, the women toned, an unreal race that Hitler would have been proud of. Everyone eyed everyone else, a moving mating game. Not being dressed in revealing shorts and see-through vest, I was pretty far down the eye-contact food chain.

But I did manage to meet a real-life David Hasselhoff: Captain Bob Moore was the local area lifeguard chief, dressed in red shorts and flip-flops. I chatted to him near the Sea Sprite Motel as we both watched the sun set. He explained that Hermosa Beach was one of the first places in the world to have a lifeguard service, back in 1920.

I remarked upon his uniform – red shorts, flip-flops, a walkie-talkie.

'We don't do things in southern California like they do elsewhere,' he grinned with the easy arrogance that seems to lie in the drinking water in this part of the world.

'If you do get into trouble, Jim,' he said, evidently marking me out as someone whose seaworthy rating was on a par with a Philippines ferry service, 'don't panic. It'll be a rip tide that's got you. You just got to swim parallel to shore. You'll be okay. If you're in trouble, we'll see you and come and get you.'

He seemed much more reassuring than David Hasselhoff, but admitted to quite liking *Baywatch*.

'Well, Jim, any publicity is publicity. A lot of people didn't know we're here 365 days a year. I enjoy the fact the TV show got the word out that we do the job.' One of the original writers of the show is a part-time Hermosa Beach lifeguard who still works with Captain Bob at weekends. 'The only thing I would say is that we don't jump out of helicopters in full uniform. In fact we don't jump out of helicopters.'

I could imagine. Bob wouldn't like jumping out of helicopters. He'd lose his flip-flops.

That night I had a sausage at Brewski's, where a waitress called Suzanne took pity on me and chatted for a while. She was fresh-faced and very Californian, if by Californian you mean remarkably attractive, athletic and vacant.

'I was like living in LA. So like, I had to like get closer to the beach. I like how laid back, kicked back it is. You can just like mill around.'

Every so often there was a chug-fart of Harley-Davidson beyond the palm-lined avenue and a lanky youth in floppy hat, goatee, and Quicksilver T-shirt would come up to Suzanne and say, 'Hey babe,' and they'd kiss. I felt like joining in – Suzanne's lips were far from unkissable – but I didn't have a goatee and my T-shirt was from British Home Stores. Instead I gave her a ten-dollar tip, smiled and said, 'Thanks,' which was as cool as I could muster.

I spent the next day on the beach. I rented a surfboard and tried for a couple of hours to catch a wave, but eventually gave up after seeing a group of seven-year-old girls laughing at me. When it became too hot and my skin began to resemble a radish, I wandered around the cluttered little shops that displayed proud little signs declaring their antiquity – 'Woody's Surf Place – Est. 1971'.

I was trying to find the Either/Or Bookshop where Charles Bukowksi used to prowl, pulling out his own books and scribbling a cartoon and autograph in them for unsuspecting purchasers. But it had, so someone told me, been turned into a Dunkin' Donuts, which seemed a bit of a blow against American literature.

In the local community office I read some newspaper clippings about local events, seeing what might entice me for the rest of the day. The most impressive of these was held every Independence Day – the Hermosa Beach Iron Man contest, otherwise known as the Independence Day Chug-A-Thon. In this illustrious and Olympic-standard event participants have to run a mile, swim a mile, then chug a six-pack of beer. The rules dictate that the beer must be kept down for twenty minutes. As the article concluded, 'Most competitors fail that test, bringing cheers from hundreds of observers.'

Independence. I wondered what that felt like.

Mary agreed to meet for dinner. She sounded tired. Maybe she'd been out on a hot date, with a non-whiner who didn't mention that he'd recently asked the love of his life to marry him. I waited for her as the sun was swallowed by the Pacific, not far from a memorial to the crew of the Space Shuttle *Challenger*, which exploded on 28 January 1986, killing all seven astronauts, including local boy Greg Jarvis. The inscription read, 'His indomitable spirit is ever with us on the Strand.'

I hoped it was. It was a fine spot to spend eternity.

Perhaps the spirit of Greg Jarvis was with me that night. Mary looked more like Meg Ryan than ever. We ate at Boccaccio's Italian restaurant and she told jokes and I laughed in all the right places and we drank wine and I felt like I was at the beach, which I was. Beyond the surf hissed gently, a serpent gently tempting.

We went on to a bar, Cafe Boogaloo, where we drank large cocktails out of large glasses while a large band played large rock. By 1 a.m. we were plastered. We staggered out on to the street, winding our way past a police car, which eyed us with careful disdain.

The sand was surprisingly cold. A spring breeze blew, promising new beginnings. Seagulls sat like small ghosts in the darkness.

We sat, apart, in the sand for many minutes, watching the moon play over the water. I was drunk, confused and in a beach frame of mind, all of which I would plead in my defence.

'Well, are you gonna kiss me?' asked Mary suddenly.

Of course the thought had crossed my mind. But I hadn't kissed a female other than Angie in a situation where tongues might be involved in seven years. That, in the lip business, is a long time. I sat, she moved closer, I moved closer, and, we, well, kissed. Adam and Eve, Antony and Cleopatra, Queen

Elizabeth and Prince Philip. As natural, almost, as breathing. Fortunately tongues were not involved. That would have been too complicated.

It was a good kiss, I think. Slow, a little moist. About a seven.

WHAT WAS I DOING?

The surf hissed again, she withdrew and smiled, then kissed me again, hands running up my back. Strong hands for a thirty-nine-year-old. Or a weak back for a thirty-year-old.

The gulls rose suddenly in a great spectral cloud, shocked and embarrassed.

She took my hand, placed it on her breast, causing me great surprise and consternation since I wasn't expecting such forwardness and I hadn't touched a breast, even Angie's, in over a year (it's hard to grab a mammary across 3,000 miles of ocean). But despite what Pamela Anderson fans might tell you, all breasts are pretty much the same, and it's amazing how some skills you never lose.

We petted – an expression I'd always associated with poodles, but which seemed perfect for our fully clothed sand-filled grapplings – during which Mary reminded me that women sometimes like you to bite the back of their neck by moaning, 'Bite my neck, bite my neck.'

Our petting continued for what seemed like hours, but was probably a matter of minutes, and tongues were at some stage involved and it was not as complicated as I'd feared, until suddenly and inexplicably Mary pushed me away. I lost balance and rolled over into the sand.

She sat above me. A divine Meg Ryan. 'I've got to go away tomorrow. A conference in Vegas. I've got to get home now.'

I looked up at her, Isaac to Abraham. 'Okay.'

'Then I'm going to Florida to see my brother. Vacation time.'

'Okay.'

'If you were heading that way, maybe we could . . .'

'Okay.'

She wrote out her brother's number in Tallahassee, shook some sand from her hair, adjusted her bra straps and walked slightly ahead of me to her car. The police car watched us angrily.

'Thanks, Jim,' she said, with a smile.

'Okay.'

'Why not come to Florida?'

'Okay.'

She kissed me, softly on the lips, sand grits and Wrigley's spearmint.

And as the white Accura purred out of the parking lot and away down the street, passing under a streetlamp, I noticed Mary had a nice red lovebite on the back of her neck.

Some skills you never lose.

My last excursion into Los Angeles was to the final venue on Sebastian's list, the most offbeat of the three. It seemed a fitting end to my time in the City of Angels.

I felt an emptiness as I drove north through the smog into the Santa Monica Hills. Not the Pit, but its malign opposite, the daze. I felt light, as if a small tornado could whip down suddenly from Mulholland Drive and whisk me away, like eggs.

I was alone. No one, in the middle of nowhere.

Just north of Ventura Boulevard lies the grotty hamlet of Calabasas, which looks a lot like it sounds. And there, hidden discreetly behind a disused factory, lie the thirty-eight acres of the LA Pet Memorial Cemetery, run by S.O.P.H.I.E., Inc., or 'Save Our Pets' History in Eternity'.

In the car park I met Donna, the cemetery warden, astride a bright white golf-buggy. 'Have you recently suffered a loss?' she inquired, accusingly. I thought for a minute, wondering if she'd somehow heard of my break-up with Angie and my subsequent dalliance with Mary.

'Er . . . no. Can I just have a look around?'

'Sure. Climb aboard.'

There are fewer experiences more scary than hurtling around the pristine lawns of a pet cemetery on the back of a golf-buggy driven by a large woman with a fascination for dead animals.

Donna is evidently a caring and thoughtful person, especially if you're not a human being.

'We have many celebrities buried here. Stars of stage and screen, as well as the children of some of the most famous names in Hollywood today.'

Children?

Donna's tour lasted fifteen minutes. She was proud of the cemetery, which was immaculate, rolling lawns, shady trees, sprinklers and worrying notices every ten yards – 'Beware of the Snakes' (dead or alive they did not say). Flowers adorned each minuscule grave, with the odd cuddly toy or worn tennis ball as a memento of past joys.

Founded in 1928, the cemetery hosts some of the most illustrious dead animals ever to be buried. There's Tawny the MGM lion, Sparky the dog from *The Little Rascals*, Tonto's horse Chief Thunder Cloud from the first Lone Ranger series, Hopalong Cassidy's horse Topper and Jiggs the chimpanzee, who once acted Ronald Reagan off the screen and whose funeral was attended by Hollywood's elite, including Bing Crosby.

'The horses take some burying,' explained Donna. 'That's when we bring in the hydraulic lift.'

Then there are the pets of Hollywood's nobility. Dogs who once caught sticks thrown by Humphrey Bogart and Gloria Swanson. Mae West's pet monkey. And Rudolph Valentino's Great Dane Kabar, whose legend almost rivals his owner's. Valentino, it seems, took the dog everywhere with him, except on his last trip to New York where he died, at the age of thirty-one, from peritonitis brought on by a perforated ulcer. Kabar, sensing something was amiss, escaped from Valentino's house in LA and made his own way 3,000 miles to the Big Apple to find his master dead in the morgue (or so its agent claimed). He then accompanied the body back to LA, and gave a moving oratory at the funeral.

Both dog and master are still together as Hollywood's favourite ghosts, often seen hanging out in Rudolph's favourite haunts, such as Falcon Lair – his house off Benedict Canyon, Room 2210 of the Santa Maria Inn in Santa Maria, and the costume department at Paramount Studios, where he is said to be the spirit who roams the catwalks above Studio 5.

Kabar, not to be outdone, is the most lively resident of the Pet Cemetery, at least according to Donna. He has 'been caught panting and licking several visitors', despite having been dead for eighty years.

Donna became less helpful when I inquired about more recent residents. 'Our policy is to protect our clients. No one wants this to become like Beverly Hills with a map and all.'

So I wandered the grassy graves alone. The gravestone's were deliberately unrevealing. I did find a Stanley Jean Pfeiffer (yes, fellas, just imagine being Michelle Pfeiffer's poodle) and a plot belonging to Amy Irving, Stephen Spielberg's ex-wife. Following acrimonious divorce proceedings it seems that Spielberg insisted his dogs be exhumed from Irving's plot and reburied elsewhere in the cemetery. I tried to locate them, but no names seemed to connect the graves to the creator of ET.

The Spielberg story seemed to illustrate a lot about the Hollywood psyche. In a world where you trust no one, a producer's best friend is often his dog/cat/budgie. The grave inscriptions were painfully intimate:

'Buffy – Our little piggsy-tailed girl, you showed us the meaning of true love.'

'Ben 1990 – Jeff and Shanna's first child.'

'Pooky – Of all the souls that I have known, his was the most human.'

Which, if you've ever met a Hollywood producer, is not such a wildly implausible claim.

On my way out of the cemetery I stopped to collect an information pack. Included in the glossy brochure were price lists – $1,323 for a forty-eight-inch metal coffin, $300 for a laser engraving of your horse (head), rabbit (full body) or Boston terrier, $1,190 for a Texas Red gravestone, and pamphlets from two psychologists offering 'pro-bono therapeutic support' for grieving owners, sorry, parents.

Diane Kelley, Ph.D., was trained in 'pet grief therapy'. She had been profiled in *Cat Fancier* magazine and offered 'practical strategies for bringing an emotional closure to your pet's death'. She boasted two offices in Los Angeles and Manhattan Beach, which goes to show that pet grief therapy is not only good for pet owners.

Her pamphlets included an account of Cindy's cat, Sparkle. Cindy blamed herself for the death of Sparkle whilst she was away on business. Apparently the maid failed to give Sparkle necessary medication and food and he died a day after Cindy's return. As Dr Kelley explains, 'I taught Cindy specific techniques to help ease her anguish. She sent her friends handmade cards that included a poem she wrote about Sparkle. After two months of working through the grieving process, she was ready to accept another cat into her household.'

The final stage in Dr Kelley's therapy was 'the creation of a memorial to Sparkle' (which explained why the pet cemetery allowed her to advertise in their information pack).

Dr Maurice Resnick seemed less mercenary. He at least admitted to having lost two dogs of his own. And his advice must strike a chord with the heartbroken parents of every Sooty, Gunner, Angel, Little Cabbage and Honey Cinnamon Rolls to have gone to the great studio in the sky.

'Don't feel guilty my friends because you sense that you grieve more for your pet than for a person. The loss of a pet, in many cases, can be even more emotionally overwhelming.'

'BOLLOCKS,' I shouted to the world.

I said goodbye to Sebastian.
    'So Jim, how do you like LA?'
    'Great. It's been good.'
    'Any news from Canada?'
    'No. I'm going to call her.'
    'Do you think that's wise?'
    'No.'
    'Wisdom, Jim, is merely hindsight.'

'Thanks for your help Sebastian.'
'Sure. Anytime. I'm sure she will see the error of her ways.'
'I hope so.'
'If not . . .'
'You have a pool and a hot tub.'
I caught the plane to Jacksonville.

4

Wendy – Florida Dolphin Trainer

America is reassuringly big. I looked out of the window of the Boeing 777 (better than a Boeing 666 any day) easing across the continent from Pacific to Atlantic. Below was land, great tracts of land rolling, stretching, stampeding to the horizon. In England we no longer have land. We have fields, gardens and science parks, but not land like America – this untamed vastness that is geography, not sociology.

There were mountains, rivers, forests, deserts, plains, single roads as thin as hair strands that extended for hundreds of miles, alone in the wilderness. There were farmhouses as small as pinpricks, towns like plums, cities no bigger than a medium-sized steak. It's no wonder the Americans are a loud people. They have to shout to fill up the space.

I was going to Florida, the playground of America, because I hoped to play.

It was a revenge thing, I sensed without really admitting it to myself. Two Christmases ago Angie had flown from London to Florida for a holiday with her mother. She sat on the beach in a bikini for ten days over Christmas and I sat in Archway watching the rain vomit from the sky.

I was jealous. I pictured her meeting tanned, muscled American men (the complement to the European male's irrational attraction to American women is an irrational envy of American men). I pictured her going to clubs, drinking towering cocktails with umbrellas and celery sticks, dancing frenetically and slipping out with Biff or Brad or Randy for a stroll along a moonlit beach and a bit of how's your pop on the sand.

If you think I was an obsessive, and she's much better off without such a jealous mistrusting partner, you may well be right, but I'd challenge anyone to experience their own beloved going off for ten days by themselves to a sun-drenched beach resort renowned for its loose morality and looser clothing while you sit at home in the pouring rain, and not feel a mite insecure.

And now I was going to Florida, to the land of looseness, and I had the telephone number of the brother of a woman who looked vaguely like Meg Ryan.

There was one more reason for wanting to visit 'the sunshine state'. Beneath all the emotional stuff there was also a desire that dated from childhood: I wanted to see a place we as Keebles were as far away from getting to as Mars. Other kids went to Disney World for their summer holidays and came back with huge plastic Donald Duck watches that sang or quacked or recited Shakespeare. We went camping in mid-Wales and came back with mould between our toes.

Jacksonville airport was small and new, unlike Jacksonville itself, which is large and new. Named after US General Andrew Jackson, the town was one of the nation's top winter holiday spots in the late 1800s and a mini-Hollywood just before the First World War, when over 300 silent movies were shot around the city. Now it's vast, covering 841 square miles, and is a centre for insurance companies and the US Navy. As such, I decided to get out of it as quickly as I could.

At least the airport was bright and cheerful. I used to love airports: the fast bright sheen of travel, the foreign people, the hustle-bustle, the McDonald's Happy Meal because there were no other restaurants and Dad couldn't be bothered to argue.

Then I started going out with Angie and airports became places of intense drama. The heart-thumping joy of getting on a plane that would take me to her. Of getting off in Toronto and knowing that beyond the glass of the baggage hall she would be there, always dressed up a little but not too much, always a little make-up but not too much, always a hint of perfume. I'd not look at the glass – I didn't want to glimpse her with this barrier between us – I'd wait, my heart pounding as I queued to get through customs.

'No, I do not intend to visit a farm whilst in Canada,'

and through, searching, questing, desperate for her face among the throng. And there she'd be. A smile. And my heart would explode.

The alternative was almost as good – waiting at Gatwick (it was usually Gatwick – cheaper charter flights). I'd always get there early, just in case the plane was early (who ever heard of a plane being early?). I'd watch the arrivals board, the clicking of letters and numbers signifying the advent of people, loved ones, hated ones, indifferent ones, the air electric with anticipation. And then her flight would click through: CRAP-AIR. LANDED.

People would start filing through, families reunited, sons greeting fathers, lovers kissing briefly, not wanting to go too far too soon, the thought of beds beyond Gatwick yet to come keeping their hands from ripping blouse and trouser.

And I felt warm inside, as part of this human community, coming together from the four corners of the world, or at least Lanzarote and Toronto. I'd try and spot baggage labels, to see if the Crap-Air flight was out of customs yet. The first people would pass, tired but excited and then, miraculously, she was there, flicking a strand of hair from her face, walking towards me as if in countless dreams.

'Hello.'

'Hi.'

And the first kiss, hesitant, soft, strangely foreign yet strangely familiar and we'd walk to the train, barely yet wholly touching, thinking of a bed beyond Gatwick.

Needless to say, the return leg was a vile nightmare. Saying goodbye. The tears, the clinging to each other like parasites. Her walking away past the red postbox to passport control, not wanting to look back, but she would, and she'd be crying and I'd be crying too.

At Toronto, me going away towards passport control, trying to be strong, knowing she was watching me. I'd turn and wave, she'd wave and turn, and we'd be apart again, the walls being rebuilt between us with every step.

'Welcome to Gatwick.'

The three worst words in the English language.

At Jacksonville airport I stepped off the plane into a crowd of families and lovers and the human communion that has been going on forever and will forever go on.

My excitement at the prospect of finally seeing Florida deflated instantly. I sat down, hurriedly, on an orange plastic seat, and watched the crowds. There were far too many couples. Young honeymooners perhaps, arm in arm, hand in hand, lip on lip. Middle-aged couples, with children in tow. And old couples, grey-haired and impressively doddery, but still together, side by side. I wanted to ask them, 'You're married. How did you do it?'

What were their stories, I wondered? Perhaps their paths to married bliss were not as straight as their impassive, bored faces suggested. Had there been rejections, letters, trans-Atlantic crossings, fights with rivals, fights with alligators, bended-knee protestations, large cash bribes, abortions, pregnancies, sex changes, incest?

I'm sure, once you are married, that you start forgetting the story that got you there. But I was still in my story. In the middle of it.

I wanted to ask them, to find some sort of hope that Angie and I might, despite our seemingly hopeless situation, find our way back together again. To being side by side, one day, married and bored in a Florida airport.

Had some of them proposed, and initially been turned down? Had they run off to America for a few months, called one day to find their loved one in tears and desperate for their return, rushed back to Canada, made love preferably in a secluded wood, and got married the next day? Maybe one of these couples had such a story – now, forty years on, all but forgotten. If only they could tell it to me, give me a glimmer, a diamond sliver of hope.

If I was a goatherd in Eritrea, having to eke out existence eating maggots from a bowl of dust, I'm sure I would be far less obsessed with romantic love and marriage. But I am a middle-class, middle-of-the-road, middle-way kid. What else is more important in life?

I stopped at the bookshop and bought *Men Are From Mars, Women Are From Venus*. Self-help books, I was learning, can become a dangerous addiction. There should be books to help wean yourself off them.

Chapter Four
HOW TO MOTIVATE THE OPPOSITE SEX
Women are motivated and empowered *when they feel cherished.*

As I head towards the exit, I pass the payphones. My heart starts thumping, sudden and emphatic. Women are motivated and empowered *when they feel cherished.*

I'm going to call her. I'm going to call her. I'm going to call her.

I call her sister Tina.

'You've got to stop this, Jim. It's over. You have to face it, get through the pain, move on. There will be others.'

'But I don't want others. I want Angie.'

'Don't call her. It's harassment Jim. She could get the police on to you.'

Great. The Mounties would ride down to Florida like a posse after Butch and Sundance and arrest me for telephoning a Canadian citizen without a permit. Or corner me at Harvey's Burger Shop on Highway 10, from where I'd run, ketchup bottles blazing, only to end in a sepia freeze-frame as 100 men in red tunics blasted me to death with maple syrup.

She'd get the police on to me. The woman who nine months ago slept in my arms with a smile on her face.

It's probably time that I own up to a degree of culpability. Confession, so the self-help books tell me, is good for your bank balance.

Angie, I've alluded, had her reasons. There were the classic Bridget Jones, Nick Hornby reasons pertaining to the male stereotype – my failure to articulate emotions, my inability to spell let alone embrace the word commitment (one 't' or two?). But there were other reasons. More visceral:

1. Whilst Angie lived with me in London I had telephone and writing contact with another woman. No sex, no clandestine meetings, just an ex-girlfriend with whom I remained a little too friendly, perhaps because it made me feel liberated in some perverse immature way. Angie found out, and her confidence was shot. She went back to Canada and it took months for her to feel she could trust me again.

2. We'd broken up two years before. On the Wednesday she'd said she couldn't go on with the long-distance heartache, the bank-breaking telephone calls, the loneliness. On the Thursday I got on a plane to Toronto (hang the expenses, which were vast), waited for her in the coffee shop beneath Sunnyside Photographic and surprised her. She was shocked, but intrigued. We went for a drink and I asked her to marry me. I didn't have a real ring, just a crappy £12.99 job from Camden Market. She said nothing, but we booked into a hotel on the lake and the next day she was all happy and said yes and then I got scared and said hang on, maybe we shouldn't just yet, and went back to London.

3. I once said I wanted to be with someone who had a career they were really into. At the time Angie was confused, anxious and completely depressed about what she wanted to do in life. I forgot my words as soon as I said them. Angie didn't.

So yes. It was my fault too.

*   *   *

As I sit in a rental car office outside Jacksonville airport watching a large man from New York City lovingly caress the keys of his shining rental car, I think about John Steinbeck and the clitoris, a connection that is literary rather than erotic. Following Steinbeck's travels around America with his dog Charley, he concluded, I think approvingly, that the American male knows more about the workings of the Ford motor car than the clitoris.

'Come on honey . . .' the large man from New York City croons to his morose-moose faced wife, who looks like she's lived Steinbeck's aphorism every night of her married life, '. . . we've got a brand new Taurus.'

I decided to rent a Ford Mustang convertible, expensive, but I didn't care (I heard Oprah Winfrey whooping in the background shouting, 'You Go, Guy! You Go!').

The Ford Mustang is the ultimate American car. Like National and Debt, Gun and Death, Ford and Mustang are two words that combined reek of America. It's going to be perfect, I tell myself – America's car, to explore America's playground.

Then, as I swung out of the car park, the heavens opened and it began to pour with rain.

It's not supposed to rain in Florida. Except that it does, the state getting fifty-three inches of rain a year, which is twenty-three inches more than Dublin and nineteen inches more than Manchester. The rain is prehistoric, pelting the earth and palm trees with primeval vigour. Fat bedraggled travellers in shorts hold plastic garbage bags over their heads like yamulkas.

'Can't believe it,' said the man at the Amoco gas station. 'Been here five years, never seen it rain like this. It's a record.'

Happy to be participating in a little bit of history, I continued onwards along Highway 10 west towards Tallahassee, the capital of Florida (glad you didn't have a bet on that one?), and one of those US names that Americans employ to get back at us for making fun of their mispronunciation of Leicester and Edinburgh. You try and spell it.

I was heading for the Panhandle, which as regional nicknames go ranks up there with the Bog Country (western Ireland). The rain hammered down and I realised that God was angry with me for spending too much money on a Ford Mustang convertible. I drove on, the windscreen wipers clucking like worried chickens, streams of water running from the ill-fitting roof into my lap.

This, I mused, was the American Dream. Florida, the promised land, a land of milk and pina coladas, where time is measured in Caesar salads and golf swings, where shopping is a pastime and weekends don't exist.

Old people in cars the size of boats were hunched over their steering wheels, heads barely above the dashboard, driving at ten miles an hour in the fast lane, trundling relentlessly through the rain. Their license plates spoke of snowbound winters – Minnesota, Illinois, Michigan. It was a Biblical image, the lost tribe of the frozen north who, having slaved all their lives to build the pyramids of American commerce, had finally escaped to the land promised them by God, or at least Walt Disney, to die in tanned comfort.

One thousand people move to Florida every day. It's the fourth most populous state in the Union, but only the twentieth in terms of size, with a population density of 215 people per square mile (California's 187, Wyoming's 4.6 – although where you get 0.6 of a person without a chainsaw, I don't know). And most of these people crowd along the coast, leaving large swathes of inland Florida populated by snakes, raccoons, alligators and huge white men who look like their uncles.

Highway 10 cuts across this region, a wet wilderness, mangrove, figs, trees that seemed alive, reaching out to strangle passing cars. I expected an alligator to cross my path at every turn. According to a New York Times report, there's no shortage of them. Recently, just northeast of Orlando, a three-year-old boy was killed by a gator while picking waterlilies for his mother. Which just goes to show, never give your mother flowers.

Trappers had been brought in and officials were beginning to worry that the Florida alligator has finally lost its fear of human beings. Which is scary, since from what I could see the human beings of Florida were among the most fearsome on earth.

On the road the selection of dead animals was becoming increasingly more exotic, their blood running with the rain. I spotted armadillo, turtle, coyote, porcupine and a large snake, all mashed. It felt like driving through a wet blanket.

On the car radio, Phil Collins sang for the fifth time in an hour, then the news talked about a man shot dead in Tallahassee that morning as he held a knife to a cab-driver's throat. As an afterthought the weather forecaster announced the possibility of a tropical storm building in the Gulf of Mexico.

The highway headed deeper into the jungle and the only radio station I could get was Rooster Country 107. Rooster Country, apparently, is a place where men are men, women are gals and music involves a guitar and a slap on the thigh. 'We're from the country and we like it that way.' The songs all sang of love, usually lost.

'At the time it seemed like the right thing – breaking up, saying goodbye,' sang someone called Billy-Crud.

'I want to feel that way again, I want to hold you in my arms, let a candle burn down till I feel your breath on my skin,' sang someone called Tammy-Tits.

'I come from a place where girls look like Sunday and treat you like Saturday night,' sang someone called Lindy-Baps.

I felt sick. I once had a girl who looked like Sunday and treated me like Saturday night. I have never been as happy to hear Christian radio. Suddenly even Rooster Country 107 vanished, with a crackle, as if zapped by the Almighty.

'Do you need a friend to be with you to the end?' boomed a voice. I swerved, skidding in the wet. 'May I recommend our Lord.'

For the next twenty miles the only voice in the world was a preacher on Sweet Joy 97.3, 'commercial-free Christian Radio', if you don't count advertising for heaven as a commercial.

'We have a mission, God's great commission.'

'Tis so sweet to trust in Jesus.'

'Stand up, you're a child of God, washed in the blood and dried in his love.'

Followed by a crazed female voice that sounded as if it came from a woman who had just bitten off her own foot urging me to 'Dial 1-800 Psalm 23' – 'DIAL! DIAL! DIAL! And remember brethren, doing right is never wrong.'

Isn't that what Goebbels said?

As I drove I looked beyond the highway – American roads are so long and so straight you can gaze at the scenery as if on a tour bus, at least until you plough into a granny driving a boat or a large reptile – to the thick forest, to the darkness between the trees, the swampland where alligators, rattlesnakes and vast snapping turtles lurk. It is a place where a belief in a benign force controlling your destiny would be a big relief.

Peering into such murky primeval bayou I was struck that Americans aren't as simple as we like to think. We make fun of them for their religious beliefs, for their naive Christian fundamentalism, but considering much of their landscape I think I too might come to believe in the earthly embodiment of good and evil, in a devil incarnate living in the swamps who can only be assuaged by the offering of rattlesnakes to the Lord (as they do in West Virginian churches), gospel-singing aerobics (LA on a Sunday morning) or large contributions to anti-gay senators of the Republican Party (most Southern states).

Because in some ways America is a medieval place, where medieval religious thinking abounds. It is a place where the elements still kill people, where many are dependent on the land, and where much of the population has little idea what goes on in a city a hundred miles away, let alone on the other side of the world. And it's a place where many still think might is right, and that those with better weapons are better off (40 per cent of Americans have a gun in the house, 9 per cent regularly carry a handgun away from the house). The only difference is that medieval folks didn't pay one dollar fifty cents for a gallon of gasoline – this precious natural resource is the same price as Coca-Cola.

As I crossed the Suwannee River, a murky stream where devilish creatures undoubtedly breed, the preaching ceased and the news came on. Not just any old news, mind you, but 'Family News In Focus', a station whose politics seemed to suggest another famous F-word.

This 'public information' began with a list of the names and addresses of US senators with supposed 'gay-group backing' and an instruction to write to, call and generally harass them into rescinding such un-Christian views. Next came an impassioned plea by Charlton Heston for more young children to be given the right to bear arms to defend themselves against evil (presumably embodied by the other young children who bring weapons to school). The bulletin concluded with an attack on the organisers who've introduced a bikini component to the Miss America contest.

'Why can't we have the Miss America the way it used to be?' pleaded the announcer before the hymns begin again.

You know it's scary when Phil Collins comes as a relief.

I neared a footbridge, the first landmark in forty-five minutes, defaced by graffiti that read 'Trust Jesus'. As I passed under the bridge a car overtook bearing a bumper sticker that read 'Bitch Goddess'.

I reached the outskirts of Tallahassee by lunchtime, stopping at an Applebee's restaurant and having a burger with six couples in their eighties. They looked at me strangely, a single man under thirty-five. I had to be a serial killer, or at least an IRS inspector. My waitress, Cindy, was cutish and got very excited when I confided that I was not from these parts, but from England. She had just returned from a school trip to Paris. 'I have to say what I found shocking was that homosexuals held hands in the street. They even kissed. I don't know how they can let them do that with kids around. I mean, kids are impressionable. Their morals can go out the window.' Especially in American suburbs, where guns are kept in the kitchen.

Cindy brought me a burger and leaned close enough for me to smell her chewing gum – cinnamon.

'Sometimes I get sick of the old people,' she whispered. 'I

have to tell them to take out their false teeth before eating the ribs.'

She had a point. There are now more than 70,000 Americans aged 100 or more, twice as many as ten years ago. Most of them live in Florida. Most of them are eating in Applebee's.

Above the bar, the three TVs were all showing the weather channel. Outside the rain continued to beat down like a Charlie Watts drum solo. The weather forecaster looked cheerful as he announced the tropical storm was building in intensity, the first of the year.

'You might want to get down to Home Depot and buy that four-ply. This one could tickle a few windows.'

I sat in Applebee's for much of the afternoon watching the rain stream down and the old folks taking out their teeth. Despite the blue-cheese bacon double-egg burger I'd consumed for lunch, I felt disturbingly light. Like most eighties university students with any pretension to being pretentious, I had read Milan Kundera's *The Unbearable Lightness of Being* (actually, I may just have watched the film, but hey, isn't film the new literature?), but I'd never really grasped what Milan meant by 'lightness of being'. Until now.

Basically it means you feel like you have vertigo in reverse. You're looking up from the earth and there is nothing to stop you floating away. It's a feeling I could trace back to childhood dreams of being in a large room that keeps getting bigger, until it is enormous and intangible.

Maybe this is why we need ANOTHER. A lover. A love is a force that acts against the vertigo. Love grounds you, binds you. Maybe that's why we get married. Because otherwise we are alone in a very big room.

I called Mary's brother. The telephone mouthpiece smelled of false teeth and spearmint mouthwash.

'Seymour cannot come to the phone right now. Please leave a message and I will endeavour to reach you at my earliest possible convenience.'

'Hello, this is Jim Keeble from England, I was hoping to meet up with your sister for a bout of passionate but meaningless sexual intercourse that would restore my self-belief. But I'll call back later.'

Cindy the waitress suggested I head on to the sea, since in her eyes Tallahassee was 'full of dull boory-crats working for the goovernment'.

'It's real fun down at PCB. They got the biggest nightclub in America. And the best beach.'

The best beach and the biggest nightclub. You can't argue with that, even if you like listening to Family News In Focus.

PCB, or Panama City Beach to cartographers, is a resort on the Gulf of Mexico, an hour from Tallahassee. It had immediate appeal – reclining on the beach, a glass of fluorescent cocktail with a celery stick in my hand, awaiting the arrival of a woman from LA who looked like Meg Ryan. A fine dream, worthy of the American constitution. And if somehow Angie could find out, she might get jealous, just, at least enough to rekindle the embers of desire which I could then pour lighter fuel on.

I turned off Highway 10 on to Highway 205. Signs appeared offering peanuts in various stages of preparation – green, boiled, sugared, fried, buttered. If you're dieting or allergic to groundnuts the Panhandle is not the place for you.

Other signs suggested I invest in 'crickets and worms', although whether this was a dietary staple or catfish bait was not clear. Sidetracks led from the highway to small dark shacks where large pickup trucks sat menacingly and mid-size dogs snarled at nothing in particular as if practising for the Nastiest Dog in America contest, held annually in Birmingham, Alabama and usually won by a pitbull from Texas called Sick.

I neared the sea. This I could tell because the air began to taste a little less of peanuts and a little more of salt, which was not an unpleasant combination. Along the roadside, trailer parks appeared, then houses of the low-slung, clapboard, dead-relatives-still-in-their-rocking-chairs variety, and then there were laundromats and ramshackle drinking dens and nightclubs, everything you need for a weekend by the sea.

Panama City Beach is accessed via Panama City, although thankfully not the one in Central America. PC is far from pc, with its lines of bars and stripclubs with fading neon signs that wink 'Exotic Dancers' at you like some dirty old man. One read 'Nud hows', which almost tempted me in, if only to see those nuds how.

The road became a bridge, sweeping majestically over the lagoon and beyond I could see the sea and it shone in the afternoon sun and the world seemed warm and welcoming and I rode into Panama City Beach like Napoleon into Acapulco.

PCB is a classic American resort, by which I mean it is designed by Americans for Americans. There is none of the Germanic efficiency of Disneyland, nor the Japanese neon of Las Vegas, just a wide avenue lined on one side with low-rise concrete motels and on the other by knick-knack shops the size of factories and amusement parks with names that were probably hip in the fifties, like the Coconut Creek Family Fun Park and Pirate's Island Adventure Golf. There is nothing subtle or complex about it. It's the sort of place you go to not because you want to be thrilled or surprised or challenged but because you know exactly what you're going to get. The restaurants all offer steak dinners. The more sophisticated restaurants offer steak and lobster dinners.

The motel car parks were half empty, this being early in the season, but those cars present were all from Georgia, Tennessee and Alabama. The coast, I later learned, has the nickname the Redneck Riviera.

I should have figured this out for myself from my fellow guests at the Happy Waves Motel – large wide men with necks that could launch ships and women with big hair, big shorts and fat arms that made jiggling noises when they walked, with children who seemed destined to be even bigger, dressed in the sort of clothes whose labels read 'one sack fits all'.

'Cw'mon, Bubba,' Paw shouted to Junior.

'Cw'ming, Paw,' shouted Junior to Paw.

The Happy Waves Motel was concrete and painted a pink that seemed designed to look like leprous flesh when it peeled, which it had. Plastic artificial grass led down the corridor to the swimming pool complex where more big people from Southern states lay on their stomachs trying to live up to their nickname. Many of the necks on show were already a deep crimson colour, the sort of hue certain middle-class couples in London paint their living rooms. I thought of a new colour that I'd sell to Dulux – Bigot Red, resonant of the American South.

I sat at the bar, sipped a Coke and daydreamed further, contemplating the sign by the swimming pool. I'm not an habitual sign-ponderer, but this one seemed to contain a sudden and profound message: 'You're free to use the pool, but you do so at your own risk.'

In this one line, it struck me, was contained much of the American psyche. The first half was full of welcome, hospitality, and abundance. The second half was a qualification, a warning, even a veiled threat. It says freedom comes at a price, and if you think we will help you if you suffer as a result of exercising your freedom, think again Buster.

Such is the careful balance of American society, an exuberant, irresistible liberty, which a zillion-dollar service industry pampers to twenty-four hours a day, offset by a sub-conscious fear that if something screws up there will be no one to help and no one to blame but yourself. Perhaps, I wondered, caffeine coursing through my veins, my neck already racist-rose from the Florida sun, it is more this fear of failure, of the isolation if you screw up, that drives the American economy, rather than a lust for success and riches.

I departed the pool and walked along the beach, whose sand was the whitest I'd ever seen. It looked not unlike like powdered ivory or poor grade cocaine (I saw a picture once), thanks to the quartz that's washed from the Appalachian Mountains to the sea. My footsteps crunched as if walking on icy snow while pelicans swooped overhead. The sun grew fat and dwindled into the Gulf of Mexico and along the beachfront stereos started playing 'Sweet Home Alabama'. Honest.

I walked with the large people, sea licking my toes. In contrast to my experience at Jacksonville airport, I felt heavy. The Pit had returned once more, a parasite and a partner. Angie was there again, or rather the lack of her was there, like the empty place under the TV where a stolen video once stood.

The sunset was undeniably beautiful, the sand silken, the palm trees tropical; this was the sort of place Angie would have loved.

But she wasn't here. And I was. Finding that you can feel miserable in a beautiful place.

I tried to think of Mary, as those lost in the desert try to picture Perrier. But she was not a strong enough force to fill the emptiness that weighed in me. I didn't love her. I liked her, sure. Maybe I was even 'in like' with her. But that was it.

Mary was thirty-nine. And a sandy tease. And she had an annoying habit of looking elsewhere when she spoke to me. It was clear, even to me, that my pursuit of her was simply a banal bid to boost my own ego, which for some time since Niagara Falls had been in intensive care.

I ran back to the Happy Waves and called her brother's number.

'Who's this?'

A good question. And one I didn't readily have the answer to. 'Er, I'm a friend of Mary.'

'Mary?'

'Your sister.'

'Yes?'

'She gave me this number. She's coming to Florida? To stay with you?'

'Yes?'

'Do you know when she's likely to arrive?'

'No.'

'Oh.'

'She's calling me tonight from Las Vegas. Why don't you call back tomorrow.'

'I will.'

Silence.

'What part of Australia are you from?'

'I'm English, actually.'

'Oh.'

'I'll call back tomorrow then.'

'That would be best.'

'Fine.'

'Cheers.'

'Cheers.'

Fortunately for my travel insurance company (I get £10,000 in case of my own death, although I'm not sure it includes suicide by pina colada) that night I found Captain Anderson's seafood restaurant.

Located on the PCB estuary, Captain Anderson's is an historic landmark in these parts, dating back to 1955. It is regularly voted the Best Seafood Restaurant in the South by readers of *Southern Living* magazine who, I'm assured, are a pernickety lot. And anyway, I don't care if you eat there or not, I'm just pointing out that other people think it's good, as well as me. People who actually eat seafood, for a start.

In the parking lot bumper stickers read 'Proud To Be Dixie', 'Southern Gals Do It With Style' and 'Abraham Lincoln Was A Communist'. Inside the 650 seats were filled with enormous people, the air thick with the scent of frying fish, garlic and the humming buzz of voices, the lilt and twang of Southern accents.

I ordered some chicken, which shocked and appalled the waitress, but she rallied and with typical Southern hospitality inquired whether I knew that fish and seafood were the specialities of the house.

'Oh, yes,' I replied. 'But I'm an English Protestant. I never eat from the sea on Thursdays.'

She smiled sweetly and soon the manager was at my table. I thought he was coming to chastise me for not trying his scallops, but it transpired he wanted to say hi because I was English. Which is not uncommon in America. It must be the one country in the world, including England, where people are genuinely happy to hear you are a follower of St George.

'Gee,' Americans say, 'that's really cool.' And just for a moment you believe they might be right.

Jimmy Patronis Jr had more reason than most to like the English. He must be the only man from the Florida Panhandle to have worked at the Palace of Westminster, having spent a year as an assistant to Coventry Labour MP Robert Ainsworth as part of a university exchange program. 'It was great. I loved the way the House of Commons bar was open after hours. Kind of ironic don't you think? That those who make the laws about drinking hours don't have to keep them? I took a girl there one time, she was so impressed.'

I had the feeling Jimmy Patronis Jr was used to impressing girls. He looked like a Greek Tom Cruise.

'To begin with the MPs saw me as a backward redneck from Florida, but I soon changed their minds. When the Scott Report came out I was one of the first to get a copy. In fact I kept it. It's here in Panama City Beach, at my house.'

Which conjured up a nice image of the Patronis family gathering around the air-conditioning unit as Pops read to them all about Matrix Churchill and illegal arms shipments to Iranian ayatollahs.

We chatted about trans-Atlantic differences. He said the thing he appreciated most about England, apart from the curry, was the fact that things were not open all the time. 'I liked the way things stopped. The way you couldn't get what you wanted when you wanted it. It kind of made you think about whether you really did want it in the first place.'

I said I liked the way things in America were always open. The way you could get anything, at anytime, even if you didn't really want it.

He offered me an array of fish that would have made the late Jacques Cousteau weep with joy had they been swimming amongst coral rather than in Jimmy's frying pans, but I had to explain that coming from an island had made me wary of anything that originated in the sea.

'Shame,' said Jimmy. 'We've got some of the best big-game fishing in the world. Best time to cast your rod is when the hurricanes are in. One guy caught a thousand-pound tuna during Hurricane Opal using just a cane and a piece of string.'

I asked him about the tropical storm in the Gulf.

'Nothing to worry about. Could grow to a typhoon, nothing more. If the wind blows, should be a good party.'

'Party?'

'Sure. Best party I ever went to was during Hurricane Opal. People board up their windows, stock up on vodka and get on down.'

I asked him about the redneck image of his home town. He laughed, in a way I imagine I might laugh if an American asked me about the Cockneys of Islington.

'Call them redneck if you want, I don't think it's a negative thing. These people are hard-working, they save up all year for a summer vacation, eat at our restaurant six days in a row, generation after generation. People here are ritualised.'

'Good food, good friends, good living,' was my waitress Tammy's summary of the Southern experience. Or as Bob Valentine, a retired chef and local bon-viveur put it, 'We're ten years behind the rest of the state. But I think that's in our favour. This is a great place to live, it's real safe. We're stubborn at times, but good people.'

After a few more glasses of wine, I was beginning to feel they were good people. In fact I was beginning to feel everyone was good people. Even the Iranians. And the Welsh.

Then Bob asked me if I was married.

I looked at my sorbet. 'I asked this girl, she turned me down.'

Bob smiled. He was about to offer advice, and I knew I didn't want it.

'What you need is a night at La Vela.'

'What's that?'

Jimmy laughed. 'The biggest nightclub in America.'

We reached the biggest nightclub in America at 11 p.m. In the taxi from the restaurant Bob explained that in recent years PCB had become better known for its spring break party than its rednecks.

Spring break is an ancient American tradition whereby universities have a week's holiday in March so their students can study for April exams or more usually go to Florida with their parents' credit cards and drink until they're covered in vomit, in prison, dead or all three. Apparently, after Fort Lauderdale and Daytona Beach kicked out spring breakers in a bid to appeal to a more family market, family-orientated PCB had welcomed them with open arms and very liberal local by-laws concerning public drunkenness.

This, combined with La Vela's 7,000 capacity, brought in large numbers of credit-card-toting Northerners to dance like banshees, and with them MTV, who now broadcast live from the nightclub during the two weeks of spring break every March.

'The world's largest collection of village idiots,' concluded Bob.

La Vela was big. It had a giant outdoor area and four swimming pools, then six dance floors inside, and they said half of it was closed because it was low season. It was so big it had its own ATM machines. It probably had a synagogue and a Turkish bath too, but I didn't find them. I didn't have time.

Whilst there were not more than 500 revellers in the club on this Tuesday night, all were in various stages of intoxication, and I was happy to swell their numbers by one.

Bob had a beer, proceeded to tell me that in PCB it was always seventy degrees on Christmas Day, then departed to see a woman called Shirley about some ear-nibbling. He made that Hannibal Lecter nibbling sound before he departed and I had to have several more beers to wash the image of his yellow teeth from my mind.

With uneasy diffidence I eyed the young women dancing. They were attractive, in a brassy, freshly permed sort of a way, but they seemed young and independent and carefree. And I didn't.

So I talked to a bouncer. Bill Waretra was large in a way only those of Samoan descent can be. He hailed from New York City but preferred Florida.

'Here we got 1 per cent of the problems we got in NYC. People come here for a good time, not to fight.'

As he talked, Bill all but purred with happiness. Judging from his slightly glazed expression, he felt he had sipped from the elixir of the American Dream. 'It definitely beats New York. Winters here are nice and mild. I've got a pool in my backyard. I took up golf.'

That's Florida for you. Even the Samoan bouncers play golf.

The young women continued to dance while Bill talked of birdies, back-swing and Calloway five irons. I eventually excused myself on the pretext of extreme boredom (okay, I said I needed a pee) and after a couple more beers found the courage to talk to two girls who were standing next to me.

Me: Hi.

The girls: Hi.

Me: Having fun?

The girls: Yup.

Me: I'm from England.

The girls: Yeah?

Me: Yeah.

The girls: That's cool.

Me: Ever been there?

The girls: No.

Me: No?

The girls: We went to Mexico once. But we got sick.

Me: Oh. Sorry to hear that.

The girls: Have fun.

Me: I'll try.

The girls: Loser.

The last bit I didn't actually hear, but I could tell they were thinking it. I'd have thought it. What else do you call a single English guy the wrong side of thirty chatting up two blonde nineteen-year-olds on a windy Tuesday night in America's biggest nightclub? Debonair? Sophisticated? I don't think so.

Back at Happy Waves I read more of 'Men are . . . Venus'. I went through the 101 ways to score points with a woman. Among these were:

Offer to build a fire in wintertime.

If she washes your socks, turn your socks right side out so she doesn't have to.

Write out neatly any phone messages you may take for her.

Maybe that's why Angie dumped me. No fires, no sock-turning, and my handwriting is dreadful.

I fell asleep listening to the weather channel man bemoaning the fact that the tropical storm in the Gulf wasn't showing signs of increasing to the sort of hurricane strength his ratings depended on.

The following day was windy but hot. I woke with a strange excitement in my belly and it had nothing to do with Captain Anderson's cuisine the night before. I would ring Mary's brother after lunch. He would tell me she was arriving today, late, and would see me for dinner. We'd walk the sand (beaches being our Verona) grapple a bit and retire to Happy Waves to make happy waves.

In my newfound optimism I headed along the strip of amusement parks and inexplicably stopped at Coastworld! Coastworld! was proud of its exclamation mark! And quite rightly so. It was just the sort of tackily flashy place children love and parents loathe.

I knew why I wanted to go there. Because we'd never have been allowed to go there as children. Whilst the other kids went to places like Legoland, Bubblegum World, or All-You-Can-Eat-Cake-Mix World, we went to the British Museum, HMS *Victory* and on one memorable occasion a prehistoric stone circle in Britanny where the stones had been take away, leaving a circle of yellowing grass, which meant instead of growing up fat, spotty and ignorant (which would have been much more fun), we remained skinny and well versed in the burial rites of the Neolithic Age (which wasn't).

In the entrance to Coastworld! there were even more exclamation marks: 'Caution! All animals may bite! Please keep hands away! Thanks!'

Any place this alarming was going to be worth the entrance fee. I skipped through the gates like a six-year-old, momentarily scaring a group of six-year-olds.

To begin with I suffered from that sense of anticlimax that you're supposed to be able to deal with at the age of thirty. The exclamation marks seemed to be the most dramatic thing about Coastworld! There was a small pool for dolphins, a circular tank containing some small desultory sharks and a fat old alligator who eyed me as if viewing a pizza he couldn't quite afford.

Feeding time brought me and the six-year-olds to the circular tank while a boy who could not have been more than ten fed the sharks, which, judging from the way they pursed their lips to eat the fish, had long since lost all their teeth. The star of Coastworld! feeding time was a rotund loggerhead sea turtle, a refugee from a nearby beach who'd been incarcerated in the park for nine years (I hoped that like goldfish, turtles had very short memories) and was reliably presumed to be thirty-five years old.

Thirty-five years old. This turtle was older than me. I felt suddenly young again. Miss Liberty was her name, and she could, according to the child trainer, exert a bite of 500 pounds per square inch, which even to a non-engineer sounded like a lot.

'She'd take off your hand,' he informed us joyfully and I began to wonder about a turtle export business to Saudi Arabia, where I hear such talents are in high demand.

Next came the dolphins, who seemed to be dancing in time

to a song by The Monkees, thereby proving conclusively to me that they are not an intelligent species.

My fellow Coastworld! acolytes were a fairly sorry bunch. The six-year-olds had names like Wayne and Bud, and there was one little tike who seemed to be called Gob, whose biggest aim in life was to kick anything metallic. Their parents were inveterate chain-smokers with big bellies, short legs and mullet haircuts, the sort of cut a friend of mine came back with from Peru one year after confusing the Spanish for long and short at a hairdresser's in Lima.

Gob started booting the door into the dolphin arena with a tenacity that suggested a great future in the NFL or debt collection, and the dolphin-trainers appeared. It was at this moment that I realised dolphins aren't as stupid as I'd thought. All three trainers were female, in their early twenties and gorgeously blonde in that wholesome American way that suggests they're bred in some FBI laboratory for use in breakfast cereal commercials.

Wendy was in charge and I decided immediately I wanted to be reincarnated as a dolphin. She wore short shorts and a bikini and the chain-smoking dads stopped smoking while their wives lit up two simultaneously. For twenty minutes the children watched the dolphins bob up and down, whilst we men watched Wendy bob up and down. She was truly a great advertisement for American nutrition.

All too soon the dolphin show was over, and I contemplated waiting two hours till the next show, but a tannoy announced, 'The parrot show extravaganza – come and pet the parrots,' and the men hurried onwards, dragging families with them. If Wendy was anything to go by, Coastworld! had a highly intelligent personnel manager and the thought of petting a lithesome twenty-year-old, I mean the parrots, was a powerful incentive.

Of course the parrot-trainer was a spindly youth called Kevin with a case of acne that probably featured in several medical textbooks. At least his parrots were good – they climbed ropes, rollerskated (better than I can), swung on swings, line-danced and then raised the American flag. The flag-raising was the highlight of the show. The audience went wild, cheering and clapping as enthusiastically as if they'd just won a world war or a trip to *The Jerry Springer Show*.

It always amazes me how proud Americans are of their flag. As soon as you cross the border into the US from Canada, every house bears the Stars and Stripes, fluttering imperiously. Many houses have flagpoles bigger than the house, and some fly several flags. It's part of the desire to belong in this immigrant country. It's also, I suspect, because Americans have little artwork adorning their houses, and a flag is the nearest thing they get to the reproduction Van Gogh sunflowers that you find in most British homes.

American flags really piss off the Canadians. Crossing the border from Niagara Falls Angie and her family used to wince visibly at the first sight of a Stars and Stripes (usually at American customs, usually at least three times the size of the Maple Leaf at the other end of the bridge). Such visual over-patriotism adds to the Canadian sense of inferiority, to the extent that one year the Canadian government tried to compete by giving out free Maple Leaf flags, but people just used them to start their BBQs or as bedding for the dog. Angie's family used theirs more patriotically – her mum used to wipe the dishes with it after Thanksgiving on 11 October.

'What do you mean, you never knew Canada had its own Thanksgiving? Do you think we follow the Americans in everything?'

I drove along the strip from Coastworld!, eschewing the pleasures of the 'longest track in North Florida' at Hidden Lagoon Super Race Track, 'The Coast's Finest Mini-Golf' at Pirate's Island, and the Miracle Strip Amusement Park (where the only miracle would be if you managed to find any amusement). There also seemed to be an unhealthy number of waffle houses, which didn't seem to be the most appropriate cuisine for the high-eighties humidity of Florida, but might explain the girth of many of my fellow tourists.

Out to sea, a bank of clouds had appeared like that mist they spot in *The Fog* before being slaughtered in their beds by ghostly pirates with cutlasses. Such massacres were still some way off, though, since along the beach the sun beat down like a *Riverdance* tap-dancer.

It was one in the afternoon. Butterflies flittered in my stomach, as if re-enacting Custer's last stand. I wanted to call Mary's brother. But I didn't want to. In this Hamlet-like state I drove to the eastern end of the shoreline, where the motels stopped sprouting, and up to the gate of St Andrew's State Park.

Panama City Beach has the best beach in America, or so the tourist office tells you. In fact they're backed up by a study done for *Condé Nast Traveller* magazine by Dr Stephen Leatherman, beach geologist from the University of Maryland. I began to wonder how Dr Stephen got that title. Beach geologist. The study of beaches. He was evidently a very intelligent man.

Looking at a mixture of environmental, biological and human factors, Dr Luckyman chose St Andrew's State Park over all other American sand for the purity of its beach and the clarity of its waters. St Andrew's State Park is small (1,260 acres), but as soon as you pass through the gate (entrance fee four dollars) the resort vanishes into the swampland that people forget is what Florida really is – glorified marsh.

Because Florida is not paradise on earth. It's a place where it rains a lot in summer, where there are hurricanes, where most of the countryside is populated by things that want to eat you, and where you're more likely to die of skin cancer than any other state in the Union. Even the name is a sham. The state was christened by the aptly named Juan Ponce de León, who spotted it from a passing Spanish galleon in 1513, a sighting that coincided with Pascua Florida back in Spain, the annual festival of flowers. When he finally landed eight years later with a mandate from Emperor Carlos V to be a bit braver and actually set foot there, he found it to be far from flowery. It was, in short, a dank humid bog. Indeed, the Spanish were ready to give it up and go home until the French Huguenots started showing an interest in 1562.

The park brochure spoke of 'Original Natural Florida'. By the swamps, signs barked 'Caution alligators, no swimming' without the exclamation marks that would surely have been more appropriate here than at Coastworld! I remembered the marina's fat old alligator. It struck me now that the look in his eye was not dissimilar to that of a football manager who was once a great star on the pitch but who now contents himself encouraging those much younger to emulate his feats. Out in these swamps, the Michael Owens of the alligator world were waiting.

A more expansive sign explained that 'alligators have a natural fear of man but may lose that fear by being around people'. I got back in the car, locked the doors and almost ran over a six-foot-long black snake that I swear stopped, raised itself up and spat at me.

'Piss off,' it hissed.

It was a Miracleland-sized miracle that I survived to the car park intact. It was empty, all other visitors evidently having been eaten. I ran up on to the sand dunes, and gasped.

I wish I was a poet. If I was I'd have some super-lyrical description for what I saw, a conjuring of noun and adjective that would leave you with an image of such intense beauty that you'd sit down where you are and smile. Like I did.

Suffice to say the beach was white, the sea was blue and the two together were gorgeous.

Red butterflies completed the French flag, no doubt having escaped from my stomach.

Far beyond, in the resort, the rednecks were wallowing by their hotel pools. Somewhere Gob was probably booting the door of a Ford pickup, but here all was tranquillity. I dragged a wooden deck chair to the sea's edge and sat, listening to the hush of wave on sand. For an hour I dozed. I did not dream. My head and heart were empty. Even now I look back on this sleep with the fondness people usually reserve for love affairs, family pets or European Cup wins.

I was woken by spots of rain. The Fog had moved closer and

the wind swirled and spat at the beach, raping the sand, sweeping it, twisting it like string.

But I didn't want to leave, so I walked along to the pier where a couple stood arm in arm watching the approaching storm. They were an impressive sight – he in muscle-shirt revealing large flabby arms, a moustache Chewbacca would have admired and feet the size of penguins, she in tight hotpants from where her ample derriere protruded like a soufflé too large for its bowl. But her T-shirt is what held my attention. It read 'Jesus@pray.God'.

Jesus@pray.God. Was it a riddle? Or a subversive message? The answer to life, the universe and everything?

We stood ignoring each other as the storm danced across the sea. The rain increased. And still I pondered the message. Eventually I plucked up the courage.

'Excuse me, I couldn't help noticing your T-shirt. Could you possibly tell me what it means?'

She looked at me, eyes filled with pity. 'It means the Lord is found within God. All we have to do is pray to God and Jesus will enter our lives.'

'I thought as much. Anyway, thanks very much – have a nice storm.'

I called Mary's brother from Happy Waves, which was soon going to have to be renamed Angry Waves judging from the state of the sea.

'Oh. It's you. She's here. Hang on a minute . . .'

Mary was there. Early. Just an hour away, here in Florida was someone I knew, however fleetingly. A warm feeling of belonging eased through me like a single malt whisky.

'Hi Jim.' Her voice, as bright and shining as the Californian sun.

'I'm just down the road. Panama City Beach. I've been to Coastworld! You should see the parrot show . . .'

'Listen Jim . . .'

'They climbed ladders, rollerskated better than I can, then

raised the American flag. Americans and your flag. I don't get it . . .'

'Jim, I'm only in town for a couple of days. Work is too busy to take a real vacation. I promised Seymour I'd spend time with him and the girls. I don't think I'll have time to see you. I'm sorry.'

Rain lashed my window. For the first time I noticed a strange smell of rotten fish in the room. Or maybe in the hotel.

'But . . . I was hoping to see you. I missed you.' I had, sort of, but I hadn't realised it till then.

'Jim, it was fun in LA, but I think we're both adult enough to leave it at that. I mean . . .'

Adult enough. To pretend. To be like children, zipping from one liaison to another. What was adult about that? I don't want to be your friend anymore. Nothing had changed since the schoolyard.

'I mean, next time you're in LA, give the office a call, maybe we can have a drink.'

'Okay.'

'Did you give me your number in England?'

I hadn't. So I gave her the number of Arsenal Football Club's ticket reservation line. That would show her.

'Take care.'

'Okay.'

'Bye.'

'Bye.'

I went shopping. Maybe I have more than my fair share of oestrogen in my system, or maybe retail therapy isn't solely a female phenomenon, but I took solace in the flashing sign that read: YOU WON'T FIND THIS STUFF IN THE MALL!

Shipwreck Ltd is the sort of place that the word emporium was invented for. I wandered, dazed and listless down aisles of beanie babies, swimsuits, surfboards, rubber sharks, alligator toe necklaces and gold lamé thongs.

Outside rain pelted the streets with Biblical wrath. I thought about buying a gold thong and an Old Testament – aisles seven and ten respectively. At least I'd be well prepared if, as looked likely, the Flood came.

On the Old Testament aisle were a row of T-shirts emblazoned with the letters WWJD. In small print this Talmudic code was explained – it stood for 'What Would Jesus Do?'.

I don't know. What Would Jesus Do?

I asked the pretty girl at the counter what it meant.

'It's a T-shirt.' She had a point.

'Why, What Would Jesus Do?'

'Some people like it.'

'I see. But what does it mean?'

'It's a T-shirt.'

I bought a rubber shark.

Back at the motel the car park was empty. I went up to my room to find a note posted on the door. For a heart-shattering moment I thought it was from Angie. She'd found me. She'd be inside, lying naked on a bed strewn with rose petals. Then I thought it was from Mary, apologising. Then I realised I was in a state of delusional shock, and read the message from the management that said they were closing the motel since the tropical storm was said to be growing to near-hurricane strength and beachside properties were being evacuated. Guests were being moved to Happy Waves' sister motel, Joyful Glades, seven miles inland on Highway 98. I got my bags, said goodbye to the dead fish, wherever it was, and drove off into the storm.

The family resemblance between Joyful Glades and Happy Waves was remarkable. Only Joyful Glades was clearly the elder sibling – the pink paint had peeled even further, revealing damp concrete, like an old man's sweaty armpits.

My room was dark, even with the curtains open. It smelled of cigarettes and cheap perfume and was the sort of room where they find kidnapped women in Raymond Chandler stories, tied to the bed with an icepick in their neck.

I sit in the hollow in the middle of the bed and watch the blank TV. Right now an icepick to the neck doesn't sound like the worst thing in the world. Water dripping in the bathroom, drip, drip. Outside the wind is performing Beethoven, sha-boom, sha-boom.

Back in school we read Thomas Hardy and none of us, with all the literary expertise of fourteen-year-olds, liked the way he used weather to indicate mood. Pathetic fallacy it was called, and as far as we were concerned they were right about the first bit, because weather never suited mood. I've been to funerals on the most beautiful day of the year. And the first time Angie and I went out in Canada it was minus five and as bleak as Antarctica and we had the best time of our lives.

But on this occasion I forgive Thomas Hardy, because the weather suits my mood. In fact the weather is my mood. Black, torrential and depressed.

I turn on the TV and watch *Oprah*.

She's standing in front of a half life-size model house telling the mainly female audience that it represents 'our stock of self-awareness'. The idea, so Oprah tells me, is to climb out of the basement of low self-esteem and get on up there to the second and third floors. It's difficult, I feel like screaming, when the basement door is locked.

I turn over to Jerry Springer.

Jerry is berating some poor girl for still loving her man after he's admitted to sleeping with prostitutes.

'But he's a dog!' bellows Jerry.

'But he's my dog,' whimpers the girl.

I like Jerry. He's the only ex-mayor of Cincinnati I've ever had any time for. His show is so unreservedly American, illustrating perfectly my theory about the prime motivation for American life – the fear of failure. We all watch it with a shiver of terror – there, but for the grace of God and a few more neurones, go I. It is a show that revels in the most horrible of human failures, and that's why we like it. It's catharsis, easing our own fears about washing out. It's also great drama. Shakespeare would have loved it, all that internecine rivalry and fisticuffs, with Jerry as his Puck. If Jerry had been around in the sixteenth century he'd have had those

Capulets and Montagues on his show in a second, and they'd have fought live on TV.

'And so in conclusion, perhaps we can draw hope from the tragic deaths of this young couple, Romeo and Juliet. We can see that love is not constricted by mere human boundaries, but flourishes still in the hearts of the young people of Verona.'

I remember reading an interview with Richard Dominick, executive producer on Jerry's show. It was the purest argument for entertainment I've ever heard, and as sick as they come. 'I don't think I can be shocked. If I could execute a criminal on air, I would do it. If a serial killer is gonna die and Huntsville, Texas says you can kill him on your show I would kill him on our show. I would show him in every second of his death throes. And I'd have them from every camera angle. So there's no line to cross. If I think it's good TV I would do it.'

Jerry ends and Judge Judy comes on to mediate in an argument between two failed lovers. The woman is suing the man for causing her to eat too much after they split up. She now weighs 290 pounds.

I go to the bathroom and weigh myself. I've put on eight pounds in four weeks.

I pick up the phone and dial Angie's number. It rings for a second before I slam the receiver down.

WHAT AM I THINKING?!!!!!!

This needs more exclamation marks than Coastworld! More exclamation marks than 'Get Your Way! Needs! Desires! Explained!'.

BUT I NEED TO TALK TO HER IF WE'RE EVER GOING TO GET BACK TOGETHER!!!!!

Where is Jerry to tell me to believe in my love? Where is Oprah to tell me to get to the loft attic of self-esteem?

I pick up the phone – the angry buzz of the dial tone seems to say, 'Make up your mind buddy, I'm tired of this pissing around.'

I'm gripped, instantly, by heart-pounding fear. She's found someone else. That's what they say isn't it? No one just splits up with someone because of them. They split up because there's someone else.

An Italian.

She always wanted me to be more Italian.

But she never liked Italian men.

I'd call, he'd pick up the phone, confirming all my fears, laughing down the line. 'So you're the *mangia-cake*. The English cake-eater. Angie's told me all about you. So it's true about Englishmen in bed, hey Jimmy boy?'

Thunder shakes the Joyful Glades, the lights crackling off for a moment then fizzing back on. Thomas Hardy could not have written the storm better. It is pathetic pathetic fallacy.

I dial, the phone rings. And rings. So distant and so near.

'Hello?'

My heart stops. 'Please, Angie, don't put the phone down. Just let me talk . . .'

Silence. I can't even hear her breathing.

'I miss you so much.'

Nothing. Perhaps she's put the phone down.

'I'm so sorry for the past, but I've changed, I know my feelings now, I know how much I love you, you are the most important thing in my life.'

Still she is silent. I keep going, the condemned man pleading for his life.

'I was wrong, in the past, I denied my feelings, I sensed my love for you but wouldn't let it out, I will listen to you, I will share everything with you, I'm yours.'

Thunder once again. I wonder if she can hear it.

'It's funny, Angie, ironic maybe, that I'm more the man you always wanted me to be now, now that you don't want me anymore.'

'I can't want you, Jim. I can't. I can't go through the pain any more.' Her voice. That I've heard so many times in my head, now real.

'I won't hurt you ever again.'

'I can't know that, Jim. I can't believe that. Maybe there's just some things you have to let go.'

I can't breathe, the room so stifling, charged with demonic spirits, electricity snarling in the air. I'm crying, I can't help it, sobbing gulps of heavy humid air.

'Why? Why do we have to let it go? Seven years of our lives. We were so close. You wanted it, I fucked it up, now I know I want it more than anything, and you don't want it any more.'

'I'm so sorry Jim. But this is the last time. I'm moving, leaving the city and I've told everyone not to tell you where I'm going. I need to make a new start. I wish you well, Jim. You'll find someone.'

'I DON'T WANT SOMEONE! I WANT YOU!'

'Goodbye, Jim Keeble.'

I sit on the verandah in the rain, tears streaming, rain streaming and hope that this is the Flood, the end of it all, because that would be better than how I feel right now.

I feel like Florida. A damp, rotten swamp of a man.

There is only one thing for it: to get up and stand in the middle of the parking lot with a twisted coat hanger and hope that lightning strikes. Or to call Almost-Married Stan.

I called Almost-Married Stan.

5

Madeline – A Washington Single

There are more single women per capita in Washington, DC than any other city in America. Or so Almost-Married Stan told me on the phone.

'Get on a plane, Jim. I personally know six women who would swoon to dine with you. It's going to be all right.'

Stan is American, a lawyer and he makes more money than Al Gore. And he's almost married to long-term girlfriend lovely Meg. Which makes him a lucky man and if he wasn't an old friend from University days I'm sure I'd have no problem hating him. But he's practical and compassionate, and has supported me through the lofty peaks and deep dark holes of my relationship with Angie.

Whilst the thought of staying with a lovestruck couple on the cusp of marriage filled me with self-pitying dread, it had to be better than dying in the Joyful Glades Motel. When they wanted a cuddle, I could just go for a long walk. Like Captain Oates, or a dying elephant.

I got on a plane, which in America is as easy as getting on a British bus – you turn up, pay for your ticket and get on the next one that arrives at the stop, only American planes are more frequent.

In the airport, the *Jacksonville Times-Union* had a headline about a local couple who had the first kiss of their lives on their wedding day.

'It just brought us together. It was wonderful,' said the bride-groom.

'We found other weddings we went to lacked something special, because the couple had kissed before,' said the bride.

'In this age, I think it's weird,' said the bridegroom's mother.

The plane ride from Jacksonville to Washington was bumpy, in the same way hurtling down Ben Nevis on a tea tray is bumpy. The pilot informed us we were being buffeted by 100-mile-an-hour winds, which I suppose was meant to reassure me by providing a scientific answer for why I was now covered in weak American coffee.

For someone who's rationally scared of flying (what's irrational about the fear of plummeting 30,000 feet to your death in a tin sausage accompanied by fat men in suits, I ask you?), I was strangely calm. The prospect of imminent demise in a blaze of screaming mutual fund managers didn't seem so bad. Death itself, as the man Hamlet once pointed out, would at least mean the pain would stop.

Whilst stewardesses staggered past, wrestling drink-carts as if they were alligators, I sat, silently staring at my *Washington Post*. One advert in particular held my attention:

Super Shag Sale! Today only 20% off.

Super Sex Pill. Herbal V 'featuring the Ultra Pleasure Delivery System'.

You just take two tablets one hour before sex and BINGO! The night of your life!

SHAG LIKE A PRO BABY!

A middle-aged man grinned out at me from the page. His name was Tyler, or Brad, or Webster. You could tell. He lived in the suburbs of some nondescript East Coast town and his idea of a fun night out was a trip to the local Roadhouse to hit on college girls who'd laugh in his face by the end of the evening.

In ten years' time, Webster would be me.

I finished the *Washington Post*. The plane skipped and dived. The stewardesses tangoed with coffee-carts.

I began to flick through the magazine that you find in every

US airplane, always more prominently displayed than the safety instructions – *Inflight Shopper*!

Inflight Shopper is a miracle of our age – hundreds of helpful consumer durables carefully crafted to make our lives a little bit easier, dozens of small plastic items to ensure the twenty-first century surpasses all others.

Can't live without air-conditioning? Wear a Personal Cooling System™! You place a few ounces of water in our specially contoured necklace and a tiny quiet fan creates a gentle breeze and evaporative cooling. Your entire body enjoys up to four hours of relief. Only $49.

I ordered three. After all, summer was just round the corner.

In Washington they'd changed the airport's name. National airport had now been christened Ronald Reagan National airport after several years of heated debate in Congress, during which time major healthcare legislation was understandably put on a back burner. The irony of one of the country's major air-traffic hubs being named after a man who couldn't remember where China was seemed to be lost on everyone but me and Almost-Married Stan.

'It's just an encouragement to every dumb-ass actor in America. It says, get your lines right and we'll name a national institution after you. What next? The Barry White House? The Rock Hudson River?'

It was good to see Almost-Married Stan.

We drove from the airport along huge freeways clogged with traffic. Everyone in Washington seemed to be driving a Sports Utility Vehicle with tinted windows, except those who were driving limousines with tinted windows. Such tintedness reeked of secrecy – a not inappropriate scent for the powerbase of the most powerful country on earth.

We passed a turn-off for the Pentagon, then drove through leafy glades to suburban Bethesda, where the powerful people who work in the powerbase of the most powerful country on earth live. The houses were all huge, hidden down tree-thick lanes. Large dogs barked presidentially. Big lights flashed on and followed our car.

My first night with Stan and Meg was full of human warmth and kindness.

'She's a bitch. She doesn't deserve you.'

'You're much better off. Now you can find a nice girlfriend.'

'Canadians. What did they ever do for the world?'

Invent basketball, give us Jim Carrey and the woman I love, I said to myself, trying not to cry myself to sleep for fear of waking the cat.

The next few days I rose late, stared at the telephone and imagined my finger on the numbers that would connect me with Toronto.

Progress report: I only dialled twice in two days. Oh, and a third time, which I let ring and ring until someone picked up the receiver. 'This number is no longer in service.'

This relationship is no longer in service.

Over several beers that night (who said American beer is pisswater? Five pints of Samuel Adams dark ale screws you up as much as any mega-strength Carling or Fetid Dog Bitter), Almost-Married Stan told me I had to cut myself off from Angie. His theory went something like this:

'You move on in life. Leave the past behind. It's like chicken-pox. You can't have it again. Any relationship that broke up, I made a point of never seeing the woman again. Over, finished, period.'

'It's easy for you – you're going to marry the woman you love.'

'When it comes to failed relationships, nostalgia is bad for you.'

'Failed?'

'Well . . . put it this way, she's said she never wants to see you again, she's left town and refused to tell you where she's gone. As a lawyer I would have to advise you against associating your present situation with the word "success".'

He was right, of course. I had to accept the grim reality. The death. The finality. The word 'failed' has never been one of my favourites.

When do you realise there's a point at which you cannot go back? At which you cannot resurrect the past? At which you have to go on, regardless? It's different for different things. A pilot crossing the Atlantic knows exactly the map reference from where he or she has to fly on to America rather than turn back to Ireland. In football it's that moment towards the end of the season when you realise your team will be relegated even if they win their last five games 33–0. The soldier getting off the boat on to the D-Day beaches reached the point of no return pretty quickly.

But relationships are different. There are no obvious map references, points differentials or bullets flying over your head. It's murky, blurred. It still felt, at least to me, that my love with Angie could be repaired. Like a damaged boot. Or a defective heart. But even I had to admit that in the league of love my team was going down even if they signed a Brazilian centre-forward with a free-kick like a donkey's willy.

I spent a happy five days of despondency being nourished and nurtured by good friends. Stan and Meg cut back heroically on their snogging, partaking in semi-private canoodling around corners, behind closed doors, by the car after I'd waved them off to work, apart from that time in the kitchen when they thought I was out and I wandered in to find them exchanging tonsils by the popcorn-maker.

'Sorry.'

'Sorry.'

'Sorry.'

My one solace, apart from long walks in the spring sunshine seeing how many large dogs I could annoy to the point of wrapping their leashes and ultimately themselves around birch trees, were the commercials on daytime TV. If you want to understand America, you could do worse than study these.

'The days of wearingpoor protective underwear are over. Buy Depend Protective Undergarments.'

'Invest with Honestblum Brokers Inc. of New Jersey. Save for the future, or your children will die of starvation or at best have to sell their organs to pay for college.'

'Easy-Ass Hemorrhoid Cream. Sit pretty every day with Easy-Ass.'

'Massivecost Mutual Funds. Because the way this country's going the Government won't pay for anything by 2015.'

As far as I could tell, and I admit I was doing a lot of Vitamin C, Slush Puppy, Ginseng cocktails at the time, daytime commercials fell into two categories. The 'let's not be embarrassed about our shitting problems' commercials, and the 'you will die penniless and ostracised and so will your family especially the little ones unless you invest heavily with our dodgy company' ones.

Late-night TV was no better. To my great disappointment there was little or no sex. I'd expected, from a nation so forward about its arseholes and adult nappies, that late-night shows would be full of talk of orgasm and nipple creams. Not a jot.

Americans, in my most humble opinion, are repressed when it comes to confronting sexuality. Topless sunbathing is an all but executable offence and many states have banned breastfeeding in public. Even art shows in New York's finest galleries are picketed for showing erect penises. THERE'S 275 MILLION OF YOU! MOST OF YOU HAVE BY DEFINITION SEEN AT LEAST ONE ERECT PENIS!

After my five days of television, dog-baiting and snog-avoidance, I needed to get out, to see the boulevards and law temples of the capital of the free world. But most importantly I felt like seeing scandal. To see how other people had messed up their lives, and perhaps to learn from the tragedies and mishaps of others. We fuck-ups need to stick together.

Almost-Married Stan had suggested it. 'Scandal Tours. You see all the tourist sights, but you get the dirt at the same time.'

I took the subway downtown.

I didn't find it surprising that there was scandal in Washington, DC, nor that there was a tour of it – this is, after all, a country where top TV producers happily admit they'd broadcast executions live on prime-time. If people will buy it, sell it! Just be sure to add exclamation marks!

Scandal Tours was founded in 1988, inspired by Gary Hart (remember him?) and his fling with Donna Rice on the Florida yacht *Monkey Business*.

During the sleaze-packed ninety-minute bus tour I began to realise that American politicians might not do as terribly in the Sleaze Olympics as I'd feared. Okay, perhaps they wouldn't get as many golds as say the French, the Russians or indeed the UK Conservative Party, but they'd be in the top half of the medals table. Bill Clinton wouldn't even have made the subs bench when compared to some of the more athletic philanderers whom the great American public has elected to public office.

'Washington, DC – drugs, theft and prostitution, and that's just the Senate,' began an actor dressed as George Bush. 'This nation's capital was built on a swamp, and corrupt creatures continue to rise from the muck.'

The tour started in the Willard Hotel, where President Ulysses Grant would sit in the lobby getting drunk and demanding that 'those damn lobbyists', as he called politicians coming to ask him for favours, be removed from his presence, thereby coining a term and profession that makes Washington what it is today.

Then there's the city's namesake himself, George Washington, who never fathered any children, and was, according to another actor dressed up as Janet Reno, infertile. 'That's right folks. General George shot blanks!'

The majority of passengers on the tour were American, and reacted with mild shock to this revelation (impotency being evidently far more scandalous than, say, selling weapons to Iran to fund right-wing insurgents in Nicaragua).

Washington scandal dates back to the first years of the eighteenth century, when the British Empire's envoy to America, Lord Cornbury, lived up to his job title as the Queen's representative when he turned up to his wife's funeral in a dress.

George Bush, aka scandal manager John Simmons, happily blamed me for his country's sleaze in front of twenty nodding

Americans. 'It started back then when the British sent over all their freaks, nutcases and philanderers. It's all your fault.'

Ignoring the temptation to point out that Americans pride themselves on taking British ideas and improving them, I smiled sweetly and listened to further infamies. There was Jefferson's illegitimate black children by his slave Sally Hemings. Lincoln's demented wife Mary Todd, who once ordered herself 300 pairs of kid-skin gloves out of public funds and then paid for a state banquet by selling off a shipment of manure that had been ordered by the White House gardeners. And Lyndon Johnson's Chief of Staff Walter Jenkins, who was caught entertaining a young man in a YMCA basement, single-fistedly changing Johnson's election slogan from 'All the way with LBJ' to 'Either way with LBJ'. Then there was congressman Barney Frank, whose boyfriend Steve Gobie ran a male brothel out of Barney's townhouse, and DC Mayor Marion Barry, caught on film snorting cocaine in a local hotel room. And one-time Ways and Means Committee Chairman, Republican Wilbur Mills, who, when stopped for drink-driving on Kutz Bridge, was found with a stripper – Fanne Fox the Argentine Firecracker – performing in his lap. Fanne jumped off the bridge into the tidal basin to escape police, although 'unlike Teddy Kennedy's dates, she floated to the top'.

The more famous Kennedy was also mentioned on the tour (American sleaze without JFK being like American Foreign Policy without Saddam Hussein). As the bus paused at the Kennedy Centre for the Performing Arts, Marilyn Monroe came on the tape singing, 'Happy Birthday, Mr President.' For the first time my fellow Americans fell strangely silent, perhaps out of nostalgia for another, more noble time, before all this crass sensationalism, when presidents at least had some standards about who they bonked behind the wife's back.

Feeling cleansed by so much muck, I returned to the suburbs with a lighter heart.

Almost-Married Stan and I went jogging, the air warm with the promise of summer and his impending wedding in Minnesota.

'How did you know Meg was the one?' I asked, candidly.

'I knew I'd be happy spending the rest of my life with her. We'd be happy with kids, happy in old age. The whole enchilada shebang.'

The whole enchilada shebang. So simple. But I'd known I'd have been happy spending the rest of my life with Angie. I just failed to realise it soon enough and tell her.

As they say at the Olympics, timing is everything.

Stan arranged for single women he worked with to meet us for dinner at various restaurants in Bethesda. There was Kathy, a small nervous lawyer with a nice smile and a passion for English novels, most of which I'd never read.

'I love George Eliot.'

'Yes. Mmmm. Indeed.'

'I think Emily Brontë is, how can I put it, tantalising.'

'Of course she is.'

There was Shelley, a Jewish accountant with a rip-roaring laugh that started in her belly and ended at the tips of her fantastically frizzy hair. I loved her hair, but sadly her nostalgia for the Reagan–Bush era turned me away.

We went to the Rio Grande Mexican restaurant – favourite of George Bush and Chelsea Clinton – although rarely together – with Bill and Linda, who were about to have a baby. As far as I could tell, American women don't have babies. American couples have babies. They talk of 'our pregnancy', 'our birth'. I wondered if, during conception, they'd talked of 'our hard-on'.

Probably.

Bill and Linda were brimming with fertility, their faces flushed with happiness. I tried not to envy them, stuffing my face with chicken burritos. But I felt gutted. Not in a metaphorical, Alan Shearer 'We should have won and we're gutted' way, but in the way a large fish must feel shortly after arriving in a restaurant kitchen. No insides. Empty, even though I'd just ingested the carbohydrate equivalent of a rugby ball.

I hadn't realised it until meeting Bill and Linda, but for the first time in my life I wanted to have children. I wanted to have children with Angie. Little dark-haired olive-skinned kids who'd run around saying, 'Forget about it,' and 'Capisce,' while their bemused father tried to teach them about marmalade and free education.

I felt my eyes dampen.

'Are you okay?' asked Linda, her hands resting on the Spacehopper that was her stomach.

'Too much chilli.'

To feel better, I went to look at space rockets. Space rockets are a male thing. They please the male psyche in many ways, not least because of their phallic associations, but there is a more complex connection. Rockets allow us to feel like we're in charge of outer space. Until we receive the inevitable visit from the seventy-storey spaceship filled with superior beings that look like wine gums, our flying dongs are state-of-the-art when it comes to space transport.

And men like to feel in charge. They like to feel they control their elements, that everything can be classified, contained and stuck into a stamp album. For some strange reason women don't seem to have this desire to box up the world and put it in the basement, but are much more able to go with the flow, to perceive and adapt. They don't need to know exactly how many miles it is from Cambridge to Southampton, and how many minutes you can save by taking the A414 to Junction 21A of the M25.

Unsurprisingly, the National Air and Space Museum was full of men being boys and boys trying to be men. There was a satisfying array of inter-planetary penises. I stepped into a lunar module no bigger than my bedroom (hey, wouldn't that be cool, if your bedroom really was a lunar module? I bet you'd pick up women just like that). I stared into the eyes of an SS20 sabre intermediate-range ballistic missile that could carry three independently targeted thermonuclear warheads (great terminology – another male delight) and watched a live transmission from the Discovery Space Shuttle mission showing scenes from NASA HQ of a bunch of bored men in shirts and ties sitting at desks, as if at the office. Which I guess they were.

But the highlight for me, and something that made me inexplicably happy, was the piece of moon rock.

I have a great personal affinity with the moon. It is said that as Neil Armstrong stepped off Apollo 11 on 20 July 1969, so I took my first step on the shagpile in our living room. 'One small step for Jim. Oh dear, did you hurt yourself, Jimmy?'

On display in the Air and Space Museum was a lump of lunar rock brought back by the Apollo 17 mission in 1972. And you can TOUCH IT!

This is what America is all about. Gratification. In Britain you'd never be allowed to touch a piece of the moon. Only the Queen would be allowed to. She'd keep it by her bed, and have a quick stroke every night before retiring.

But in Washington, DC, anyone and everyone can reach for the moon and have it. The rock is 4-billion-year-old basalt, which is old. It feels very smooth and slightly cold. Which is pretty much how moon rock is supposed to feel. I stroked the rock long and hard, glaring at small boys who intermittently approached to cop a feel.

'Get away! It's mine. All mine.'

Out on the Mall it was a lovely spring day, the sort of day when people meet and fall hopelessly in love, at least until October. People were jogging in shorts, showing off white flesh for the first time in the year. The cherry trees were quivering with excitement, anticipating the next few weeks when they would reassume their role as national treasure during the blossom period and presidents, kings and movie stars would wander beneath their boughs marvelling at the age-old festival of rebirth.

I found myself at the foot of the Lincoln Memorial, wondering what Abe did when he found out about all those kid-skin gloves Mary Todd had ordered. He probably donated them to the poor. Abe was an unscrupulously honest man. No wonder they shot him.

Beyond, spring flowers were sprouting by the Vietnam Memorial. 'No running,' said the sign, but these boys, whose names seemed to go on for weeks along the shining granite memorial wall, should have done.

One of the small carved names: Augustus Edwin Keeble Jr. Born 14 October 1944. Died 28 February 1969.

Timing is everything.

I called home from a phone box on Pennsylvania Avenue.

'We're so sorry,' said my mum, which made me feel like crying.

'Is there anything we can do?' asked my dad, which made me cry.

The grapevine had offered up a bumper harvest. I told them the bare essentials. That Angie had turned me down, that I'd come to America to get over it, and that Stan and Meg were looking after me.

'Are you all right being with people who are about to get married?' asked Mum.

'Yeah,' I said, courageously. 'They try not to kiss too often when I'm around. I'll be fine. I just need a little longer . . .'

'You'll find someone else, Jim. You're a lovely person.'

Thank God for mums.

I spent the afternoon at the FBI, not trying to track down Angie's whereabouts (although the thought had bossa-novaed across my mind) nor checking out the marital status of French actress Emmanuelle Béart (although the thought had cha-chaed across my mind), but going on a tour of the Bureau's J. Edgar Hoover Building, a concrete beehive covering an entire city block, with all the charm of a multi-storey car park (much like J. Edgar, from what I read).

Arriving at 2.30 p.m. I joined a large queue. *The X-Files* has been good for business at the FBI. We shuffled on to wooden benches, an odd bunch of truth-seekers comprising several American families, some swarthy Europeans and a few Brits. And one dishevelled fellow with mad staring eyes who seemed to be the sort of person the FBI was set up to protect America from.

While waiting, we watched videos outlining the Bureau's activities, all of which seemed disappointingly unglamorous. Where were the exploding aliens, the Muslim super-terrorists, the flesh-munching serial killers? Instead there were crusades against computer, bankruptcy and insurance fraud, toxic waste and unpaid student loans.

The most interesting video was a highly instructive course on how to launder money. It was meant to show what a good job the FBI did in uncovering money-laundering operations, but in reality it was a step-by-step guide to the process, from 'placement', through 'layering', to 'reintroduction.' I thought about making notes, but then it occurred to me that maybe this was one of the FBI's famous 'sting' operations, and a camera would record my deceit and they'd get me on my 1991 student loan default.

After a two-hour wait (someone needs to investigate the FBI's organisational skills), I entered the secret building. Our tour guide was called Marlene and she looked suspiciously like a Martian. Her knowledge of FBI history was impressive, confirming her Martian status.

The Bureau, we learned, was founded in 1908 by Theodore Roosevelt as an offshoot of the Department of Justice. In 1924, twenty-nine-year-old J. Edgar Hoover was appointed Director to wage war on gangsters such as Al Capone and John Dillinger. Later the FBI moved on to Nazi and Cold War spies, and now terrorists in the form of the Oklahoma Bombers, the Unabomber and Eric Rudolph, chief suspect in the Atlanta Olympic Games bombing, who is still on the run in North Carolina.

Strangely enough, the tour fails to mention the FBI's merciless persecution of hapless Atlanta security guard Richard Jewell, the first person to be charged with the Olympic bombing. The accusation made by the FBI against Jewell was that he planted the bomb, then made a phone call a couple of miles away, before running back to the scene of the crime in a time that would have been four times faster than the world mile record. If convicted, they would surely have had to release him in time to join the US team for the Sydney Olympics.

Display cases consistently failed to illustrate such cock-ups – the inability to decipher exactly what happened to TWA Flight 800, and who was responsible for a series of fires in Southern black churches, and why *Titanic* made so much money. Instead the history on display brimmed with macho glory – from John Dillinger's death mask (with the FBI bullet exit hole visible beneath his left cheek) to present-day impounded terrorist weapons including a 9 mm MAC 10 sub-machine gun, a hand grenade, a mercury switch bomb and a lethal-looking nail bomb.

All this we viewed with much joy, especially the young children who stared at the guns with wide-eyed fascination. In another cabinet was an array of drugs from marijuana to heroin and LSD, to the delight of an elderly English couple who had evidently enjoyed such items themselves in the 1960s.

'Look. Amphetamines.'

'See the barbiturates back there?'

Elsewhere we viewed the Bureau's famous Top Ten Most Wanted list.

'Anyone recognise any friends or family, let us know,' said Marlene, half joking. Admittedly one of the mass-murdering drug dealers did look a little like my Uncle Andrew.

Top of the list was Ramon Eduardo Arellano-Felix, a Mexican drugs baron, followed by Olympic bomber Rudolph and the Libyan Lockerbie suspects. Each looked highly dangerous in their pictures. Each seemed in desperate need of a new hairdresser.

To be honest, the tour became increasingly more dull. Forget the movies. Working for the real FBI must be as interesting as a job with Glaxo-Wellcome, only with less free drugs.

Upstairs we peered into the DNA labs frequented by Scully in *The X-Files*, the largest criminal labs in the world, carrying out 800,000 tests a year. The equipment seemed authentic – computer terminals blinking, steel freezers undoubtedly containing human heads, super-viruses and dismembered alien torsos. But there were no people.

The labs, mysteriously, were empty, as indeed was most of the building we saw. Whilst one explanation might be that most of the FBI's real work gets done at its Quantico, Virginia base, I had a feeling there was a more sinister explanation, probably involving Marlene's Martian background.

She was explaining that the FBI can now take 'lip prints' from food left at the scene of the crime. 'People often eat or drink items during robberies,' she explained, and this being America I believed her – 50 per cent of adult Americans are overweight and by definition that means a sizeable percentage of American burglars must be overweight. Of course they'd eat on the job. I wondered if the lip-print test could be developed for home use. You could test your partner's lips each evening to see if they'd kissed anyone that day.

'I knew it. You're snogging Reverend Jessop!'

The final displays on the third floor included 5,000 guns the FBI uses to test ballistics, stacked behind glass like so many toys for Christmas. In a neighbouring office a woman was showing her newborn baby to a colleague. Guns, for Americans, are normality, everyday, as human as birth, and of course death.

The highlight of the tour was saved until last. Downstairs we sat as if in a cinema, in front of black curtains. With a fanfare, the curtains drew back to reveal – a firing range behind thick glass. This is, after all, the land where you're free to choose your weapon. The kids in pushchairs were trundled to the front for a better view.

Into the range strode Special Agent Samantha Barnum, more glamorous in a white trouser suit and coiffured blonde hair than Scully ever was.

I FELL IN LOVE AT ONCE.

She was gorgeous. I hung on her every word, which coincided with a most agreeable rise and fall of her breasts.

At the age of thirty-four, Samantha had been an FBI agent for twelve years, and seemed very much at home with fire-arms.

'A gun should be used to save a life,' she said before picking up a 9 mm Glock pistol and shooting a fist-sized hole in the heart of a man-shaped target.

'90 per cent of gun battles take place within twenty feet,' she explained, before picking up a 10 mm MP-5 sub-machine gun and blasting a melon-sized hole in the target. Which, to my worried surprise, I found incredibly sexy.

'Wow,' whispered a small boy. 'She's good.'

'Wow,' I whispered. 'She's a fox.'

Special Agent Barnum took questions afterwards.

'Can I have a go?' screeched one small child.

'Is there much of a kick with the MP-5?' asked his dad.

'Can we get a hotel room?' I ventured. In my mind.

Actually I stuck up my hand and nervously inquired what Samantha thought of *The X-Files*. She laughed a laugh that ricocheted through me.

'I only saw one, where they were chasing a big lizard. You know, the Bureau has 250 responsibilities, but UFOs are not one of them.'

She said she'd drawn her weapon on occasion, but never shot it. Then the mad-staring eye man put up a quivering hand.

'Are you trained in head shots? Because I heard there's an FBI killing triangle between the eyes and the mouth.'

I tried to get closer to Special Agent Barnum as mad-staring eye man cornered her with an FBI application form and his theories on killing people instantly with a bullet through the nose. 'Their whole nervous system shuts down immediately. I've tried it with mud rats.'

'I'm sorry sir, you need to speak to the personnel office about your application. They'll give you the address at the office by the exit. Now, if you'll excuse me, I have to get ready for another tour.'

With that Special Agent Barnum turned on her Prada heels and sashayed off through sliding doors leaving only the hint of gunpowder and Chanel lingering in the air.

Mad-staring eye man turned to me, eyes madly staring.

'Women shouldn't be allowed round guns,' he spat. 'Too unpredictable. The menstrual cycle . . .'

I found myself nodding out of extreme fear, and stood back to let him stomp off towards the exit office where I hoped a couple of large female FBI agents would take one look at him, lock the door and rough him up with a bumper packet of Tampax.

It was exactly seven weeks since the ice of Niagara Falls. Spring was gripping America like a flowery vice. Peculiar bright birds appeared, squawking with passion – red cardinals, blue popes and green archbishops, or something like that. Buds the size of golfballs budded, exuding the sort of sticky stuff usually associated with burst extraterrestrials. Everywhere jars of maple syrup appeared at roadside stalls as if by governmental decree.

Spring in America is nothing like spring in Britain. It's bigger, better and more springy. The transition from winter to spring is like two consecutive episodes of *Sesame Street*.

'Today is brought to you by the colours brown and grey.'

Then, the following morning, 'Today is brought to you by the colours green and bright green.'

It's as if someone, probably the Chief of Staff at the Pentagon, presses a button and the whole land surges into a state of fertility. Shoots shoot forth like missiles, trees sprout leaves like armour and flowers stand to attention like gay soldiers. Animals emerge from wherever they've been hiding during the cold winter – deep burrows or Florida – and start fervent mating. I saw an alarming number of small creatures screwing – rabbits, raccoons, skunks and a pair of squirrels that fell out of a tree, so energetic was their bonking.

With all this sap coursing through veins, I wondered if I might miss Angie less, if I might be swept up in the spring dash to mate. I made an attempt. I inquired of Almost-Married Meg, 'Where does a single man meet women in America?'

'Forget bars. The discerning woman hangs out in bookstores. Try Barnes and Noble.'

'You're sure?'

'Stan used to go there all the time.'

Meg was right. The Bethesda Barnes and Noble was sprinkled liberally with liberal young women. I ordered a nettle and bratwurst tea, grabbed a leaf-bark flapjack and settled into a sofa as big as a mini-bus to ogle.

It was, to be honest, disappointing. The sartorial elegance of the average Washington woman, as far as I could see, stretched to a black dress that looked like it had been fashioned in prison, accompanied by white tights and running shoes, making them look like a cross between Florence Nightingale and sprinter Florence Griffith Joyner. To cap it all, none of them seemed wowed by my pretence of reading *Ulysses*.

But I didn't care. I was secretly overjoyed to be back in a bookshop. My pulse quickened, my breathing shortened.

After a quarter of an hour I strolled nonchalantly towards the self-help aisle like a junkie towards his pusher. I couldn't help it. All those lurid colours – pinks, yellows, oranges, like so many exotic pills, calling out to me from the shelves.

I started with the more emphatic tomes, flicking through *Getting over getting older!*, *You can heal your life!*, followed by *Get your way!* and *Cure by crying!*.

Next came the blatantly over-ambitious *14,000 things to be happy about!*, and then the more elliptical *Don't stop at green lights!*, *One day my soul just opened up!* and an interesting thesis entitled *Why Zebras don't get ulcers!*.

But my enjoyment dissipated as I became aware of a more sinister sub-group of books. Among the happier, shinier volumes, lurking like plague-carrying insects, were dozens of highly threatening titles:

Men Who Can't Be Faithful! Nasty Men! The Myth of Male Power! It's A Guy Thing! Men and Marriage! What Men Want! 101 Lies Men Tell Women!! Men Are Just Desserts! What Men Won't Tell You But Women Need to Know! Men Who Can't Love! How To Make A Man Fall In Love With You!

Men, the books screamed, are useless. Not only are they useless, but they're nasty, mean, cheating, lying, retarded gits. One book in particular caught my eye – *10 Stupid Things Men Do To Mess Up Their Lives*, by Dr Laura Schlesinger. As I flicked through it, Dr Laura screamed at me about the stupid mistakes I'd made with Angie. Of my stupid ambition, of my stupid independence, of how I'd ignored Angie, of how I hadn't seen her feelings, her needs, her love at all.

'You were stupid, Jim,' she seemed to be writing. 'Always have been, always will be.'

I was saved from beating myself to death with Dr Laura's book by the appearance of Almost-Married Meg, who wanted to know if I'd found a soulmate in the cookery section. We sat and drank mud and blueberry infusion.

'Here,' she said. 'This'll cheer you up.' It was an email that she'd just received from a friend in a downtown law firm:

```
-----Original Message-----
Subject: FW: 'serious and systematic' guy or
total freak? Hello friends - This is an email
that a wonderful friend of mine received the other
day from a guy she knows nothing at all about.
She met him while out dancing and gave him her
email address. When he emailed her, she emailed
him back with a few get-to-know-you questions
. . . like 'What's your last name?' This is how
he responded:

   I am at a stage in my life where I'm looking seri-
ously and systematically for someone I can share
my life with. You seem like a nice person, and I
don't mean this as baldly as it might sound, but
I don't have time for twenty questions by email.
I met five girls Saturday night, have already
booked a first coffee with three of them, and meet
more every time I go dancing . . . and I go dancing
at least three times a week. I immediately rule
out women who put up too many barriers. I don't
do this because I think there's anything wrong
```

with them, nor do I do it because I'm arrogant. I do this simply to economize on time. I know that dating in this city is difficult and scary for women. But keep in mind it's that way for the guys, too. Most of all, remember that you're competing with thousands of women who don't insist that the man do all of the work of establishing a connection. And they live closer. Now, maybe you'll find someone who's so taken by a single dance with you that he's willing to negotiate by email for a chance to trek to your suburban hideout to plead his case. But you might not. And if such a person does exist, and you do happen to cross paths with him, what do you imagine a guy that desperate would have to offer?

'So, you see Jim, compared to most of the bastards out there, you're an angel.'

'Thanks. I feel much better.'

But, of course, I didn't. Which is why, the very next day, I signed up for the *Washington Post* Singles Party.

It was a rash decision, I know. There I was, sitting with a coffee reading the English soccer results and pretending to understand the political pages of the *Washington Post* when the advert caught my eye. It was two pages on from Larry Flynt's full page ad offering $1 million to anyone who could provide 'documentary evidence of illicit sexual relations with a Congressman, Senator or other prominent officeholder'.

'Don't stay Single! Come to the *Washington Post* Singles Party!'

A singles party. In Washington, DC. Where there are more single women per capita than . . . Yabadabadoo.

I'd never been to a singles night before. Was there a dress code? Would I be expected to have sex on a first date? If I got married to a woman I met at the party would I owe the *Washington Post* a bonus payment on top of the forty dollars that I was about to slap on the Visa?

I called the booking line. The party, said the woman on the end of the line, was to be held at the Washington Hotel.

'Where's that?' I asked.

'Don't ask me. I'm in North Dakota.'

She gave me a toll-free number, which I called.

Beth was in Minneapolis. She didn't have a clue where the party was either.

The Almost-Marrieds were sceptically encouraging.

'Should be fun.'

'Just be yourself.'

'But Jim, you must beware of GHB.'

'Do you mean GBH?'

'No. What's GBH?'

'Grievous bodily harm. A criminal charge in Britain. What's GHB?'

'Gamma-hydroxybutyrate. It's a nutrient found naturally in every cell in the human body, but taken in strong doses it weirds you out. It's the date-rape drug.'

'The what?'

Almost-Married Stan looked at me as if I'd just admitted I thought the world was flat. 'The DEA list GHB as one of the most prevalent drugs in America. People slip it in your drink, and – bingo – it increases dopamine in the brain, thereby making you more open to sex. Strong doses can make someone pass out in fifteen minutes and fall into a coma within half an hour. That's when they get drilled.'

Apparently dating had changed since I first sidled up to a girl at Shelford Rugby Club disco and mumbled, 'Wanna dance?' while George Michael whined 'Careless Whisper'.

They say you know you've been given GHB because of the side effects, which are listed as nausea, amnesia, hallucinations, altered heart rate and convulsions. Much like sex itself, in my experience.

I am on the Metro's red line, heading downtown on the first hot night of the year. Men try to hold their thick woollen coats while simultaneously loosening their ties. Women dab their cheeks as mascara melts. Children are thinking about ice cream, women about bikinis and men about breasts. The scent of sweat mixes with a dozen cheap deodorants. It's the sort of night men take out their saxophones and sit in apartment block windows playing a lazy blues, the sort of night you step out of your clothes with your loved one and dance naked in the dark. Or so I'm told.

I am a single. I'm going to The Great Night of Sadness (my title, not theirs), to my first ever singles party. I am 'coming out'.

What sort of desperate, hopeless, bag-over-the-head loser would pay forty dollars to go to a party full of other lost causes? Forty dollars where I come from is twenty-five pounds. I'm not sure I'd pay twenty-five pounds to see Emmanuelle Béart naked, let alone to just chat in a mindless way with someone I'll never want to see again.

I exit the subway feeling nervous. The way people were looking at me on the train, they knew. They knew where I was going, what I was admitting to.

THIS IS NOT ME.

But, here, now, tonight, it is. I make my way to the Washington Hotel, the erect white column of the Washington Monument shining through the darkness – a warning, or encouragement?

As I enter the hotel, a cab pulls up and three middle-aged women in evening dresses and pearls get out. The ballroom is downstairs. Which is where the three women totter. I'm wearing a scummy leather coat, jeans and a short-sleeved shirt. I look like I've come to fix an unruly boiler in the basement. As I hand over my coat, I notice large holes in the sleeves. The man checking in alongside me is wearing a Rolex and I have a suspicion it's far from fake. The bright-eyed twenty-year-old at the desk looks up, trying to hide his pity.

'Hi there, Jim. Welcome. If you'd just fill out this name tag and wear it. It helps with introductions.'

I take the sticker and stare at it. I want to write 'I'm doing this for a bet' or 'I'm a journalist undergoing serious journalistic research'. Instead I write 'JIM'.

It doesn't take long for me to realise I've made a mistake. Out of a few hundred people there are maybe six of thirty and under. Most are middle to late forties.

Out of 300 'guests' (or schmucks as the retail trade likes to term them), 70 per cent are male. Here they are, in the capital of the most successful country on earth at the beginning of a new millennium, probably some of the richest people in possibly the richest city on earth, and they're desperate.

Jennifer is in charge. I feel slightly uneasy about handing over my future to someone called Jennifer. She's mid-twenties and looks as if her high-school photo had the caption 'Most Likely To Succeed'. The fact she's organising a *Washington Post* Singles Party obviously goes against her projections for this time in her life and she's full of bitter energy.

'Right, I'm giving you all a playing card and you have to join up with the other three suits of your number. But only when I say.'

All around her Jennifer's earnest twenty-three-year-old helpers gaze at us all as if to say, 'Please, dear God, I haven't believed in you until now, but don't let me become as sad as these people.'

There are no windows in the room, so thankfully no one can see us (this is underground), but there are four massive chandeliers, hanging as if in judgement. On a large round table in the middle of the room is a food buffet consisting of Brie, Cheddar, grapes and a marshland of damp petits fours. Some sort of ornamental fountain rises above the buffet to give it a bit of sparkle, but it sounds like someone with prostate problems taking a piss. The whole thing looks like a bad wedding buffet, which must be a bit sad for those here tonight who've had their own bad wedding buffet.

It's only 8 p.m., but since many of my co-singles are older people, raised in an age when, if it said 7.30 p.m. on the invite, you arrived at 7.30 p.m., the place is packed. There are grey-haired old men. Older women still wearing wedding rings, as if to say, 'See, I was desirable once.' A few are dressed up to the tens, nervously trying not to eye up every member of the opposite sex, anxious not to give away their secret, which is a secret we all share here tonight, that we are nervous and vulnerable and wishing we were somewhere else with someone else.

The men are mainly on their own, the women in little bands, like muggers, two or three to a gang.

I have a horrible thought. These people look like my parents. I imagine my parents going to something like this and I can't think of anything sadder. Except perhaps my parents' son going to something like this.

It is then that I start to chug the free wine as if it's some secret potion that will bring Angie down the ballroom steps and into my arms. I spot a man in a cowboy hat and feel vaguely encouraged. Butch and Sundance would know what to do. Butch would wisecrack and charm, and Sundance would sit in a corner and the prettiest girl in the room would walk up to him and say, 'How about it, gunslinger?'

I wander towards the dancefloor with two plastic glasses of wine. The band are called Spiceband and they play a lot of old music, but then the average age here is pushing forty-five.

'Ohh, won't you stand . . . stand by me?' sings the black diva on stage. Is this Americans being ironic, I wonder?

'When a man loves a woman . . .'

I chug more free wine, which is becoming increasingly more tasty, and realise the only women here I fancy are the twentysomething workers from the *Washington Post*. They scurry around like Santa's elves, encouraging the sad old farts (us) to fill in *Washington Post* personal ads. We can do two for free. Any more and we have to pay.

This is when I cease to wonder about the *Washington Post*'s motivation for hosting such a gathering. Firstly, they must be making a tidy sum out of this night, knowing full well that us singles are liable to throw cash where our self-esteem should be. But secondly they're also attempting to get us all hooked on personal ads in the hope we will continue to write them long after the party (and since we're all hopeless losers, we'll never find true love, so we'll just have to keep paying for more and more ads).

I have to admit, writing personal ads is somewhat addictive. Jennifer's helpers provide us with a helpful orange sheet with guidelines on how to attract a mate through prose. We are to treat ourselves like a new product, and thrust ourselves on the unwitting public.

'Find a positive way to describe yourself instead of "exaggerating" the truth. Maybe you have freckles because you love being outdoors. Or you're a few pounds overweight because you'd rather sit and read a good book – making you a fascinating conversationalist.'

What about, I wonder, if you're a few pounds overweight because you like to stuff your face every night with chantilly cream and cheesy puffs? Or if you're butt ugly because your parents were butt ugly and so were all their cousins?

'Being specific actually spices up your ad. For instance, saying you like music, sports, and sunny beaches is less compelling than saying you have a passion for Gregorian Chants, the Boston Celtics and Acapulco.'

Best I reveal my love of 'The Smurf Song', Southampton Football Club and Sheffield balti houses.

'Nothing catches a reader's eye like a good beginning. So don't be afraid to try something like "Urban Cowboy", "Dashing Dentist" or "Ms Right".'

I begin my ad: 'Hung like a Donkey . . .'

I write five ads, mainly under the pseudonym of Matt Le Tissier, Southampton Football Club's star striker, then choose two to go into the paper the following Sunday.

They read as follows:

English man with love of wine and madness, 30, quests after Mediterranean princess to share deranged times. 25–35 preferred but exceptions for Royalty.

English gentleman hopes for fun/insight with happy woman. Interests from Sartre to soccer, tequila to *Trainspotting*. Passport holders only.

At my particular table our *Washington Post* helper is called Maxine. Since she's Hispanic and pretty and all the other women writing ads with me are over fifty, I find myself becoming swiftly attracted to her. She laughs politely when I say, 'Does this personal ad have to be personal?' I sense an 'in'. I try to remember the advice from the Barnes and Noble self-help section.

'Use a line like, "I couldn't help myself, I just had to come over and tell you your smile was keeping me from concentrating."'

'Take the ice from her glass, throw it on the floor, stamp on it and say, "Well, that's the ice broken, how about a kiss?"'

Or as Duncan, a friend from Sheffield, used to put it, 'Nice frock. Want a fuck?'

I tell Maxine I'm new in town and ask her what Washington nightlife is like. She seems appalled, as if some professional contract has been broken. The hypocritic oath between Singles Party organiser and single.

'I'm sorry, er . . . Jim is it?'

Yes it is, Maxine, because that's what it says in big letters on the sticker on my coat.

'I'd love to chat, but we've got to get ready for the prize draw.'

The prize draw comes and goes; some old couple randomly thrown together win a trip to Barbados. Spiceband plays 'Guantanamera'.

For a brief wine-drenched moment, I have an out-of-single-man-body experience. I stand, distant, watching the ebb and flow of attraction and detraction. It's like viewing a television documentary about dating. White-haired minx pretending to laugh with silver-haired foxes. Two black women talking to the only black man in 300 guests.

Then Madeline walks up to me. Suddenly, I'm back in America, a country where strangers take delight in accosting you and vomiting out their life on to your shoes. Americans, it must be said, are the least shy people on earth.

Madeline, in the first thirty seconds, tells me she's recently divorced, loves England, and goes Spanish dancing every second Tuesday. She says she's thirty-five when she obviously isn't. She says she teaches immigrant kids English. She pushes the point that she's been to London. And then smiles, waiting for the gift of a monologue in return.

'Like a glass of wine?' I stammer.

We sip wine, chat about England, then about America, then about London, then about Washington. Then Madeline smiles her winningest smile, takes a swift sip of wine and says, 'So, Jim, how about dinner tomorrow night?'

I stay quiet, like the accused, or an idiot child in some Dickens novel. Madeline seems a category A, prime-time nice person, but I don't have an ounce of attraction towards her. Not a milligram. I haven't the energy. Maybe it's an excuse, but I know it would be a waste of our time and self-confidence.

'Oh well,' she sighs in a practised sort of way.

'Sorry,' I mumble like a mollusc and move away, leaving her stranded, alone in the middle of the dead-flesh carpet, shipwrecked.

I feel like shit. Spiceband plays 'Stand By Your Man'. Jennifer introduces her 'find the other cards' game. I locate the other three nines – a middle-aged man called Wayne with a paunch and a taste for Looney Tunes ties – and two older women – a svelte velvet-clad dame called Lucy who throws her head back to laugh, showing gold fillings all the way back to her tonsils, and Sammy, a small dumpy woman in her thirties with a necklace Mr T would have envied. We smile, bashfully, chat superficially, then part.

I stand by a pillar finishing my twenty-second glass of wine and think. These are good people. These are nice people. Why are they by themselves?

IT'S NOT FAIR.

It's advanced Darwinism. The survival of the fittest (as in 'she's a fit lass'). Someone needs to get David Attenborough to come with his TV crew and specialist cameras to film such events. *Dates on Earth!* The new twelve-part series from the BBC

159

Natural History Unit. They'd put cameras in the canapé tray, and hide for days under table ten waiting for a rare sighting of a couple of Singles actually having fun together. And perhaps David Attenborough could answer why these poor *Homo sapiens* are by themselves, wearing stickers with their names on at the age of fifty, having to put their self-respect on the line at a time when they should be curled up on a super-deluxe American sofa with their loved ones, trying on each other's dentures.

It's heartbreaking, like watching defenceless antelopes getting mauled by lions, or leaves fall off a tree.

I look at them all, us poor people. I mean, maybe we have terrible psychological problems or predilections for bestiality, but it's more likely we just live in an age where if something doesn't work we replace it rather than fix it. Out with the old, in with the top-of-the-range forty-four-inch active-matrix shiny-knobbed satellite-compatible partner.

Us singles, we just outlived our sell-by date.

Two hours into the evening, I am legless, which is when Betsy and Paula come up to me.

'Hi Jim.'

They know my name because I'm wearing a large sticker with my name on it. I think their names are Betsy and Paula. To be honest, I've drunk so much wine I can't read their name tags, but they seem relatively pretty, late twenties and they look like a Betsy and a Paula.

'We expected a younger crowd,' says Betsy.

'There are only two good-looking guys here,' says Paula, suggestively.

'You didn't talk to anyone all night,' says Betsy, suggestively.

I am the Sundance Kid. I try to grin cockily, which seems to alarm them, so I ask, in my best slurred English, what they're looking for from this night of humiliation.

'To meet a good-looking, fun, intelligent guy,' says Betsy.

I try to look like Robert Redford.

'No,' says Paula. 'Me, I'm looking for the badaboom.'

'The badaboom?'

'Yeah. The instant connection. Like turning on the light bulb.'

The badaboom. Of course. I look at Paula with reverence. She is there, like an angel before me, a messenger from beyond.

'The badaboom. Does it exist?'

'Sure. You've just got to keep looking.'

I left the *Washington Post* Singles Party shortly after. How many others left alone, I do not know. Some were clearly destined to go home together, the way they were clinging to each other on the dancefloor like fighting pitbulls while the Spiceband played 'Lady in Red'. How many of them woke up happy together?

To my great lack of surprise, there were many better-looking, more interesting people on the subway home. Here, I realised, I had just as much chance of finding true love for $1.75.

In a neighbouring seat I listened to a man talking to his female work colleague.

'You have to enjoy spending time with yourself, or no one's going to enjoy spending time with you.'

The woman disagreed. 'I once went to a bar by myself. I was so sad.'

I nodded. There's no way round it. It's sad being single. It's a label, like wearing a rainbow badge if you're gay, or a seal cub if you're in Greenpeace. America, the land of the free, loves to give you a label.

Us singles are a minority, with our own codes of practice, our own meeting places. And as a minority we have our own rights (the right to stand at a bar and glare at the couples).

I came out tonight and it felt like shit.

On the last day in May, I take the Almost-Marrieds to see one of their favourite singers, Lyle Lovett, in concert, to thank them for keeping me alive. Lyle is on good form, and seems little affected by having once been married to Julia Roberts. I try to forget that Angie loved Lyle and that she played his songs every weekend, and most evenings, at least when she was in a good mood. We'd sit, sip Corona and listen to *Pontiac*, especially her favourite, 'Give Back My Heart'.

The past choked up through me like a fast old train, but I was brave. While Stan held Meg's hand tight, the music uniting them, drawing them together and easing them forward towards a honey-dipped future and their wedding at the end of June, I gritted teeth and concentrated on the present like a death-row inmate. The here, the now.

Lyle Lovett took the applause. 'This one is for every man who's ever been dumped by a woman.'

I smiled, despite the world. Summer was just around the corner.

6

Vanessa – A Croatian-American Girl in Virginia

Americans are good at summer. They have a head start on most of us: vast tracts of countryside to be summery in, not to mention 95,000 miles of coastline on which to frolic, plus more ice cream flavours than anywhere else in the world. The range of American ice cream flavours is mind-expanding, derived from combining unctuous, teeth-destroying desserts found in low-cost supermarkets to make indecipherable yet irresistible flavours. Because Americans, like five-year-old children, are never afraid to combine many ingredients in one blazing inferno of taste. My favourite American ice cream flavour, after much testing, was dark-chocolate-double-chip, honeycomb-waffle cinnamon bubble-gum flavour. Mmmmm. You're high for weeks.

But mainly, I suspect, Americans are good at summer because they're very serious about having fun. Along with the right to bear arms and the right not to know where the rest of the world is comes the right to play hard. You see it come the first warm days of the year. Vast hordes of picnickers, barbecuers, SUVs dragging huge boats, jetskis, horse-boxes, trailer-mansions and space shuttles. Because Americans are almost alone in the world in having lots of cash to spend on simply having fun.

Thankfully, the Almost-Marrieds had spent time in Britain and seemed to have obtained a somewhat Anglo-Saxon view of materialism – 'fun objects' are evil, spending is only justified on household items, necessary nourishment and property. They did, however, own the biggest television set I'd ever seen, but apparently a local Maryland by-law forbids you from having a screen less than fifty-two inches wide.

So it was that we drove to the beach, minus jetskis or caravan the size of Chipping Norton. We had, of course, packed a picnic, which would have happily fed Somalia. We drove three hours south of DC to Norfolk, Virginia and on to Virginia Beach.

'You're tapping into history,' said Stan. 'The first English tourists arrived on these sands 400 years ago.'

'God save the Queen.'

We resisted the temptation to head further south to spend a day in the cheerily named Great Dismal Swamp and after a merry hour or so stuck in traffic in Norfolk's prehistoric road system, we burst forth like a cork from a bottle towards the sea.

We pulled into Virginia Beach behind a station wagon sporting a bumper sticker that read 'Whatever!'. I liked the exclamation mark. It seemed an answer to the self-help book brigade, and neatly summed up my mood.

I was all wept out. I was numb, neutered, nullified. My emotions had retreated, as if into a small cave somewhere in my chest that even small, very thin potholers wouldn't be able to reach. I felt neither happy, nor sad, nor excited, nor bored. I found I laughed little at jokes, television or even cats trying to cross a road. Equally the sight of a Canadian flag or an Ontario licence plate drew little more than a nostalgic sigh from me. In short, I was blah. Blah. Blah. Blah. Which I suppose was better than being heartbroken.

Oh, and no one had called my *Washington Post* personals ad mailbox.

The sea at Virginia Beach sparkled like orange-peel Baskin-Robbins sorbet. The main boulevard, imaginatively named Atlantic Avenue, was bristling with cars and soccer players. I blinked, twice. There were footballers everywhere, bouncing Nike soccer balls, stretching hamstrings, pulling on lurid soccer shirts.

'Oh dear,' said Almost-Married Meg.

'I'd forgotten,' said Almost-Married Stan.

'What?'

'The Annual North American Sand Soccer Championships.'

Of course.

Every one of the 11,000 hotel rooms in Virginia Beach, it seemed, contained at least two soccer players. They were all shapes and sizes, from the smallest weediest Steve McManaman lookalike, to men who looked as if they pulled tractors with their teeth for relaxation.

We cruised up and down Atlantic Avenue three times, until Stan noticed a sign that read 'Unlawful to pass this point 2 times in 3-hour period'.

Opposite was a sign that read 'Be kind – live the gift of love'.

Finding a stretch of sand not inhabited by puffing men kicking balls proved difficult. We wandered along the three-mile board-walk watching the soccer games. To my surprise many of the players seemed as skilful as Brazilians, probably because, judging from their skin colour, they were Brazilians. There were overhead kicks, nutmegs, knee juggling, soaring volleys. Many of the players spoke Spanish, or Italian, or Croatian, or Greek or Russian. With such a huge immigrant pool to choose from, and more organisational skills and money than the English Football Association will ever have, it's difficult to see America being crap at soccer for much longer. In a decade, I'm prepared to bet my collection of 1974–5 season Topps Chewing Gum Football cards that the USA will have conquered this last bastion of non-American culture, and so they will finally and inevitably be the best at everything (except modesty).

We ate an eighth of the food we'd brought and dipped our toes in the sea. Our left-hand neighbours were a slender sculpted couple who seemed to have stepped from the pages of *Mr and Mrs Gym-Muscle*. Our right-hand neighbours were a family of flabby, happy souls with six picnic hampers who seemed to have stepped from the pages of *Carbohydrate Weekly*. There is, I mused, a balance about so much of America. Extremes oppose each other to produce a strangely solid equilibrium: Excessive gun deaths, set against the strictest drink-driving laws in the world. The world's most powerful superpower, in which dwells the most unworldly populace on the planet. More Nobel Prize winners than any other nation on earth, and most high school students don't know where Canada is (lucky them).

By mid-afternoon, Almost-Married Meg's Scandinavian ancestry was beginning to show in the sunburn on her arms. We packed up the remaining 87.5 per cent of our picnic, lugged the two-litre bottles of Coke, Cherry Coke and Sprite to the car and drove back towards Norfolk.

The state of Virginia made me feel homesick for the first time – everywhere there were signposts with British names. The first settlers, fresh off the boats, were a far from original lot. Having escaped religious persecution, famine and men wearing tights you'd have thought they'd have wanted to turn their backs on the motherland and create fresh, unique names for their rudimentary settlements, like Screwkinggeorge or Dazzle. Instead they simply created a little Britain.

Amongst Virginia's counties there are: Suffolk, Norfolk, Surry (sic), Cumberland, Westmoreland, Middlesex, Essex and New Kent. There are other counties named after British towns: Buckingham, Southampton, Portsmouth, Chesterfield, Stafford, Gloucester, Lancaster, Halifax, Bedford, Bath, Northampton, York.

Confusingly, there are also towns called Dorset, Isle of Wight and Britain. Not to mention those towns that mimic exactly British counterparts, such as Newport, Ivor, Chester, Grimstead, Richmond, Buckingham, Rugby, Derby, Fife, Belfast and Dundee.

Whilst the Almost-Marrieds discussed wedding seating plans in the front seat, I pored over the road maps. To my relief it seemed that later settlers to Virginia evidently grew tired of aping British geography and went for more way-out nomenclature.

Thus Virginia welcomes you to Welcome. It also gives you Benefit, Charity, Wilderness, Cuckoo, Fox, Dolphin, Clam, Oyster, Allnut, Fries, Ebony, Java, Casanova, Nora, Belinda, Tiny, Looney, Modest Town and of course Bland County. Not to mention my favourite Virginia place name, Hydraulic, which is not far from Overall, just across the state line from Mechanicsville, Maryland. Look at a map. You couldn't invent this.

We had dinner in Norfolk, a soulless city of concrete and roadworks, which had a strangely medieval feel to it, being dominated by the might of the US Navy on one side, and the might of Christian fundamentalism in the form of Pat Robertson's Christian Broadcasting Network on the other. These twin foundations of American society – the military and the religious right – seem to be directly descended from medieval society, no different to the France of Charlemagne or the empire of Suleyman.

Except the Norfolk version of Chartres Cathedral or Istanbul's Blue Mosque is the Waterside Shopping Mall. We sat at the Crabshack restaurant, where the Almost-Marrieds shared crab and I ate a 'singles plate' of chicken, by myself. The evening was curtailed by a fire that broke out in one of the second-level boutiques, sending us all scurrying out to stand by the waterfront.

As the fire trucks careered our way, small smoke coughing from the roof of the Waterside, I watched the waitresses from Hooters exit their restaurant. Dressed in orange bikinis (hence the restaurant name) they tottered forth like painted chickens, and huddled on their own, suddenly startled and embarrassed by their removal from the safety of the Kingdom of Titillation. Out here, in the wilds of the real world, surrounded by mothers and young girls and old women, their mystical mammarian power had been usurped.

I stared anyway, their magic for me at least still lingering.

'You have anything like that in Britain?' asked a Crabshack waiter who'd earlier served my solitary chicken.

'What, breasts?'

'No. Hooters.'

I told him sadly that I believed we British had yet to reach such a civilised state of affairs, but that I'd suggest it to Richard Branson on my return.

'How d'you like Virginia?'

'Great. All the British names make me feel a little homesick though.'

'You been to Tangier yet?'

'In Morocco?'

'Naw. In the Chesapeake. Tangier Island. They speak your funny English there.'

'Funny English?'

'Yeah. Like the Founding Fathers. Like on the *Mayflower*. Like in Shakespeare. You should go. Make you feel at home.'

Forsooth I thanked the knave and merrily didst progress on my way.

Neither Stan nor Meg had heard of Tangier Island, but it did exist, at least according to the *Rand McNally Road Map of the USA and Canada*. It lay in Chesapeake Bay, close to the eastern shore of Maryland, a three-hour drive from Washington. It looked like a fish-hook. I was caught.

To give my friends snogging space, I decided to take a short break. Meg happily lent me her car, trying to hide her excitement at being able to walk around the house naked once more and kiss her fiancé while he did the hoovering.

I headed out of Washington, DC to 95 South and crossed the huge bridge just after Annapolis, passing over Kent Island, the first English settlement in Maryland, dating back to 1631. I stopped off in Cambridge, as I stop off in all Cambridges around the world, as a mark of respect for my home town.

As Cambridges went, it was about a 6. It was pretty enough at first sight – rows of clapboard houses, flowers, a park with a memorial to Roosevelt, who came here once – but a closer gawp showed the decaying wood, the crumbling brownstone and a main street on which numerous shops were closed. Grass grew amidst forgotten railway tracks. Old people shuffled around in the sunshine. It felt like a place abandoned because of some chemical leaking from the earth, a town dying because its veins – main highways, airports and suburban rail links – had been cut off, like so many once thriving American towns now separated from more cost-effective infrastructures.

But it did have English's Restaurant, a place no English person should ever pass without stopping: 2 pancakes. 2 sausages. 2 eggs. $2.22. In America, as Almost-Married Stan always likes to point out, you are never far from simplicity.

From Cambridge I dipped through Oxford (much smaller, just as crumbling) and spent the next half-hour admiring the ineptitude of Maryland's first town-namers. They were obviously comfortable replicating names of towns back in Britain, but their attempts at originality were far more dismal than their Virginian counterparts. I passed signs for Stumptown, Indian Bone, Gum Swamp and American Corner. And one of the more unfortunate town names in a nation of unfortunate town names: Crapo, Maryland.

I reached the port of Crisfield by mid-morning, in plenty of time to catch the summer-season cruise-boat to Tangier at 12.30. In winter the only way over is by the daily mail-boat. Or a twelve-mile swim.

Crisfield bills itself as the 'Crab Capital of the World', but my guess is that's the same world that comprises the 'World Series' of baseball. There are a lot of crab pots, crab boats and Wind-Up Happy Crabs for $2.95, but nothing about Crisfield makes it feel like a world-beater.

Chugging out into the bay, the cruise-boat skipper set the scene. There were 800 souls on Tangier Island, he said, which has a school of 115 children and 14 teachers. There were two registered nurses, a doctor and dentist came twice a week, and there was one full-time policeman. There were hardly any cars – people walk, cycle or use golf-carts. The island itself is tiny – two and a half miles long and a mile and a half wide, and it's four feet above sea level.

'If too many people in Washington, DC flush their toilets it'll go under,' he giggled. He went on to talk about the island's distinctive lingo: 'Many islanders still use words and accents that would have been familiar to the Elizabethan English. Most people have the same family names as the first settlers from Cornwall.'

It all sounded tantalisingly un-American. I mean what could be more un-American than a place of Cornish surnames where they speak like Shakespeare and there are no cars. Yet Tangier's history is umbilically linked to that of America itself. Ruled by the Algonquin for who-knows how long, the first 'white' man to stop there was Captain John Smith in 1608. He named the island Tangier, perhaps because he saw broken Indian pottery that reminded him of the Tanja pots of Morocco, or perhaps because he was sick of people naming places Cambridge and Oxford.

The first settlement came in 1686, when fisherman John Crockett moved to the island with his family from Cornwall, and encouraged others to follow. Present-day surnames on Tangier include many of these original families – Crocketts, Dises, Evans, Landons, Parks, Pruitts – although Islanders fiercely deny accusations of in-breeding. Tangier men, they say, always go off the island to find a bride. Honest.

Not so, says author Patricia Cornwell, whose novel *Unnatural Exposure* is partly set on the island. 'They don't exactly rotate their crops,' she writes. 'There are maybe three family names on the whole island.' Ms Cornwell isn't altogether complimentary about much to do with Tangier. She describes locals as partaking in 'drunkenness, bootlegging, drugs', and her descriptions are not found in any Virginia tourism brochure: 'this tiny barren island where people endured the worst weather with the least beneath their feet.' She goes on to talk of 'ignorant fishermen and their ignorant families', and describes the local speech patterns thus: 'I had heard this dialect before in unspoiled mountain caves where people are not of this century ... His strange syllables and cadences sprung, tongued and rolled over each other like the water of his world. There was thur; can't was cain't; things were thoings; do was doie.'

The plot of *Unnatural Exposure* turns around biochemical terrorism, with the island being infected by smallpox. Cornwell hints that the local crabs – the historic lifeblood of Tangier – become infected with the fatal disease, something that in reality would destroy the island's 400-year-old traditions and only real source of income.

It's only fiction, but in a country where a B-movie actor becomes President and a WWF wrestler is made Governor of Minnesota, fiction often influences public perception of reality. It was unlikely Cornwell's novel was on many Islanders' bookshelves. I made a note to keep it well hidden whilst onshore.

Before long, we chugged across the invisible border from Maryland into Virginia, across the old Mason–Dixon line from Union sympathy into a Southern state that supported the Confederacy in the Civil War, a place where they like to execute more prisoners, tax your car (unlike Maryland) and allow you to purchase beer in a supermarket (unlike Maryland).

The island appeared, a thin lip of brown land in the shimmering bay. Gradually we could make out houses, which seemed to be floating on the water. As we neared, these turned out to be not dwellings but crab-huts laced with fishing-pots. Beyond was the village, a church steeple and sky-blue water tower the only buildings of note.

I was excited to be going to an island. Apart from the fact I love sea, isolation and beaches, islands are also places of great romance, at least in literature. There's Captain Corelli, Niall Williams' tempestuously romantic *Four Letters of Love*, and of course *The Tempest* itself, which Shakespeare based on a British expedition to Virginia in 1609. Setting out from Plymouth, nine ships and 500 colonists of the imperial Virginia Company headed across the Atlantic to fortify John Smith's colony in Virginia. While eight of the party's vessels securely arrived at Jamestown, the flagship, aptly christened the *Sea Adventure*, was conspicuously absent. This ship, carrying both British Admiral Sir John Somers and the future Governor of Virginia, Sir George Somers, was separated during a fierce storm off the coast of Bermuda, the legendary Isle of Devils, dreaded by superstitious sixteenth-century sailors.

It ran aground, but the island turned out to be less devilish than first feared. The colonists found shelter, food and 'wood enough' to repair the *Sea Adventure*'s wounded pinnacles. The flagship's late arrival at Jamestown, roughly a year after the Virginia Company fleet had originally set sail, was regarded as a miracle and most likely became the inspiration for Shakespeare's final play, written in 1613.

Whether I would find Caliban or Miranda on Tangier Island, was, as yet, uncertain.

Our boat was met on the wooden quay by a fleet of golf-carts. Golf-carts, I quickly realised, are the camels of Tangier – a beast used for every transportational need, from taking kids to school to moving furniture. There were a dozen at the dock, waiting to whisk tourists for a tour of the island or to the three guest-houses.

I climbed aboard with Shirley Pruitt, owner of Shirley's Bay View Inn, because she had the nicest golf-cart – it had six seats and shone like a heavenly chariot. It seemed a fair bet that the owner of the nicest golf-cart would also own the nicest guest-house.

We puttered along at five miles an hour, passing a sign that barked 'Speed Zone. Radar Control. 15 mph!'. Shirley didn't speak much, but smiled and nodded greatly. We arrived at the guest-house, which was as nice as the golf-cart – a red clapboard house and a garden full of gnomes. Shirley's silence was compensated for by husband Wallace, whom I encountered jacking up his out-houses with bricks and metal poles to prevent summer flood damage.

'At coimes ein, at goies aut again. We're used ta thart,' he said in an accent as thick as a man from Padstow. 'We've bane har on ar own so loing we got ar own way of talking,' he explained as I looked on in bafflement. Whether this was original West Country English, or the purest form of American English, as spoken by the Founding Fathers, preserved because of Tangier's isolation, God or a professor of linguistics only knew. What was definite was that it was near impossible to understand.

I was under the impression Wallace had offered to lend me a bike which I was to pick up from his sister's: 'Go darn thar by Wandar's geft shoip, it's tha bloie oine by tha fance,' but equally he could have been inviting me to a Rolling Stones concert in Dallas.

'Thar's noit a whole lat ta doie, boit poiple seem ta lark thart,' concluded Wallace. I nodded enthusiastically and set off to see the island.

I found a bike lying against the fence by Wanda's gift shop, so the Stones gig was probably off. The bike was unlocked. Security on Tangier is better than the Vatican – everyone leaves their doors open, kids wander freely. Unlike most American towns, no one's ever been killed on its main street, and the policeman, Darren Landon, seems to spend most of his time giving people lifts in his blue pick-up.

Everyone seemed friendly enough, calling out 'Hoi thar,' as I cycled by. I stopped at Wanda's gift shop and chatted with Wanda herself as she sat under a maple reading *Country Living*.

'We love visitors, most everyone speaks to everyone,' she said. 'But don't get me wrong. We still depend on the water to make a living. Outsiders are making rules and regulations, but the watermen know the right way. That's their livelihood, all they have to depend on.'

As local tourist literature says, 'Traditionally a boy on Tangier grows up with the sea; a girl grows up with the home.'

Tangier is all about tradition. These are a strictly religious people, who would consider the Archbishop of Canterbury a libertine. As Wanda told me, 'They give me the devil for opening on a Sunday.'

It's also a teetotal island. In 1998 the island council rejected Warner Brothers' plans to shoot *Message in a Bottle* there because of a scene in which Paul Newman would drink a beer. The location scout for Warner had declared, 'It's like *Children of the*

Corn over there. There's no separation of church and state. It's grassroots fundamentalism gone totally out of control.'

The cruise-boat took day-trippers back to Crisfield at 4 p.m. and the island sighed with relief. People began to mow their lawns. I headed for the Chesapeake House, one of the island's three restaurants. I had to be quick. They stopped serving dinner at 5 p.m.

The food was hearty, a pioneer meal of all-you-can-eat ham, coleslaw, beets, potato salad, corn custard, clam fritters and crab cakes, all for $12.95. I later read a 1973 *National Geographic* article in which the menu was exactly the same. Things on Tangier seem to progress about as quickly as icebergs.

It was the first time I'd finished dinner by 5 p.m. since I was ten. There were still four hours before darkness, so I cycled to the beach, where in 1814 Tangier's local reverend, Joshua Thomas, preached a sermon to 12,000 British troops, in which he warned them that they'd lose their war against the Americans, despite a vast numeric advantage. With imperial arrogance the Brits laughed in Joshua's face, went off to attack Baltimore and were soundly thrashed.

Oh say, can you see, by the dawn's early light,
What so proudly we hail'd at the twilight's last gleaming?
Whose broad stripes and bright stars, thro' the perilous fight,
O'er the ramparts we watch'd, were so gallantly streaming?

The night after Reverend Thomas' sermon, the battle ensued, viewed by a local man, Francis Scott Key. The next day, the American flag was still flying over Baltimore's Fort McHenry, and Scott Key was so overjoyed that he did as all true patriots should under such circumstances and wrote a poem:

And the rockets' red glare, the bombs bursting in air,
Gave proof thro' the night that our flag was still there.
O say, does that star-spangled banner yet wave
O'er the land of the free and the home of the brave?

First published under the title 'Defense of Fort M'Henry' and later as 'The Star-Spangled Banner', it became a popular song sung to the tune 'To Anacreon in Heaven'. 'The Star-Spangled Banner' became the national anthem as late as 1931.

What I hadn't realised is how much it slags off the British. Take verse three for example;

And where is that band who so vauntingly swore
That the havoc of war and the battle's confusion,
A home and a country should leave us no more?
Their blood has wash'd out their foul footsteps' pollution.
No refuge could save the hireling and slave
From the terror of flight or the gloom of the grave:

Foul footsteps? Hireling and slave? What about Kenneth Branagh? David Niven? The Beatles?

And the star-spangled banner in triumph doth wave
O'er the land of the free and the home of the brave.

On the beach in Tangier, a dyke built by British sailors still remains (our digging, as elsewhere, surviving longer than our empire). I sat on it and watched the sun dazzle the bay, accompanied by six large women who admitted they often came to the beach to escape their husbands. 'Gets a little claustrophobic on the island at times,' one admitted.

I saw what they meant after dark. There was nothing to do, except go to church. There was a prayer meeting on, and the street outside the church was full of parked golf-carts. It hardly seemed like grassroots fundamentalism out of control. Judging from the flickering lights coming from the houses beyond, those who weren't in church were glued to their television sets. As Wallace had warned me, 'You coime oiver and try n' taike ar talavasions yar goin' gat yar hands cut arff.'

The only souls outside were a couple of kids riding round and round the island in a golf-cart, rap music blaring. Their blond hair shone in the darkness – for some genetic reason I'm distinctly unqualified to explain, many islanders are as blond as Abba.

And many of the girls, I'd quickly noticed, were far from ugly. My pulse had raced encountering a couple of seventeen-year-olds on bicycles near the tip of the island.

'Hoi thar,' they'd chanted, before pedalling away, blonde locks flowing in the wind like refugees from a Heidi movie. Yet I had the feeling that to approach a Tangier woman might result in a dinner with, rather than of, the crabs.

So instead of heading to Lorraine's Pizza Joint, the only place on the island open after 5 p.m., to chat up seventeen-year-old blonde girls, I went back to my room to read about crabs.

That night I learned more than I'd ever wanted to about crustacea. About the two ways of crab-fishing, or 'progging', as the watermen of Tangier call it. There's 'scraping' or dragging nets over the sea bottom, in summer, then dredging up buried crabs in winter. I learned the local terminology, of 'jimmies' (male crabs) and 'sooks' (female crabs), about 'ketching a rank pailer' – catching a 'peeler', a crab about to shed its shell. I learned that a sook lays 1–2 million eggs, but only two or three survive. As one crab fisherman wrote, 'Sooks'll spawn a million little crabs. If they all survived the world'd be et up by crabs.' Eighty-five per cent of island men are watermen, still earning a living from 'progging'. As one wrote, 'The sea is our life, our highway, our farm, our prison.' 'What cows are to cowboys, crabs are to the men of Tangiers,' said another.

It's a hard life, by all accounts. The blue crab of Chesapeake Bay has a two- to three-year lifespan. During this time it will shed its shell several times. Just before shedding, its claws have a white edge to them, which goes pink, then red a day or two before the event. When it sheds its exo-skeleton, it's called a 'buster'. The idea is to catch a load of 'peelers', then keep them in the crab-shacks in trays of water and watch them day and night for the moment they become a 'buster'. They must be removed from the salt water immediately, since the new shell starts to harden within an hour.

At night along the wooden wharf crab-shacks are lit by swinging fairylights, like rows of Santa's grottos, while the men of Tangier stare at their crabs. Softshell crabs earn eight times more than a hard shell crab. It pays to stare.

Next morning the island was empty of men, who had gone out to check crab-pots at 3 a.m. I walked from one end of the island to the other (about an hour) in warm, early-summer sun. I sat on the beach and flicked through the major literary discovery that is *Something Fishy From Tangier* by E. Frank Dize. In this book about crabs, crabbing and crab recipes there are intermittent nuggets of wisdom:

'Anger is the ill wind that blows out the lamp of intelligence.'

'America is a tune – it must be sung together.'

'A paper plate glued to the bottom of a paint can is more convenient than spreading papers when painting.'

Unfortunately, there was nothing in *Something Fishy* about mending a broken heart.

I wandered across a bridge on to Cantor Island, the larger of the two islands that make up Tangier. Here the houses were bigger, boasting two golf-cart garages. At Pam Eskridge's New Creations hairdressers salon a sign urged me to read II Corinthians 5:17 – 'If anyone is in Christ he is a new creation' – as good a verse as any to take with you to a hairdresser's.

The biggest event of the day was when a helicopter arrived to carry a woman with an inflamed appendix to the mainland for treatment. The entire island turned out to watch. I stood and gawked, along with fellow tourist Jim Campbell, a doctor from Ohio.

'I love this place,' he admitted. 'It's got a real island community and culture. It seems that tourism is coincidental. You have to come here to appreciate it. A lot of people in the US wouldn't believe there are places like this.'

One person who couldn't believe it was Betty Smith. I went to have tea with her. I had no choice. Everyone on the island had urged me to pay her a visit.

'You're English? You have to go and see Betty.'

Betty is the island's only 'English resident', originally from Lydney, Gloucestershire. She married an American serviceman in 1947 and moved to the United States. The flight took eighteen hours. She had thought her new husband's home town was in the suburbs of Washington, DC, but it turned out to be on Tangier Island.

'I didn't know it was an island. Men forget to tell you things sometimes.'

Her first years were hard. 'On Sunday morning I used to hear the church bells, and I'd stay in bed and cry because they reminded me so much of home.' It struck me, suddenly, that perhaps I might not have been completely happy married to Angie and living in Canada.

Eventually Betty's ailing mother came over from England to the island to be looked after by Betty. She died in the small clapboard house, buffeted by Atlantic gales.

'She looked at me, said, "Is this Cheltenham?" and died,' said Betty, a suspicion of a tear in her eye. 'I still miss the hills and fish and chips,' she concluded.

As she talked, this seventy-two-year-old woman, who'd been on Tangier Island fifty-two years and still missed battered cod, made me feel homesick. I felt a pang for custard, *Sports Report* at 5 p.m. on Saturday, and the expression 'dual carriageway'.

It was then that I knew I'd have to return home sometime. To start again. Like a salmon struggling across the Atlantic to wriggle up the stream of its birth and mate. Or a defeated heavyweight champion.

But not just yet, because Betty's twenty-two-year-old granddaughter Judy had arrived from Crisfield. She was blonde and bright-eyed, slightly well fed but with a rippling giggle that jiggled into the summer afternoon. She offered to escort me to Lorraine's that evening. I accepted even though an engagement ring the size of a tarantula sparkled on her finger. I couldn't face another night reading about crabs.

As it is the only place on the island open after 5 p.m., I'd expected Lorraine's to be packed. Instead, it turned out to be a small wooden shack by the wharf, not unlike the other wooden shacks by the wharf. There were four booths, a formica counter and packets of breakfast cereal on the shelves. The special was crab with fries and drink for $4.25. Crab, it must be said, figured quite strongly on the menu.

Judy was greeted by the owner, Lorraine, with a cackle and, 'Hoi thar short stuff.' The other customers were two old men who looked like they'd been recently carved out of wood, a teenage boy with acne for skin and a man in wellington boots.

We sat in a booth and I ordered a beefburger, which brought disdainful glares from Lorraine and the man in wellington boots. Judy ordered oyster cakes and a glass of milk. She was definitely a woman unafraid of calories.

'How do you like the island?' she asked.

'It's amazing. It seems so cut off from the rest of America.'

'That's what I love about it. I'd love to move back here. I'm getting married in August, but he's from Baltimore, and he doesn't want to come and live on Tangier. "Backward" he calls it. But it isn't. It's just more simple. It has a rhythm that is out of step with the mainland. The mainland's always rushing ahead, pushing forward. Here, we stop, look around and listen.'

We ate our food, and Judy told of learning to catch crabs with her grandfather, the ex-marine, of helicopters dropping supplies when the island is cut off by storms, of knowing everyone in every house in every street.

'It's like we're a family; if someone dies we've lost a part of the family.'

Yet today, it's the traditions of Tangier that are dying, as Judy went on to explain. In the 1990 census, a third of the island's households reported earning less than $10,000 a year (the national average is $37,500). Times are difficult for the crab fishermen, with new crabbing limits, reductions in crabbing permits and the Pfiesteria micro-organism killing stocks. Young people have two choices – work on the water or leave. 'There's nothing else to do.'

Judy had left the island, and I sensed she knew she'd never live there again. Her emigration, mirrored in thousands of small towns across the United States, the curse of post-war America.

I walked Judy back to her grandmother's house. 'See that swing? I had my first kiss on that swing. Cousin Wally.' She paused, looked around her. 'But you can't marry your cousin.' We shook hands, and I wished her all the best, this woman who, in an age of digital television, supersonic flight and military satellites, just wanted to live in the house where she was born.

I walked back to the wharf, and sat on the wooden quay, still warm from the day. All was quiet. It would be another five hours before the watermen would rise and take their boats out into the pre-dawn darkness of the bay.

I sat on the dock watching the lights from the crab-shanties and thought about this world of golf-carts, crab-boats, and prayer meetings. Where the green light at the end of the harbour is the end of the world.

It was a strange place, but strangely reassuring. A sign that things continue, whether we want them to or not.

Summer became more summer, which was a surprise to an Englishman used to summer becoming spring and then winter, then summer again, all in the space of a day. In America summer, once it starts, seems set to carry on forever. The sun comes out, the temperature stays at eighty degrees and the insects buzz louder than lawnmowers. American insects, I'd quickly discovered, are huge, probably genetically modified by all those pesticides, or the Three Mile Island nuclear accident, or the CIA to defend the country against communists in the event of Iraqi nerve gas killing all human beings.

I dialled my *Washington Post* Personal Plus mailbox. There were three messages.

'Hi. I'm Jackie and I love English accents. I like reading, travel and the movies. I'm thirty-six and sporty. If you like I'd love to meet up for coffee.'

'Hello, Englishman. My name's Vanessa. Madness is my middle name. If you'd like to meet Royalty give me a call.'

'My name is Angie. I love soccer, my brother's at school in England and I follow Manchester United. I'm twenty-nine years old and work in publishing. Hopefully we could meet up.'

I swear. She said Angie. Which one did I contact? Well . . .

Initially, I called none of them. I made Almost-Married Meg listen to their voices, to see if feminine intuition could tell what they looked like.

'Number one is athletic but she's not cute. Two is a lawyer. No doubt. Probably thinks she's better looking than she is. And three, well, she's homely and probably a virgin.'

'Thanks Meg.'

'Any time.'

I called number one. Jackie. She laughed on the phone, a practised laugh. I got the impression this was not the first blind date she'd been on.

'We'll meet at Starbucks on K Street. It's near my office. 6.30 okay by you?'

'Yes. Great. See you then. You know I've never done this before.'

The last sentence uttered after the phone clicked off.

I was in Starbucks on K Street at 6.23 p.m. I held my copy of the *Washington Post* like a shield. My heart pounded as the espresso machine steamed. I ordered an Earl Grey tea in a booming baritone that said, so I thought, 'I'm here for a date. With a woman.'

It was amazing. That a woman, a member of the female species, had actually planned part of her day around coming to see me. She'd leave her work, maybe tell her friends she was going on a date with an Englishman, get in her car, or walk, imagining me, thinking about me, planning a date with me. Okay she had no idea what or who 'me' was, but the concept of me was enough to alter the pattern of her day. I mattered.

Jackie turned up at 6.43 p.m. She was short, with a neatly cropped bob, a trouser suit and briefcase. She looked like she was in her early forties.

'Hi. I'm Jackie.'

'Yes. Hello. I'm Jim.'

'You don't sound very English.'

'Oh. Don't I?'

'Not so much.'

'Oh. Maybe . . . maybe it's because I've spent the last seven weeks in America. And I was going out with a Canadian . . .'

Oh dear. Thirteen seconds into the date and I'd already mentioned Angie. Jackie laughed a practised 'Let's cover up his embarrassment' laugh and ordered a double decaff mocha with low-fat milk.

It didn't get much better. Jackie had been on too many dates. Her patter was so practised, so wooden, I felt like I was sitting through an episode of *The Bold and the Beautiful,* only worse.

'Yeah, I love Italian cuisine, especially Tuscan specialities, you know Jim, like *prosciutto di Parma, agnoletti, bistecca alla fiorentina* . . .' She pronounced the Italian words with exaggerated flourish. Perhaps this impressed WASP accountants from Ernst and Young, but I'd known a real-life Italian-Canadian family for seven years . . . '*Spaghetti alla chittare, fiorentino con fegatini* . . .'

As Jackie talked and I nodded, deflecting her with questions whenever the conversation lulled, I felt sadder and sadder. I drank three cups of Earl Grey, looked at my watch, coughed and said, 'Well, I'm sorry, but I've got a really early meeting in the morning . . .'

Jackie looked at me with contempt. 'You're going?'

'Er . . . I've got this meeting.'

'Fine.'

'Okay. Well, er . . . it was great. I'm really sorry I've got to go. Here's my number, maybe we could have dinner sometime.'

She took the piece of paper I'd carefully written out on the subway and glared. I walked from Starbucks, my stomach sloshing, awash with Earl Grey. It was 8.04 p.m.

Sunday night, me and the Almost-Marrieds sitting on the sofa, in front of the fifty-two-inch television. We're watching *Butch Cassidy and the Sundance Kid* on some obscure cable station (Channel 334 out of 467). Paul Newman and Robert Redford have just been chased by Lefors and his posse, escaping by jumping into the river. They turn up at Etta's place. She is cardiac-beautiful. I wonder whatever happened to Katharine Ross.

Etta says, 'They rumoured you were dead . . .'

Sundance says, 'Don't make a big thing of it . . .'

Etta nods, turns to go, and Sundance says, 'No . . . it's okay; make a big thing of it.'

And they kiss.

On Monday morning I called Vanessa.

'How you doing?'

'Fine. Great. So . . . I was wondering, would you like to meet up?'

'No. Sorry. I prefer Irishmen.'

'Oh.'

'It's a joke, Englishman. Sure I'd love to meet up. Have anywhere in mind?'

'Er . . . well, I don't really know Washington very well.'

'Where are you?'

Good question. A bigger question than it sounded. A life question.

'Bethesda.'

That much I knew.

'I'm in Chevy Chase. Do you know the farmers' market on Old Georgetown Road?'

'I'll find it. That'll be great.'

Farmers' markets in millennial America are basically very expensive supermarkets. Instead of charging $2.99 for a bag of apples, they charge $6.99 for a bag of 'Happy Orchard Organic Red Crusties! Grown in our historic 250-year-old orchards! As eaten by Thomas Jefferson!' Farmers' markets sell olive oil for $37.55 and balsamic vinegar for $62.44. A lettuce costs you more than the all-you-can-eat salad bar at Pizza Hut.

It was a hot Saturday. Kids were eating ice cream from dawn, and the radio played Chris Rea's 'On the Beach' from breakfast onwards. Everyone in America was wearing shorts, khaki, from The Gap, exposing yards of flesh that would make certain Papua New Guinean tribes lick their lips with delight. On such a day if the CNN camera was to pan down from the President's face, it would reveal a pair of Ralph Lauren shorts and two very knobbly knees.

Vanessa turned up on time. 11.30 a.m. She was tall, with black curly hair, a round moon face and bright red lipstick. She was probably late twenties. She wore shorts. Her legs weren't bad. I tried not to look at them, but failed and she knew it.

'Good morning.'

We sat on a bench and had coffee. Coffee is the American dating drink, which is strange, since it only serves to quicken the heart rate, make the hands shake a little more and the eyes stare that much wider.

Vanessa seemed supremely confident. She crossed her long legs and sipped her mocha as if on television. I asked her why she'd answered my ad (I'd prepared questions in advance – she was, after all, a lawyer – Meg was right).

'Well, let's say I've answered one or two over the last year. Why not? You seemed different, snappy, funny . . . at least your ad did.'

She smiled.

'Want an ice cream?'

She had vanilla. I had dark-chocolate-double-chip, honeycomb-waffle cinnamon bubble-gum, which seemed to impress her very little.

Vanessa was Croatian-American. Everyone in America is Something-American, like Stan (Russian Jewish-American), Meg (Norwegian-American), and Mary (German-American). Vanessa's family had emigrated at the outset of the First World

War. She'd never been to the Balkans, didn't speak a word of Croatian and had never heard of World Cup goal scorer Davor Suker.

'Soccer? Very un-American.'

Yet she described her family as Croatian-American. Because this is how you survive in the States – by asserting an individual label within the whole. Everyone needs a brand name.

I found myself liking Vanessa. She talked long and hard and told stories about her law firm and the 'anal-arseholes' she worked for, of her love for her Toyota Miata convertible, David Bowie and Chinese food but no monosodium glutamate, no sireee, and she wolfed down her ice cream before I'd even reached the level of my cone.

She asked me about England, and seemed to listen to the answers.

'So they have a weather guy called Michael Fish?'

'Yes. He always gets it wrong.'

'What a weird name.'

I didn't bring up CNN's Flip Spiceland.

'So, why did you place the ad?' she asked as we ordered more coffee.

'Er . . . I . . .'

I wanted to tell her about Angie. But something in the sunniness of the day, in the laughter from the kids at the other table, in the way she held her plastic Starbucks mug, stopped me.

'I thought it would be a laugh.'

We chatted for another hour, before she departed to go shopping in her shiny blue Toyota Miata convertible, which she drove away, at speed, with the tiniest of waves.

She called four days later.

'Englishman. I'm heading to the country this weekend. Since you're a tourist and have yet to witness the beauties of rural Virginia, I thought you might like to come.'

'I . . . er . . .'

'Separate bedrooms, so don't get any ideas.'

A weekend away with a woman. I hadn't done that in two years. I tried not to think of the last time – Angie and I in the lake country north of Toronto where we felt sad in each other's company. We spent one afternoon in an espresso bar in Huntsville, Ontario staring out of neighbouring windows. Silence. Perhaps that weekend, looking back on it, was the beginning of our end. The first tremble along the fault line that would lead to the terrible quake.

Vanessa seemed happy enough to see me. She drove northwest of Washington, DC into Loudoun County. Beyond the housing subdivisions there were rolling hills, oak woods and, to my astonishment, dry stone walls, not to mention fields of very British-looking sheep.

The 'Cotswolds of America' opines one tourist brochure, and it's not a bad comparison, apart from the lack of Japanese tour buses. It all looked so English. I tried to persuade Vanessa to drive on the left, but she declined.

We chatted as she drove, about the weather, her car, her job (again) and her horse.

'I just wanna say hi to Buffy, if that's okay by you?'

'Your horse is called Buffy?'

'She lives in Middleburg. It's a real cute town. You'll love it.'

We stopped in Leesburg, a place that likes to think it's old. Because it likes to think it's old, the only amenities in Leesburg are antique shops and tea rooms. We stopped and had tea, probably because Vanessa thought that would be an English thing to do.

'I wanna show you a museum,' said Vanessa in a tone that suggested this was an non-negotiable situation.

On a beautiful hot June day we went inside to a museum. Morven Park is a stately home left to the nation by Westmoreland Davis, one-time Governor of Virginia (1918–22) and millionaire turkey farmer. This latter fact might explain why he was also

America's number one fox-hunting fan. Morven Park, you see, contains a museum of American fox-hunting.

'Isn't it neat. Very British, huh?'

'Fox-hunting? In America?'

'It's so cool. I just love the red jacket. And the fox hardly ever gets killed.'

'You go fox-hunting? With Buffy?'

A Croatian-American fox-hunter. Just what the world needs.

The Museum of Hounds and Hunting is housed on the ground floor of the damp old mansion and traces the history of American fox-bashing. There's a hunting horn dating from 1731, hunting costumes and accounts of fox-hunting American presidents, including George Washington and Thomas Jefferson (Washington's diaries abound with accounts of hunts, including one occasion when Congress was in session as hounds neared the Capitol and several congressmen jumped on horses to join the chase). There's also a series of pictures of a foxy Jackie Kennedy fox-hunting (she's falling off her horse and still looks foxy).

And a *Titanic* exhibit. The connection, in this instance, between the iceberg and fox was local huntmaster Clarence Moore, who went to England in 1912 to purchase the best horses and hounds he could find. Being a man 'whose style could not be called conservative', according to his biography, he booked his return on the world's finest ship, and perished along with Leonardo DiCaprio. The fifty hounds were never found – legend has it they can still be heard baying across the North Atlantic.

I tried to show interest. Vanessa beamed with pride. It was a reaction I'd seen before amongst her fellow Americans – the eagerness to ally themselves with something, anything histori-cal, with 'tradition', to anchor themselves to a past however disconnected to them. In this country that constantly rushes headlong into tomorrow like a bull towards small Spanish men, anything that slows down the future is greatly cherished.

I did salvage one thing that amused me at the fox-hunting museum. It seems that at the turn of the century there was a fierce rivalry between US and English fox-hunters over who had the better hounds. This culminated in American hunter Harry Worcester Smith challenging the great English huntmaster Henry Higginson to a contest – Smith's American hounds (slighter, more streamlined) against Higginson's English hounds (heavier, wider head) 'for love, money or marbles'.

'The Great Foxhound Match of 1905' was avidly followed in England, and was reported on the front page of *The Times*. Smith's American hounds finally defeated Higginson's English hounds in a hotly fought contest. Neither pack of hounds actually caught a fox, but the American mutts won because the judges considered that they had done 'the best work', as Americans are wont to do.

We walked out into the boiling sunshine.

'Neat, huh?'

I tried to nod. Out in the grounds there were men on horses, preparing for a dressage competition. The horse, Vanessa insisted, is to Virginia what plastic surgery is to LA. It was the state's equine expertise that helped the South win important battles in the region during the Civil War. As Theodore Roosevelt wrote in an 1886 article, if fox-hunting had been as much a national pastime in the Northern states as it was in the South, 'it would not have taken us until the middle of the war before we were able to develop a cavalry capable of withstanding the shock of Southern horsemen'.

Next stop, Vanessa decreed, was a Civil War site.

'You're a tourist,' she reasoned.

As the sun wept from the sky, we trekked to Ball's Bluff just outside Leesburg, site of one of the hundreds of bloody battles that scarred Virginia during the American Civil War. As often with battlefields, I found it to be a beautiful spot, all the more so after Vanessa skipped away to call someone on her carphone. It was a peaceful place – the woods silent, the Potomac River sliding by at the base of the bluff. The only thing to disturb me was a large snake – an unfortunate feature of American summers – which slithered by looking for small children.

I lingered for a few minutes at the lonely gravestone of Colonel

Edward Baker, a life-long friend of Abraham Lincoln, and gave thanks that I've never had to fight anyone more serious than the taxman.

We got to Middleburg in the middle of the afternoon. We went to see Buffy, who lived in what seemed to be a five-star hotel on the edge of town. Buffy was big and snorted a lot. For some reason I recalled the first time I'd eaten horsemeat, on a French exchange at the age of fourteen. It hadn't tasted that bad, at least with a nice mustard sauce.

'Isn't she wonderful?'

I nodded. A fillet steak, with relish or Roquefort dressing.

Vanessa made me pat Buffy's nose, which was wet. The horse didn't like me. Perhaps it could read my stomach.

Vanessa spent two hours with Buffy. She seemed to have forgotten about me, and trotted round the arena like Liz Taylor in *National Velvet*. I drank coffee from a machine and sat in the sun trying not to feel doleful.

I still missed Angie. Almost ten weeks had passed. She was still inside me, a gasp, a flutter, at times an ache. Vanessa, before me, ignoring me, was so disconnected from my life she might as well have been Liz Taylor in *National Velvet* on my TV. Angie, a good 2,000 miles away, felt so close I trembled with despair.

Middleburg was very pretty in a well-scrubbed, old-fashioned clapboard Stars and Stripes way. It was evidently very wealthy, since it had even more antique shops than Leesburg, and there were foxes everywhere. Grocery stores, clothes shops, even the library were adorned with fox images – door knockers, flags, stuffed animals. We stopped at the Red Fox Inn, a red-bricked place on the main street.

'I booked you a room,' smiled Vanessa, who, it must be said, smiled a lot.

'Thanks. Do we share a bathroom?'

'Oh, I've got a room at the stables. I hope you don't mind. It's just there's an early-morning ride tomorrow . . .'

'Sure. No problem,' I lied.

The eighteenth-century Red Fox Inn was a favourite hang-out

of George Washington. As such, it's remarkably expensive. I was shown to my room up rickety old stairs and gasped quite loudly when I checked the price hung on the back of the door of my small but admittedly comfortable room.

$150. Oh God.

You pay for history in America. And not only did George W. get drunk here, but the Red Fox Inn was a favoured canoodling spot for JFK and Jackie when Jack wasn't Marilyning. Americans will pay serious cash to dance with history, but they'll pay silly cash to get within even a breath of the Camelot myth.

Vanessa did deign to dine with me.

'There are 175 hunts in America and Canada,' she intoned over a thick peanut soup. 'It's getting more and more popular.'

I found this hard to believe. In America, hunting is not done on horses, dressed in stiff red jackets, chasing after a small ragged mammal. It's done in pickup trucks, up trees, up mountains, dressed head to foot in camouflage, chasing after elk with an assortment of sub-machine guns, AK47s and missile launchers. This is, after all, a country where people regularly dress up like Rambo and head into the woods to blast anything that moves – stags, bear, moose, woolly mammoth, blue whales. Where in rural Wal-Marts you can buy shotguns and ammunition in the same store as CDs and Christmas cards. Where on the nationally broadcast ESPN sports channel a grizzly man called Wayne Pearson shows you how to kill wild pigs with a crossbow. 'Find yourself the bow of a mature oak, set up a seating position, and wait. Pigs ain't clever, but they are dependable. They will come to you.'

We drank Virginian red wine (not bad, as it shouldn't be for $36.99 a bottle). Vanessa talked a great deal about equestrianism, fox-hunting, Buffy and a case she was assisting at the following week involving two other law firms.

'We're all suing each other,' she laughed, as if this was the funniest thing she'd said all day, which thinking about it, it was.

I caught her looking at her watch twice during the main course. By dessert, she had stopped talking. I tried to tell her a story about my sister's birthday party when my sister was seven and I was nine and one of her friends sat in my ice cream but didn't realise it and refused to move . . .

'Really?' said Vanessa.

'Yes. Really.'

We had coffee. It was 9.30 p.m. Vanessa yawned. She turned and smiled at me.

'Jim, I've had a great day, but the ride goes out at 6.30 in the morning. I really should get some sleep.'

I said nothing. Not that I'd fallen in love with Vanessa, or even fancied her that much, but rejection is still rejection. And it's amazing how much being turned down by someone makes you want them.

We got the bill. Vanessa paid, which was decent of her, and hopefully made her feel less guilty about enthusiastically inviting a foreign stranger away for the weekend, realising she didn't really like him and arranging a horse ride to avoid spending too much time with him.

She kissed my cheek, and departed. I went upstairs and watched TV. Taking into account the price of the room, it cost me seventy-five dollars an hour, a rate that if applied across America might get the population back to reading.

The next morning was torpid. We had a coffee at the hotel, Vanessa looking ruddy-faced and pleased with herself. For a moment I wondered if her early morning ride had been far from equestrian and involved some stableboy or instructor.

'How's Buffy?' I lied.

'Missing me already.'

She dropped me off in Bethesda, and didn't wave as the car pulled away. I knew I wanted to see her again, purely because she didn't want to see me again.

Men. I'll never understand them.

I checked my *Washington Post* Personals Plus mailbox. There were still three messages – Jackie, Vanessa and Angie who liked soccer.

I called Angie who liked soccer.

'Oh. I'm sorry. I met this guy. We're dating.'

'Congratulations.'

'Yeah. It's great. I hope you find someone.'

I was too late for Angie #2, just as I'd been for Angie #1. Like replying too late for a car advertisement. The wheels had gone.

It was turkey-roasting hot. I sat in Stan's garden on a Monday afternoon and drank half a bottle of vodka with cranberry juice.

Stan came home and woke me as insects finished devouring my nose. 'We're going to Arizona.'

'What?'

'It's my alternative stag weekend. I got an airmile award, two seats to Phoenix and three nights' accommodation. We'll be cowboys.'

I hugged him, and went inside to pack my Levi's.

7

Debbie – Ex-cheerleader from Phoenix

We arrive in Phoenix on one of the sixty-five days in the year when the sun doesn't shine. And one of the ten days in the year when it rains.

'What's going on?' barks Stan before heading off to sue someone.

I'd spent the flight west with my nose pressed to the aeroplane window like a bee to a windscreen, from the emerald Appalachians to the wide greening plains of the Midwest and finally to the aridity of the desert, gazing down at the earth, baked, the colour of dead skin. Brown, the colour of lifelessness. Crenellated crust, like some far-off planet.

As you look down from 27,000 feet, Phoenix isn't very phoenix-like. It's a massive grid, like some intergalactic game of tic-tac-toe, the squares filled with houses, like work camps, which in a way they are, housing the labourers for the high-tech factories that sprawl into the desert of the Valley of the Sun. Row after row of identical houses, line after line, but they all have swimming pools, little blue teardrops dashing the city. Welcome to the American Dream – sun, car and swimming pool. I'm not sure there's anything wrong with that.

Phoenix is a city the word sprawl was invented for: the lazy spatial extravagance of American building. The valley that it yawns into is the size of Wales. There are factory complexes in it the size of Abergavenny.

While Stan is away shouting at someone about the weather,

I stand helpless and happy in Phoenix airport. Posters urge me to 'Adopt a Greyhound' and I'm so excited I almost do. On the airport benches sit nice old guys in Western drawstring ties being nice old guys.

'Howdy, son.'

I swear that's what they said.

Stan returns, incandescent with rage, but he's procured us a car rental upgrade.

'A fucking jeep. I need traction in this weather.'

On the radio news all the reporters are apoplectic with excitement about the rain. Apparently Phoenix has just suffered the driest winter since 1956 and they need three straight weeks of deluge to replenish the aquifers.

'I'm not amused,' mutters Stan, spraying a bus queue of poor people as we hurtle past.

In our hotel we watch TV and munch room-service burgers. I recall my misery in the Joyful Glades Motel, Florida and thank Stan again for his friendship.

'How do you say in England? No worries, mate?'

I haven't the heart to explain that's Australian.

The local news, once it's got over the rain, is apoplectic about the expansion of the Phoenix telephone network. Apparently the dialling codes are changing for the third time in two years. So many people are moving to Arizona the infrastructure cannot cope.

The final news item is more serious, about a child abuser, accused of seventy-seven counts of abuse.

'If he's convicted,' says Randy Bits, the News Five newscaster, 'he could spend hundreds of years in jail.'

Stan and I look at each other then shout in stereo at the screen, 'How can someone spend hundreds of years in jail, you moron?'

The next day is startlingly sunny. There is no sign that rain has ever fallen. It's cantankerously hot by 10 a.m.

'This is about the last weekend of the season for dude ranches,' explains Stan. 'By next week it'll be so hot the horses will ignite if they're out in the middle of the day.'

'On the spot?'

'Just like that. Actually it may be a tad uncomfortable anyway. We'll have to buy hats.'

We stop at a convenience store, which lives up to its name by conveniently selling cowboy hats. I try on a ten-gallon white version with a jaunty black band.

'Butch or Sundance?' I ask my friend.

'Ronald Reagan.'

On the road south we turn the jeep's air-conditioning up to maximum. My back still sticks to the seat, but at least we have six cup-holders in the car, into which we place various fizzy beverages. This is one of the greatest things about the United States, in my opinion. You're never short of a place to park your beverage.

We follow a Camarro with a bumper sticker that reads 'Mean People Suck!'. I laugh. I feel light-headed, released. Perhaps it's the epic heat of the day, or the epic vista of the desert, the purple hills, the yellow burnt scrub, the cacti, but I just want to breathe, deeply and without rancor. It's one of those days that if it was your only day on earth, you'd be happy.

I start to hum the theme from *High Chapparal*. Stan doesn't know it, and insists the show was never broadcast in America. 'Purely for British consumption. You guys know no better.'

We pass a sign that reveals we're in a 'blowing dust area' and another that reads, 'State Prison – do not pick up hitchhikers!', so we don't. We pass an ostrich farm and drive alongside a train longer than Liverpool, then we turn off the highway on to a lesser road that leads us through forests of cacti, pencil thin, as prickly as Mrs Thatcher. The road is long and cracked and looks like it goes to Mexico, which it does.

I ask Stan what a dude ranch is.

'It's Club Med with a Western atmosphere. It's rich folks thinking they're being primitive. My friends from Beverly Hills love it.'

The word 'dude' derives, at least according to Stan, from British English. 'It was first familiarised in London in 1881 and is a revival of an older word "dudes", meaning clothes. It means, if I remember correctly "one who renders himself conspicuous by affectation of dress, manners, and speech".'

'You've studied this?'

'I'm a lawyer, remember. Terminology is my oxygen.'

In the late 1800s and early 1900s, Stan explains, Western cattle ranches were owned by rich Easterners and businessmen from Chicago. These well-fed, well-dressed townies would come to visit their ranches each summer, often arriving on their own steam trains with whole entourages of servants, mistresses and children. They'd be taken out on the range with the real cowboys and allowed to lasso the odd steer, just like on modern-day dude ranches. Upon arrival at the ranch, they'd change out of smart city clothes (dudes) and put on cowboy gear. The real cowboys so admired their masters' urbane elegance that they adapted features for their own dress, such as waistcoats and colourful scarves. So originally dude meant 'tourist', or 'city slicker'.

'Apparently dude ranches are great places for singles,' smirks Stan.

We arrived at Rancho de la Mesa in time for lunch. It was down a winding dusty track, marked by a bleached white cattle skull, leading to an ancient hacienda shaded by eucalyptus trees. It seemed old and peaceful and very un-Club Med. In fact Rancho de la Mesa contains one of the oldest buildings in Arizona, built by Franciscan missionaries in the late 1500s, which is impressively historic even for a Brit. It was Spanish, then Mexican, until Arizona became the last of the forty-eight main states (excluding Hawaii and Alaska) to sign up to be American. They didn't fly the Stars and Stripes here until 1912.

Rancho de la Mesa became a dude ranch in 1928, when a rich Chicago banker built the hacienda. Famous visitors include Lyndon B. Johnson (whether Chief of Staff Walter Jenkins brought his young men along is either unrecorded or on the files of the FBI) and Democrat nominee Hubert Humphrey. There was also a fellow called William Clayton, the Under Secretary of State, who drafted the Marshall Plan in one of the guest rooms, thereby rebuilding Europe from the Mexican border.

We were met by the owners Robert and Samantha Segal, who moved into the ranch three years ago. They were lean, late thirties and ridiculously healthy, all tans and twinkling eyes.

'Welcome,' they drawled, in unison. Americans, to their credit, are about the only race who can say welcome and sound like they mean it, even when they don't. Or especially when they don't.

Inside the hacienda the colours were bright ochre, honey and bright blue. I was in the High Chapparal.

'We didn't want anything antithetical to the nature of this place. We're kind of trying to create perfect imperfection,' purred Samantha.

'We want to have the best of Mexico and none of the bad,' growled Robert.

'You'll love it here. Europeans always love it here. The vastness of this country blows them away.'

I was almost blown away. Actually I almost fell off my horse, but not because of the scenery, which was breathtaking, but because Cisco decided I might not be the best occupant for his saddle. I was nervous of Cisco. He knew I'd eaten *cheval*.

'He minds very well,' said Robert. Cisco pawed the ground. Like most of the ranch's thirty-five steeds, he was a quarter horse (bred to run a quarter of a mile, and therefore powerful, quick and ideal for chasing down errant cows).

'A horse is as smart as a three-year-old child,' continued Robert, as if this was meant to be comforting. Personally I wouldn't like to be out in rattlesnake-infested desert on the back of a three-year-old child, but at least a horse, according to Robert's logic, would be able to get me a beer from the fridge on our return.

'If he's not happy, his ears will go back,' Robert concluded.

Stan's horse was bigger than mine and called Lucky. This hardly seemed fair. Not only did he get to marry the love of his life, but he got the best horse on the ranch. I was about to complain when I realised I wouldn't be there but for him. The bastard.

Our fellow cowpeople were a mixed bunch. Several thirty-somethings, including Danny from San Francisco. I liked Danny. When asked what sort of horse he wanted he replied, 'Dead, and gets on with all the other horses.'

There were several families – the women comparing the stitching of boots and gloves, the men talking about the size of their hats. Ted McShay and his family from Kansas were sporting the Full Chisum – hats, boots, chaps, denim shirts.

'Well you wouldn't go to the beach without a swimsuit would you?' chirped Ted. 'I wore my boots around the office for three days before coming here. I'm not going to show up at a dude ranch with brand new boots.'

Ted was the spitting image of Angie's brother-in-law Tom. I liked Tom. So I liked Ted. I asked him if he'd ridden much before.

'I rented *City Slickers 1* and *2*.'

Alongside us was Al, who was eighty-two years old. He hadn't ridden a horse since he went back to Los Angeles after the war in 1945.

'I woke up one day, said to myself "I should get in the saddle again before it's too late."' We all nodded, admiringly. It's scary what top-notch healthcare does for elderly Americans. If things carry on like this, they'll live longer than plutonium.

We headed out on the range (I've always wanted to say that). We were doing 'the run for the border' – Mexico lurked about two miles from the ranch. Rancho de la Mesa had 180,000 acres for us to ride in (281 square miles). It used to be a ranch of 3 million acres (or 3 million soccer pitches, or 4687.5 square miles, which is bigger than The Gambia or Jamaica, so there).

We were an ungainly group, not so much Wild Bunch or Magnificent Seven as the Beverley Hillbillies. Dean from Seattle looked like a true cowboy – Levi's jacket, beard, flowing locks. Ted and family looked like *Little House on the Prairie*. And Stan looked like a lawyer in a cowboy hat. Americans, it must be said, make the most and least impressive cowboys.

Our leader on this daring mission was a woman – Maya, a fourth-generation Wyoming rancher, probably late forties, with white hair down to the small of her back and a face lined with decades of galloping through some of the sunniest parts of America. She hardly seemed to move in her saddle as we went, until I realised she was moving as one with the horse. I, in contrast, was moving as seven with my horse.

Cisco stopped and started eating some grass.

'Don't let him eat!' shouted Maya. I tugged on the reins. Cisco carried on eating, but at least his ears were no longer back. The rest of the posse had disappeared over the horizon before I could get him to move on, a small victory that coincided with him finishing all the grass within twenty feet.

I caught up with the Hillbillies at the border fence, a line of rusted barbed wire. In numerous places it had been stamped or pinned down with rocks to allow people to step over. On the Mexican side the ground was strewn with ragged blankets and empty plastic bottles.

'They hide in the bushes until night, then make a run for it,' explained Maya. 'The Border Patrol gets them by the afternoon and takes them back.'

The Americans looked at the barbed-wire fence, their last protection from invasion by Hispanic hordes. There was an uncomfortable silence, which surprised me. Americans seem afraid of very little (apart from failure and knowledge of anywhere outside the continental USA), but they are afraid of Mexico.

To break the ice Maya told the story of a friend of hers whose son was caught across the border with a handful of shotgun shells in the back of his truck. 'It cost $150,000 to get him out of jail,' she said. The Americans nodded.

'You have to remember,' Stan whispered as we trotted along the length of barbed wire, 'we've been fighting Spanish-speakers for land for 250 years. There's still a degree of mistrust.'

The heat hammered down. I personally wouldn't like to hide

under a bush with no leaves for twenty-four hours in order to run into an Arizonan desert crammed full of scorpions and rattlers to be chased by Border Patrol men, drugs-enforcement officials and the Army laden with the latest in weapons technology, with the possible but improbable goal of getting a job that pays $3.50 an hour cleaning out excrement from an all-you-can-eat chilli bar in Tuscon. But then I'm not an extremely poor Mexican with a large family to support.

The rusted barbed wire, ragged shirts, blankets and crumpled plastic water bottles, were sad. Sad small reminders of desperation.

I felt a little sick. Sick that I was all right, Jack. That I was on a highly expensive holiday playing at being Butch Cassidy, while people on the other side of the thin fence risked their lives to get jobs no one else would do. My melancholy about Angie seemed very small in comparison, but then, as someone once said, we all suffer according to our means.

At the sleepy border post a man on the other side waved forlornly, looking across to paradise, the promised land. I find America opulent. God knows what the Mexicans think.

I ceased my metaphysical angst when a jumping cholla, a cactus that, according to Maya, 'will leap up and spike you with its evil needles if you turn your back on it', leaped up and spiked me with its evil needles.

'Ow!'

'I warned you!'

We rode into town. Sasabe is a one-horse town, not counting six dogs and a couple of pickup trucks. A sign read 'Never Mind the Dog. Beware of the Owner.'

This town, at the end of America, is small and poor. People here earn their money from cutting mesquite bushes; the thin wood is used to make charcoal for flavoursome barbecues from Tijuana to Anchorage. In the general store, which sold everything, a young Mexican girl served us cold drinks. She was round with bright black eyes and a smile that would launch a Trojan War. Her name was Juanita and she lived in Sasabe, USA with her aunt. Her mother lived in Sasabe, Mexico, two miles down the road, but Juanita saw her only once a week (which I suppose is better than a lot of children at English private schools).

'But I am American,' she said earnestly. I explained that I was not American, but English. When the other Americans were out of earshot she handed me an ice-cold Coke.

'I would rather be Mexican,' she said quietly, 'but who can afford it?'

We got back to the ranch around 1 p.m. The horses were drenched with sweat, and the roads were starting to melt. I climbed down off Cisco, whose relieved eyes were less those of a three-year-old child and more like those of a twenty-seven-year-old woman whose elderly husband had just died leaving her a hefty shares portfolio.

All the talk about man's affinity with horse, getting to know your horse, rider and horse as one – I finally understood it, because Cisco and I were none of these things.

Walking back to the hacienda, I also understood why cowboys are bowlegged. It felt like I'd been wrapped round a barrel for three days (try it at home and see how you cope). But it was great to get off a horse, grab a beer and sit in the sun, listening to the horses naying and the hot wind rustling in the eucalyptus and talking about a long hard day in the saddle, even when that day was only three hours long.

This seems to be what dude ranch holidays are all about. Like Stan's friends from Beverly Hills, we were all convinced we were getting back to the primitive. I sat nursing a Corona with the feeling that people had done this here for hundreds of years, that my sore legs, cactus-spiked backside and sunburn were part of a long and noble tradition dating back to the first Spanish conquistadors.

Stan went off to have phone sex with Meg. I sat in a deckchair, cowboy hat pulled low, and chatted with Maya the cowlady through the long slow hours of the afternoon.

It was her sixth year in Arizona after a lifetime in the snow and heat of Wyoming. 'Women are very much accepted in ranching in Wyoming. After all, it was the first state to give women the vote,' she stated, with John Wayne gravel in her voice. 'It's harder for a female down here though. There's still some of that Spanish machismo. But I'll tell you this: women have more patience with their horses.'

According to Maya, a good wrangler must have a knowledge of horses 'but also a second sight to pick horses for people who you've never met. It comes with experience. You have to like people. And if you don't like them you have to be a good actor.' Dude ranching is easier than working on a cattle ranch. On working ranches, recalled Maya, you're in the saddle twelve to fourteen hours a day.

'Work was part of my childhood,' said Maya, and I nodded vigorously in the heat, even though avoiding work was part of my childhood. 'Ranching was a way of life. But now the old family ranches are dying out, going belly-up. It's the Forestry Service, the Bureau of Land Management. There's stricter regulation of grazing, down to the level of the grass that cows are permitted to chew. The big shots in Washington are controlling the lives of people whose ancestors have been farming this land for hundreds of years, for whom the land is their bread and butter. Them sitting in DC have never even seen the mountains.' There was perspiration on Maya's furrowed brow. 'We don't have enough people in our state,' she said quietly. 'We don't have enough votes to count.'

I was reminded of Judy's words on Tangier Island, of the innate rural mistrust of the city. And of Americans' schizophrenia – on the one hand a distrust of bureaucracy, on the other the most complicated legal system in the world. I began to glimpse why people bought seventeen machine guns and holed up in concrete bunkers and then sued the government when FBI agents burst in and inadvertently broke their collection of vintage Star Wars figurines.

Almost.

By her third beer Maya had softened. She said she loved

Arizona for the sunsets and sunrises. She thought dude ranches were vitally important in preserving ranching traditions, the ways of the Old West.

'Most horses of this class and kind, the way the economy is, they'd be dead now if it weren't for ranches like this. A ranch gelding would get $650 a carcass from a factory in Ohio that processes meat for France and Asia. Or they'd be turned into dog food.'

I made a note to tell Cisco he was lucky to be alive.

'What makes us here so special,' concluded Maya before going to put her horses to bed, 'is we still have all the land around, and all the history. Coming here is like stepping back in time.'

The sun set, leaving a sky empty except for colour – the burning ember of the day, still hot but now gentler, a musing heat, dry and easy. This was a place where land and sky were still the biggest things around.

We sat on the steps of the sixteenth-century mission house and drank beer. Stan was brushed and scrubbed and grinning, so I assumed the phone call had gone well. Everyone chatted to everyone else, puffed up with pride at our dash along the border.

Americans, I decided, flushed with Arizonan sun, Mexican beer and the quality soreness that came from several hours astride a large mammal, are about the only people who could make a dude ranch work. Because a dude ranch will only work if its guests are (a) enthusiastically willing to make a fool of themselves and (b) friendly. Even though we'd only just met, our happy band of twenty or so desperadoes were yabbering away as if this was an old school reunion. Everyone was telling stories, even Almost-Married Stan, who usually restricted any information about himself for fear of litigation.

I found myself next to Bud, Maya's co-tourist wrangler, also an ex-rancher from Wyoming. Bud was about my age and a big man, seemingly cumbersome on land but as lithe and sinewy as a ferret in the saddle. He sported a droopy Wyatt Earp moustache and the ruddy cheeks of someone for whom the four basic food groups are eggs, beans, coffee and steak.

Bud said he found dude ranching a little strange to begin with. 'At home, if someone falls off you ride by and laugh at them. Here you stop and help.'

Over three more beers he gave me the lowdown on the history of cowboying. Cows, he said, were introduced by the Spanish in the mid-1500s, who also brought over the horse to the Americas. Whilst breeding horses, some escaped, to form the herds of wild horses so prized by cowboy films.

The first organised herding of large numbers of cattle took place in 1800, when Spanish ranchers noted the long tall grass and wide empty spaces of Texas. The first cattle drive west occurred in 1843, when ranchers noted that a cow you could sell for three dollars in Texas would fetch two hundred dollars in California.

In real life, said Bud (end of his second beer), guns were not carried openly on the range, as dust clogged up the firing mechanisms. Six-shooters and rifles were kept wrapped in blankets, like infants. Also, any visible wearing of weapons would have been likely to antagonise local Indians, who tended to need little excuse to attack. Cattle drives that passed through Indian territory had to pay small tithes to the local chief rather than brazenly hurtle into ambushes.

'You know how the term "Maverick" came about?' (third beer, first whisky).

I shook my head, because I didn't.

'Maverick was a rancher in Galvaston, Texas whose farm was on an island just offshore. Because his cows were cut off from the mainland he didn't bother with branding. But when there was a real low tide, the cattle used to escape and wander about town – no branding, nowhere to go. The locals called 'em mavericks.'

I nodded. It might, after all, be true.

Bud concluded with a flourish, 'Man and horse have been partners for 4,000 years. That relationship has only begun to break down in the last 100 years. Both horse and human can do something together that neither can do alone. The horse realises you can't do without it in the desert. I've been nine days alone with a horse in the desert. You think you get a bit goofy talking to it, but a relationship develops. You'll see . . .'

I was convinced. I and Cisco would be as one.

We sat out and ate tamales under the electric blue skirt of the Arizonan dusk. Satellites zipped overhead, but otherwise the night was ancient. A coyote whined somewhere distant.

I sat next to Old Tom from Georgia, whose wife Maddy was a keen rider. Old Tom said he didn't like horses, but he was happy 'to sit, drink, and laugh', which sounded like a fine way to spend a week. There were several families, children running round excitedly until one father or mother used the ultimate verbal sanction in southern Arizona, 'Be careful, Joey. There's snakes out there at night.'

One couple had a nine-month-old baby, who sat demurely in a baby-sized cowboy hat. I must be going soft, because I found myself smiling warmly into my burrito.

Did I want children?

Shit.

It was happening.

I was becoming my parents.

I had my last drink of the day with Ted and family. By now I was fuzzily broody. Ted's family were like Angie's cousins, and maybe for a moment I was kidding myself that they really were Angie's cousins and the break-up never happened and Angie would come down the dusty track and we'd go to the cabana and start trying for a family (which would hopefully take more than one go).

Ted and daughter Joanne and son Sean were trying to figure out how long it would take to ride Sparky, Grey and Bubbles, their dude ranch horses, back to Kansas. We figured on 1,000 miles, at about 30 miles a day. That was two months.

'Sure we could do it,' said Ted. 'Just like John Wayne.'

It then turned out that Joanne didn't know who John Wayne was. I wondered out loud what America was coming to.

'It all went wrong when Clint Eastwood started doing comedy,' explained Ted. We all nodded sadly.

Before I departed, Ted, who'd had a few tequilas along with his eleven beers, grabbed my arm.

'Listen, Jim. You've got to live for today. Look at Old Tom.'

I looked. Old Tom was giggling into his Dos Equis.

'He's eighty-five. And he's still having a ball. Isn't that great?'

Ted then told me with American candour that both his parents died young. 'They never got to enjoy what Old Tom there's enjoying. The love of his kids, his family. I want to enjoy that.'

I staggered away from worship at the mission house. All was silent, a beautiful emptiness. Even two weeks shy of midsummer, the night air was cool – we were at 3,700 feet.

'I want to enjoy that.'

I was staying in room 5, where *Gone with the Wind* author Margaret Mitchell once slept. On the bed there were seven cushions. Americans, like most imperialists, love cushions. I hadn't the energy to remove them and tumbled into the most tranquil sleep in months, dreaming that I was a baby in a nest, being mothered by Vivien Leigh.

I wake early the next day. It's still dark, but only just. Outside I hear the horses stirring, their hooves pattering the ground as gently as lapping water. I walk out into the dawn.

At the stables a donkey comes to the gate to sniff the air. A distant cockerel calls. I stand, alone, breathing in the immense stillness, the mountains behind soft orange, and beyond the bold silhouette of the Baboquivari Mountain, where according to Indian mythology, God dwells, overlooking his world.

Gradually, inevitably, the sun blossoms out of the cold mountain peak. Dogs begin quarrelling, the donkey starts to bay. The world is coming alive once more.

Vegas, LA, Washington are a long way away. And so is Niagara Falls.

I can feel the world turning beneath my feet.

I find myself walking up a small track, through the ebony mesquite trees, their chaotic branches reaching for the sun.

Warmth silking the land. I reach a small cemetery, a scattering of crumbling Mexican graves from another age. I open the gate, which creaks as all cemetery gates should, as a welcome call to the dead, and wander among the stones, the plastic flowers, the small makeshift mementoes of lives long gone.

It's the first time I've ever visited a cemetery before breakfast.

There's only one gravestone with a legible epitaph.

William Charles Davis Senior. 'Only those who dare truly live.'

Back at the ranch, breakfast is cooking. Don, the ranch foreman, is sniffing the air.

'You know, son, out of all the places I've worked at, this one is the most benign. There's something benevolent here. Spiritual.'

I smile, and sit down to gorge myself on eggs and beans.

Stan is looking tired. 'Three in the goddamn morning and she was still going on about the freaking seating plan . . .'

He decides to eschew the morning ride in favour of that other traditional cowboy pursuit – reading *Vanity Fair* by the pool.

This time we mount our horses with greater swagger. Cisco's ears go back when I come near, but I'm ready for him.

'Dog food,' I whisper. His ears go forward and I get on without further complication. I admit I'm beginning to enjoy the feeling of climbing up on to a horse. The lazy swing, left to right over the saddle, and clumph, you're in the driving seat.

I decide I've rarely felt better.

'Only those who dare' said the epitaph, and I realise I don't want mine to read: 'James Keeble. Could have had a better time'.

We ride up to Rattlesnake Ridge. There are no rattlesnakes but there are telegraph poles stretching into the distance in a highly cinematic way. I start humming the theme from *Chisum*. Across the valley drifts the scent of mesquite smoke. Butterflies are butterflying. A buzzard laces lazily through the cloudless sky.

'Looks like we got ourselves some of that famous Arizona

weather,' says Maya. By this she means it's a hot one. Last year, she tells us, the thermometer topped out at 133 degrees.

'Melted my hat.'

We stop and admire the view, wiping sweat from brow as if we're being filmed in Cinemascope. The valley is empty as far as the eye can see, to the great rock of the Baboquivari, and God him, or herself.

Ted pulls Sparky alongside. 'Okay, I'm Catholic, but I don't see how you can look at that scene and not believe in some greater power.'

I agree. A view like this makes you believe in Warner Brothers.

It seems like there's nothing for sixty miles around. Vast plains. As we amble along like some shambolic ex-posse, everyone is singing to themselves, which is a pretty good barometer of whether people are having fun (unless you're my mum and it's raining in the Lake District).

There's no talking, only snatches of song, buzzing of bees and the mewl of buzzard. It may well be pantomime, but I sense a more ancient stillness, the communion of human, horse and landscape, a lolloping, temperate rhythm of hoof on dust that stirs something strong and tranquil deep inside.

After the later afternoon ride, out amongst ragged cactus and twisted mesquite, during which Stan admits he's always wanted to be James Coburn, something he makes me swear I'll never tell Meg, I feel like I've been a cowboy all my life. All right, we've not actually encountered any cattle, but I'm convinced I'd have no trouble lassoing unruly bulls or charging down steep inclines into fast running rivers shouting, 'Geronimo!'

The first beer tastes sweet. I sit on the mission hall steps and watch the sun set, saying a little prayer to the God who lives on top of Baboquivari. Not a bad day, considering it began in a cemetery. Did I live it as if it was my last . . . ?

As if it was my second last. At least.

I see Debbie at dinner. She's arrived with her friend Mary from Portland, Oregon. Mary is a dark-haired lawyer with a cynical sense of humour and before long she and Stan are arguing about the death penalty, which Mary claims to agree with, especially lethal injection, which she champions as the most 'natural way' to dispatch a human being. Various parents are talking loudly to their children to prevent them from hearing.

I don't mind Mary's rhetoric because it gives me a chance to talk to Debbie, who tells me she's local, hailing from Phoenix. Now before anyone cackles, I must point out that I don't usually find blonde women attractive, and maybe it's the sun, or the cowboy hat, or a feeling of being emasculated by a grass-chewing horse, or the wine on top of the beer, or whatever, but right now Debbie seems, how shall we say, knockout. She must be late thirties, maybe even forty, and she's very pretty, well preserved in an expensive, fully moisturised, six-days-a-week-at-the-gym sort of way, and she has fantastic breasts, which may or may not be her own. And she's smarter than the average blonde (no, a blonde joke will not be forthcoming).

I ask her what she does for a living (cool and debonair, n'est-ce pas?).

'I'm retired.'

'From what?'

'Had my own advertising company. Sold it last year.'

'What did you advertise?' (smooth as taramasalata).

'Whatever the client paid us to . . .'

'Yes. Of course. That makes sense . . .'

Somehow, over the course of the meal I manage to claw my way back from this dismal start. I tell her about my travels around the States, and I don't mention Angie once. It turns out she's trying to write a novel based on her family (Swedish farmers from the northern Norbotten region who came to North Dakota where they decided the winters weren't cold enough, so they moved up to Hudson Bay to hunt seals).

'Ever been to Canada?' she asks.

'Er . . . not really.'

'I had a Canadian boyfriend. He proposed. But I couldn't

face the thought of those winters. I guess I'm nothing like my ancestors.'

Debbie has one blue eye and one green eye. She also has a very small waist.

Mary and Stan are still arguing about the death penalty.

'You can't play God!' exclaims Stan as children are escorted from the courtyard.

'God is dead!' retorts Mary, slugging a full glass of Saint-Emilion.

'Only because he was wrongfully convicted of first-degree murder in Texas!'

The night is long and warm. We move to the mission hall but, strangely, few people join us. Just wrangler Brad, and Old Tom, who sits at the bar and sneaks glances at Debbie's breasts. Old Tom enjoys life.

Mary and Stan stop arguing about the death penalty and start arguing about tobacco legislation.

'They should pay up. Cigarettes kill . . .' intones Stan.

'So do cars. So what are you going to do, sue Ford? General Motors?'

I tell Debbie about my first ever encounter with a horse, in the cub scouts at the age of six, when I refused to be lifted into the saddle and everyone laughed. She tells me about her time as a cheerleader.

Stan stops talking suddenly. Every man in the room is seeing the same image: Debbie at sixteen in her cheerleader's outfit.

'Yeah,' adds Mary. 'We were cheerleaders together.'

The image becomes less immaculate.

To break the awkward silence, I ask how they held their pompoms. (*Suave moi, non?*)

'That's the drill team, dummy,' says Debbie, jabbing me with a finger. I find I like being jabbed by Debbie's finger.

'Silly me.'

True cheerleaders, it appears, never touch pompoms. They are artists with no need of props, except short skirts and spangles.

'The key to cheerleading,' continues Mary, as animated when talking about high school football games as when extolling the virtues of death row executions, 'was to smile without making your eyes move.'

Debbie nods. I sit, nursing a tequila, unable to believe my good fortune. Here I am, on the Mexican border with two American cheerleaders. Ex-cheerleaders. Talk about the American Dream.

When I was an acne-ridden adolescent I'd watch American TV shows and films like *Happy Days*, *The Brady Bunch* and *Grease*, where all the girls dressed up in tight sweaters and skirts no British mother would sanction and jumped up and down in adoration of boys kicking a pig-skin around some grass. It seemed so unfair. When we played soccer, on sodden Saturday mornings, we were lucky to get an old man and a dog with diarrhoea watching us play. Where were the girls? The chants? The mini-skirts?

To the delight of the four men in the room, Debbie and Mary get up and go through a routine.

'Linden Hall, Linden Hall! Go! Go! Go!'

We applaud, as much for the past as for the present.

'It was very stressful,' admits Debbie.

'We were always on the bottom of the pyramid,' snorts Mary.

The pyramid?

'There were five levels to the pyramid,' explains Debbie. 'The short girls had it made, they were always on top, didn't matter how heavy they were.'

'You know, Debs, they all wear support hose now . . .'

'You've been following this?'

'Sally's girl just got on the team.'

Bud the wrangler looks up. 'Support hose?'

I look to Stan. He's nodding, as if he knows what support hose is, which considering he's about to be married, he might. I try to look knowledgeable by consulting the bottom of an empty tequila glass.

'You don't know what support hose is?' asks Debbie.

'Lycra bandages,' mutters Stan. Everyone turns to look at him. 'They're skin-coloured, used to help support muscles and keep cellulite in.'

He looks up at our bemused faces, as he usually gazes into the eyes of a jury. 'I had a girlfriend one time who worked in Hooters,' he admits, face reddening.

'Does Meg know?' I whisper.

'I thought I'd tell her after the honeymoon.'

'I've never been to Hooters,' intones Bud sorrowfully. 'There's a lot of places I haven't been.'

Mary snorts again. Debbie goes to the bar and pours another drink. I have a sudden, sneaking suspicion that she may once have worked in Hooters.

Later.

Bud and Debbie are country dancing, twirling around to a Garth Brooks CD. Bud is trying to get her as close as possible, which is understandable. He's surprisingly dainty on his feet. As is Debbie.

Later still.

We're talking about horses. I get some tips.

'The horse that looks fat, don't let that fool you,' says Bud. 'They're often the best.'

I get the feeling Bud is also talking about himself.

In a swift moment Debbie's hand brushes mine.

She goes to the bar. I follow, lean against the wood like Lee Van Cleef.

'Er . . . I need some air. Fancy a walk?' (*Subtle moi, non?*)

To my heart-thumping joy, Debbie says, 'sure, why not?'

I can feel Bud's sad eyes following us.

Outside the air has cooled once more. On the mission hall steps Foreman Don is standing gazing at the stars, breathing it in. He smiles at us.

'We had a couple staying here from New York City one time. I was hammering this new roof and I saw them dragging their

212

chairs closer to me across the yard. "Why are you doing that?" I asked. "We miss the noise," they said.'

Debbie and I walk out past the buildings along the sand-filled old river bed. I try not to panic that every rustle in the undergrowth is a fleet of rattlesnakes, priming themselves for attack. Beyond is the empty arch of night, the silver dust of stars.

We look up at the stars. It would be hard not to, as there seem to be at least 16 million of them. It's the sort of sky that makes you want to believe in aliens even if you don't, or want to believe in God if you only believe in aliens.

'Ever seen a UFO?' I ask.

'I don't think so. Thought maybe I saw one once as a kid in Wisconsin, but we did live on the O'Hare flight path.'

We gaze upwards. On such a night it's not impossible that a spaceship might appear, or indeed God. If this was a movie a shooting star would burst overhead, but it's not, and it doesn't.

Silence. A rustling of rattler, or something in the undergrowth. I glance at Debbie, who's looking skywards. Actually, I glance at her breasts and think it would be really great to touch them and I move closer and she doesn't move away.

Only those who dare truly live. The ghost of William Charles Davis Senior is out tonight.

So I touch her breasts, gently, and then I leap back in terror, because I realise I've just touched a Class A sexual harassment suit.

Debbie's friend, Mary from Seattle, is a lawyer and loves the death penalty. What will she demand for such blatant abuse of her oldest and dearest friend?

'CASTRATION, YOUR HONOUR, IS THE ONLY SOLUTION!'

At least that would solve one problem.

Debbie looks at me.

'I'm sorry . . . I didn't mean . . .' I stammer, guilty as charged. My pounding heart fills the galaxy.

She steps towards me and kisses me, not passionately, a

practised kiss that is far from the first or last she'll ever give. A kiss of beer, peanuts and sunshine.

My hand on Debbie's left breast and it's more solid than I've been used to among the few sets of mammaries I've had the good fortune to clutch. A shifting of matter within matter.

'Okay, so there's some enhancement . . .' grins Debbie before kissing me again, 'but it feels good doesn't it?'

My heart pounding fills the universe. Snogging an ex-cheerleader with breast implants beneath a billion stars in the middle of the Arizonan desert. If that's not the American Dream, I don't know what is.

We kiss for what may be several months, and she has a small but insistent tongue, and that's all the detail I'm prepared to impart. Except that my hand was prevented from straying too far from silicone and she did nothing to tarnish her cheerleading reputation.

Unfortunately.

'So?' demanded Stan the next morning. 'Which base?'

'Which base?'

'Which base did you get to with Hotstuff?'

'First.'

'First? You only got to first?'

'Last night, Stanley, I was just happy to get on the team.'

Debbie is nowhere to be seen. Her convertible BMW shines brightly in the parking lot, but her cabana door remains resolutely shut. She knows I'm leaving. I know I'm leaving.

I leave.

Driving north. On the map is a settlement called Surprise. Surprise, Arizona. Stan informs me there's also a Surprise in New York, Indiana, Tennessee, Nebraska and California. So coming across a Surprise is not much of a surprise.

We're on a smaller road now. No cars for a thousand miles, a single white line, stretching to the end of the world. We come over a hill into forests of slender cactus, like petrified anorexics, tall and slender, then into a cactus graveyard, dead cacti like rolls of rotten carpet, some riddled with holes, like sockets of skulls. A single cactus sits like a club stuck in the ground. Others squat like balls of barbed wire. It's a cartoon landscape, blue sky, red rocks, green cacti. All that's missing is Wil E. Coyote.

I am feeling away. Away from Angie, away from England, Canada, the rest of the world. And it feels great.

In this strange warped desert not of this planet, I feel liberated. Free. There's something about the expanse of the land, a land that hasn't changed in dozens of hundreds of years. An ancient, immutable simplicity.

I feel exhilarated, exalted, exhaled and exchanged. Redeemed. Thanks to this great, glitzy, glaring, gregarious, gigantic country, where freshly squeezed orange juice is a right not a luxury and silicone-breasted blonde women drive BMW sports cars and write novels about seal-clubbing Swedes.

God bless America.

'Have you got a suit?' asks Stan as we reach the concrete maelstrom of Phoenix.

'No. Why?'

'For the wedding. I want you to be best man.'

8

Leah – A Minnesota Girl

I was happy to be flying to Minnesota, a state famed even within America for its wide open spaces. After Virginia and Arizona, I had a sneaking suspicion my improved soul-state had something to do with broad horizons and empty vistas, and Minnesota is pretty empty. Roughly the size of Britain, it has a population of 4.3 million. And I was going to the setting for one of my favourite films of all time (just behind *Butch Cassidy and the Sundance Kid* and ahead of *Mighty Ducks 2*) – the Coen brothers' *Fargo*.

The only thing I wasn't glad about was the fact I was to be Stan's best man. I felt honoured and all, in the same way Lord Cardigan must have felt honoured to have been selected to front the Charge of the Light Brigade, but I had three concerns (terrors):

1. It would be my first wedding since I asked Angie to marry me and she said no.
2. It would be my first visit back to Canada since I asked Angie to marry me and she said no.
3. It would be my first ever best man's speech.

Minnesota is nice. Minnesotans are nice. Minnesotans are the first to tell you this. Then they tell you they're inscrutably honest.

Nice, and honest.

The deviants.

They're also outsiders in more ways than one. The rest of

America likes to make fun of their accents, their geography, hidden away near the border of some country called Canada, their predilections for dairy products and their weather – minus forty degrees in winter, plus ninety degrees in summer. With a climate like that, Minnesotans should be barking schizophrenics. Instead they're level-headed Democrats.

Because the rest of America laughs at them, every so often Minnesotans like to rebel against the rest of America in a nice, honest way. For example, you don't have to wear a motorbike helmet in Minnesota. And there's still a state law (#42.03) claiming Minnesota's right to use the weather within its boundaries for its own nefarious purposes: 'The state of Minnesota claims its sovereign right to use for its residents the moisture contained in the clouds and atmosphere within its sovereign state boundaries.' So if it doesn't rain in North Dakota or Wisconsin, you'll know why.

Most recently Minnesotans rebelled by voting in Jesse 'The Body' Ventura as their governor. I can't fault them – I'd have voted for Jesse. 'The Body' is an ex-Navy Commando, ex-pro-wrestler, and ex-radio shock jock. And he used to be a bodyguard for the Rolling Stones.

Now he's the nation's first state governor to have his own action figure doll (twelve dollars – wears both commando fatigues and dark gubernatorial suit). He's a six-foot-four, eighteen-stone Porsche driver who's considering legalising drugs and prostitution, not to mention lowering the vehicle licence fee (he has four cars), removing the surcharge on jetskis (Jesse has five) and awarding the governor's wife a yearly stipend of $25,000 (his wife's name is Terry). In his campaign he used the theme tune from *Shaft* and regularly quoted those deceased sages, Jerry Garcia and Jim Morrison. And last year he declared 15 February 'Rolling Stones Day' in honour of his former employers.

It's difficult not to like Jesse, especially when you're someone who's not affected by his governorship. And Minnesotans seemed happy enough to vote for him – he won 37 per cent of the vote in an election with America's highest turn-out – 61 per cent (which doesn't say much for democracy in the world's greatest democracy). Perhaps it was his punchy sloganeering: 'Our Governor Can Beat Up Your Governor!'

His honesty is refreshing. On cannabis Jesse says: 'Of course I've smoked marijuana. Who hasn't?'

On the homeless: 'We have charities, don't we?'

On students: 'If they're bright enough to go to college, they're bright enough to figure out how to pay for it.'

On the arts: 'I don't know. Do you want me to start painting?'

In a *Playboy* interview he admitted he would like to be reincarnated . . . as a 38DD bra. This man is not, it has to be said, Tony Blair.

I'd decided to rent a car and spend two days driving up through Jesse's land to the site of the wedding – Rainy Lake, straddling the Canadian border. The man at the Avis desk was blond and large.

'Howya dueen?' he beamed.

'Fine, thanks. You?'

'Ja. Sure.'

If you've seen *Fargo*, you'll know the accent. Descended almost entirely from Norwegian and Swedish settlers, northern Minnesotans have maintained a lilting almost Scandinavian accent and big, happy Scandinavian looks. There are thirty-eight Donald Petersons in the Minneapolis phone book.

I began my Minnesotan tour stocking up on provisions at the Mall of America. Such a title deserves to be visited. Of course it's the 'Biggest Mall in America'. Of course it's got 500 stores, a 14-screen movie theatre, 25 restaurants, 27 fast-food outlets, a mini-golf course, a 70,000-square-foot aquarium with sharks and a Snoopy Amusement Park (Charles M. Schulz, the creator of Peanuts, was born in St Paul), all in a shell the size of Wembley Stadium.

Driving up to it the building doesn't look that impressive, but when you get inside you realise what a miracle the architects have achieved – they've managed to cram a camel-load of crap into the eye of a needle.

There are statistics galore. The Mall contains 45 miles of telephone cable; 32 Boeing 747s could fit inside it, or 24,336 school buses (which I assume means up to 500,000 American schoolchildren, a terrifying thought). Apparently, if I was to spend 10 minutes in every store I would get out of The Mall of America in 86 hours or 3½ days.

I lasted 37 minutes. The Mall was a vast prison full of very loud overweight inmates, or the retail equivalent of a Las Vegas all-you-can-eat-buffet.

A 1997 survey conducted by the National Park Service and *Road Smart Magazine* lists the Mall of America as the most visited destination for US travellers. More popular than the Grand Canyon, Yellowstone National Park, the Empire State Building, New York's Metropolitan Museum and Washington's Smithsonian. Which says something about US travellers.

I bought a can of Coke. And ran.

I drove into St Paul, the smaller and more historic sibling of the Twin Cities in search of antiquity. St Paul is the political centre of the state, and its literary cradle. F. Scott Fitzgerald came from St Paul. The Great Gatsby, I recalled, was a Midwesterner.

As an antidote to America's biggest mall, I visited the Minnesota History Centre. As you enter, there's an inscription from dead environmentalist Sigurd F. Olson: 'If we can live in our modern world with the ancient dreams that have always stirred us, then our work will have been done.'

The museum exhibits illustrate the short but hard-fought story of Minnesotan life. As far as I could tell Minnesotan life had developed thus: Indians hunted buffalo and farmed in a disorganised way. Numerous Nordic immigrants arrived, hunted buffalo and Indians, and farmed in an organised way. Cereal crops were grown. Cows were raised, milk, cheese and butter made the Norse folk even bigger. And that is pretty much that.

Being of Scandinavian stock, the Norse folk were instinctively socialists and provided the Democratic Party with large amounts of votes, not to mention several failed presidential candidates, from 1968's Eugene 'Clean for Gene' McCarthy (he encouraged students to shave and cut off their long hair) and Hubert Humphrey (who was trounced by Richard Nixon) to the pasty-faced Walter Mondale. Remember Walter Mondale? No, I don't either.

Exhibits also display the personal effects of famous Minnesotan artists, from *Little House on the Prairie* author Laura Ingalls's pen collection to The Artist Formerly Known As Prince's high heels. This is Minnesota, it seems, a happy marriage of bizarre extremes. My favourite part of the museum was where you climbed up the steps of a grain elevator and launched yourself on to a conveyor belt, pretending you're a corn grain. Only I wasn't allowed to, being noticeably older than ten.

Outside the afternoon was hot. Wet hot, damp hot, moist hot, soggy hot. Minnesota means 'Cloudy Water' in Sioux, and there's no shortage of H_2O in the state – 95 per cent of the population live within ten minutes' drive of a lake. At last count, Minnesota boasted 10,000 lakes. It's rare you meet a Minnesotan who doesn't know how to swim, or fish – some can do both.

In wintertime this water in the air means snowfalls can be all consuming. The state police cars are burgundy, so they're visible if they get stuck in drifts. Because of extreme winter cold, downtown Minneapolis is laced with covered walkways linking all the major offices and shops, making the city look like an outdated Russian space station (circa 1961) that the Politburo had designed by deranged impotent scientists called Yurgi but without the technology nor the money to build it. Many of the bigger offices boast trees, shrubs and the odd patches of grass within their precincts, adding to a sense of a strange lunar experiment.

I stopped and sweated for a while by the river, which surged and tumbled over rapids and falls in the centre of town. Only as I read a rusted information sign (a bad habit of mine), did I realise the staggering truth. This was the Mississippi!

The MISSISSIPPI!!!!! What in bejesus was the Mississippi doing up here?

I've always liked the Mississippi. As a child it was one of those words that was simply fun to say. I went through a phase of saying it a lot.

'Can you pass the Mississippi ketchup?'

'I'm feeling very Mississippi today.'

'You Mississippi idiot!'

For a short while I believed Mississippi was a unit of time, as it seemed to be a universally accepted quantity used for counting during all games that involved small children scampering away to hide.

'One hundred and seventy-three Mississippi.'

It was also a great word to spell. It hardly seemed credible that a word could have so many of the same letters. It went against all grammatical training.

And, best of all, it sounded like someone having a pee.

Here I was, on the banks of the upper Mississippi, from where the mighty river surged 2,300 miles south to New Orleans. The rusted sign said the river acquired its name from the Native Americans, who called it Misi Sipi, or 'big river'. Apparently, the big river begins as a small piddle in the Lake Itasca region of Minnesota, and then drains most of America's central plains between the Rocky Mountains and the Appalachians. If it wasn't for the Mississippi, Iowa would be under water. There would also be civil war between the states of Minnesota and Wisconsin, Iowa and Illinois, Missouri and Tennessee, and Arkansas and Mississippi, since the river forms the border between them.

Old Man River. Meet thirty-year-old Jim.

I ended my visit to the Twin Cities with a drive down Cretin Avenue. It would have been rude not to.

From downtown Minneapolis, highway 10 leads north to St Cloud through rich pasture, maize fields, lakes and white picket fence houses where Stars and Stripes fly proudly against a blue sky. On the surface this seems a perfect America, devoid of violence, racial tension, garbage and Jay Leno.

It's the land of Garrison Keillor, of his stories about the fictional northern town of Lake Wobegon, where 'all the women are strong and all the men are beautiful'. Even the roadside advertising is wholly wholesome – blond children smiling down over the highway, glasses of milk in their innocent hands.

Such sweeping fields of corn, such green lawns, such fresh-leaved maples, such picket fences and sweet-toothed children put me in a fine mood, which is only enhanced when I chance upon 107.5FM, 'The Power Loon!'.

The Power Loon is a hell of a radio station. It plays eighties rock in between commercials for fishing bait and ammunition. Local boy, Rich Midget, sorry The Artist Formerly Known As Prince comes on three times in an hour.

'You don't have to be beautiful, to turn me on . . .' (but it helps).

At once Rich Midget makes me feel happy and sad. Angie and I dancing on the beach in Nice.

I still miss her (yes, I'm bored of it too). But in the summer heat, the verdant bountifulness of Minnesota, it's a nostalgic yearning, as if for childhood or a cup-winning soccer season. On the road are numerous cars with Ontario licence plates, but I feel the knot of sadness break and ease through me, until I can breathe it out, and maybe, for the first time, smile at my memories.

I'm looking forward to Stan and Meg's wedding. Meg's family have a house on a lake just across the border in Canada. They'll tie the knot at the water's edge, on a small island that is almost the exact geographic centre of the continent of North America, 1,300 miles from any sea.

And Meg has lots of single girlfriends.

North of St Cloud is the town of Brainerd. Upon seeing the sign, I start clapping my hands in glee, which causes my fellow drivers some alarm. Because Brainerd is *Fargo* country. In *Fargo* a ninety-foot-high statue of Paul Bunyan, the American folk-tale lumberjack, stands at the entrance to Brainerd. I arrive in town, and gaze up and down Main Street.

Nothing.

I drive the backstreets for an hour.

Still nothing.

How can you miss a ninety-foot-high statue of Paul Bunyan?

The convenience store clerk shakes his head, 'No sir. That statue's up in Bimidji. They stretched the truth in the film. We do have a Paul Bunyan Park, if you're interested.'

The Paul Bunyan Park does boast its own Paul Bunyan statue, albeit a much smaller version than in the film. It also has a ten-foot-high Babe the Blue Ox.

Paul Bunyan, for those of you who don't know your American history, was a Minnesotan lumberjack who was as big as a mountain. He travelled everywhere with his pet blue ox, Babe, whom he'd saved from drowning as a calf and who became so big it would take a crow a day to fly from one of Babe's horns to the other. Paul and Babe are credited with creating many American landmarks, from the Rocky Mountains to the Mississippi River. It's a nice creation myth, like Adam and Eve. The only problem is that Adam and Eve is now being taught as natural history in certain Southern schools.

Instead of consorting with Paul and Babe, I opted instead for authentic Middle America – the baseball batting cage. It was run by two boys barely out of diapers. Willie (thick set and blond) showed me how to hold the bat while Ade (thick set and blond) made sure the throwing machine was fast enough to scare the pants, socks and body hair off any lily-livered European stupid enough to think he could take on America's national sport.

They'd not met anyone from across the Atlantic before and we shook hands warmly before I entered the cage, Daniel to the baseballs.

WUTHD!

That's the sound of a baseball travelling at 100 m.p.h., narrowly missing an Englishman and whacking into the padded wall behind the batting cage.

'A little fast for me, lads . . .'

They cranked the machine down to 70 m.p.h. and the next ball nearly cannoned a hole in my stomach.

'Any chance of it a little bit slower?'

'Slower? He wants it slower?'

'Okay Ade, go ahead and put it on the infant setting.'

'You think?'

'Ja, sure.'

On the infant setting I hit two out of twenty-five balls. Ade and Willie watched in amazement, although to their credit they didn't laugh. It's difficult to laugh when your mouth is wide open.

I was a little upset. I was in a mind to drive back to the Mall of America, purchase a soccer ball and return to challenge the two of them to a game of headers and volleys, but thankfully I'm more mature than that.

'You don't have a soccer ball here do you?'

'Soccer? No. Why?'

'Oh, nothing. Nothing.'

I'm thirty. I can accept humiliation – after all, who cares about baseball? Only 275 million Americans, most of Central and South America, and all of Japan.

To conceal my shame, I asked Willie and Ade what there was to do in Brainerd.

'Oh, not so much. Baseball. Movies. Working on the farm.'

'It's kinda quiet.'

Willie explained that he would, however, soon be departing happy Brainerd to embark on his life's ambition – to be a fighter pilot.

'Yes sir. I'm gonna be a Top Gun.'

Considering Willie's two eyes had evidently never looked at the same thing at the same time since the day he was born and he walked with a limp, I was slightly concerned for his chances at America's top fighter pilot academy, but judging from the amount of American soldiers who die in 'friendly fire' incidents each year, perhaps he stood a greater chance than I gave him credit for.

I bade the lads goodbye, promising I'd send them the postcard of Princess Di they requested (I hadn't the courage to ask whether they knew she was dead or not), and headed on my way.

'Stop by anytime,' they shouted as I departed, and they meant it.

* * *

From Brainerd I took the POW/MIA (Prisoner of War/Missing in Action) Memorial Highway east. Signs pointed to Malmo, Thor, and Mora, Swedish wrinkles in the American skin. As the sun set over more green fields and more American flags, I ended up at Mille Lacs Indian Reservation and its casino.

Native Americans own more of Minnesota than any other state, and many of the Ojibwa and Dakota tribes have turned their autonomous rights into hard cash – Minnesota now has seventeen casinos (more than Atlantic City), all owned by Native Americans. Together they have a gross revenue of over $3 billion. It seems a neatly capitalistic way of atoning for past sins. It's a little like Germany allowing Israelis to set up casinos in Nuremburg. A little.

'We kill thousands of you, steal your land, turn you into drug-addled alcoholics, and then give you the right to make billions of dollars letting us lose money at cards.'

The American Way.

The Mille Lacs Ojibwe Band own two casinos at Mille Lacs Lake and Hinckley. I stopped at the eponymous version, a sparkling, glittering building that looks more like an airport terminal than a gambling den. It had a hotel. I decided to book in for the night and try my luck, as a test – to see how far I'd come since the five dollars I lost in Las Vegas.

Andrew the receptionist offered me free valet parking.

'You can do it 50 billion times and it's still free,' he grinned. This is not often said in America.

The casino serves no alcohol, by order of the Mille Lacs Band Elders, to dissuade their citizens from alcoholism. I went in with a dollar in coins and put them in a slot machine. On the last quarter, the machine started to rattle. And hum. And then jangle. Lights started flashing. And coins started spewing out like popcorn.

The coin counter kept counting. When it passed 100 I started hyperventilating. When it passed 200 I started doing a jig. By the time it stopped on 229, I was doing a passable impression of the entire *Riverdance* cast.

229 quarters. Or $57.25.

The strange thing was, nobody seemed to care. Perhaps this happened all the time.

I took my coins to the cashier and changed them into notes.

'I won it. On the machine.'

'Tens or twenties?'

'You don't understand. I won. Me. Jim. I never win anything.'

'Five tens, a five, two ones and a quarter. Thanks for playing Mille Lacs Casino.'

What I should have done at this stage was to take my sweaty notes and leave, in the knowledge that half my hotel room was paid for. But gambling is a drug, much like cocaine or gardening. I sat down at a blackjack table.

Psychologically this was more complex than it sounds. Consciously I was just excited at the prospect of winning more free money, but subconsciously it was all about Angie. Oh yeah. Because the only other time I'd been to a casino, before Las Vegas, was with her. In Niagara Falls.

It was a terrible night, right up there with the time I was sick in my lap at my cousin's christening. We argued. She flirted with other men. I tried to look cool. She sat down at a blackjack table full of leering men and proceeded to win $110, with which she bought herself a bottle of champagne and drank it. By herself.

So sitting down at the blackjack table, flushed with slot machine success, was an attempt to banish this memory and prove to myself that I could do what Angie did. Another small drawing pin in the coffin.

My first card came down. An ace. I bet three chips. A king. Blackjack. On my first hand.

To cut a long and personally very satisfying story short, I stayed at the blackjack table for an hour. I lost a few hands, but mostly I won. I can't explain it. I have no skill. My fellow players had to guide me, but this being Minnesota, they were very nice about it.

'I've got a king and a jack!'

'No son. Wait till the dealer's turned up his cards.'

My winnings totalled $100. It was late, I was tired, and it was two days until the wedding.

'$100 on this one.'

My fellow players breathed in sharply, collectively. Betting a hundred bucks on a single hand might not sound much in Las Vegas, but here in Mille Lacs I was James Bond.

I was strangely calm. Paul Newman in *The Sting*. In my humble opinion.

My first card was a seven. Not great, but if I got a face card I would be okay. My second card was a six.

'Shit.'

Thirteen. No good to anyone.

'Hit me.' Well why not.

A three.

Sixteen.

'Hit me.'

'Now son . . .'

'You're sure?'

'Hit me.'

Steve McQueen, at the very least.

The card slid on to the table like a tongue licking steel.

A five.

I had twenty-one.

I'd won. $200.

It seemed like a new beginning. Or at least a change from losing.

The next day I stopped the car at the Mille Lacs Visitors' Centre, a more spiritual experience than the casino. This small museum, illustrating the history of the Ojibwa tribe, who first settled here in 1750, related a saga of oppression, poverty and recent faltering rejuvenation. On one wall were the words of Raining Boyd, a Mille Lacs council member: 'Everything is sacred to the Indian. The grass and the water and the trees. If you stop to think about these things you would understand what the Indian is all about.'

There are 2,906 members of the Mille Lacs Band. Before the casino they survived mainly from state and federal handouts. Now the casino provides them with $20 million a year. Mille Lacs is the first Indian community in the US to use casino profits to back a development bond issue to build housing for its members. As another sign said: 'Indian gambling is not just about gambling. Indian gambling is about schools, clinics, housing, water towers and day care. It's about good paying jobs where once there were none. It is about pride and about the ability to take care of our children and our families.' These are obviously proud people. Proud to be different, yet proud to be American.

By the door there's a picture of a young Mille Lacs man. His name is Paul Moose. He looks young, the sort of kid who might do anything in life as long as it doesn't involve working in an office.

Paul Moose was the first American killed in the Korean War.

Bob at Bob's Gas Stop was less impressed by his Native American neighbours.

'This country's ours as much as theirs. Minnesota's where America began, and it's where it'll start again.' Bob was not a small man, with a beard to match. I had my suspicions that the new America Bob had in mind might have something to do with assault weapons and white supremacy, but I kept my thoughts to myself. It doesn't do to rile someone twice your size. The heart of Real America, according to Bob, was Hibbing.

Hibbing was north, on the road to Canada. Driving down Main Street, I felt like Michael J. Fox. This was *Back to the Future*. Women in beehive hairdos waddled along pavements. All the stores were brick-fronted, fading signs singing slowly in the breeze. Even the cars were old, huge boats on wheels. I stopped at the Lybba Delicatessen for lunch, where middle-aged women who all seemed to be called Mavis served sandwiches and turkey wild rice soup wearing plastic hairnets.

'Thanks for stopping by, ja,' crooned Check-Out Mavis, and she meant it.

The one person who won't be walking into the Lybba Deli-catessen anytime soon is Bob Dylan, even though Hibbing is his home town. I almost fell off my chair when Bagel Mavis told me.

'Well . . . I guess Bob Dylan would be the famous person to come out of this place.'

She said Bob was born in Duluth, but moved to Hibbing when he was six. He bought his first guitar at Erickson's Music Store. I dutifully walked in and asked the shopkeeper about the shop's most illustrious customer. (I assumed Bob was the most illustrious. It's difficult to see who could have been more illustrious. JFK? Elvis? Jesus?)

'Folks here don't really get on with his music,' she replied in a tone that invited my departure. Reading through local newspapers in the library, I came across an editorial from 1991: 'It would be fair to say that many of Dylan's lyrics don't make a lot of sense to local folks. Maybe if he did a polka album . . .'

I drove by the house where Dylan lived at 2,425 7th Avenue East, a hideous two-storey grey pebbledash square just up from the immense granite high school, a place of extreme and ugly grandeur that cost the iron-ore barons $4 million in the 1920s. Bob did the three-minute walk to the monumental building every school day for five years, yet the high school history book fails to mention his name once, even though his second band, the Golden Chords, played at the 1958 annual concert, when Dylan pounded out rock n'roll tunes on the Steinway and broke the pedal before being booed from the stage.

Robert Allen Zimmerman left Hibbing at the age of nineteen and has not returned since. He studied for a while at the University of Minnesota in Minneapolis, then dropped out and wandered to New York City, where he became Bob Dylan and did okay for himself.

In 1986 Hibbing Town Council had a vote to rename Harbor Drive 'Bob Dylan Drive'. On a Monday night the council voted 6–3 to change it. On Thursday there was a revote and the motion was defeated 6–3. It's still called Harbor Drive.

Hibbing's civic pride is reserved for 'the biggest hole in the world' – the world's largest open-cast mine, which looks like the surface of the moon and is just as big. Iron ore is the lifeblood of this region, with the Mesabi Range providing vast supplies of low-grade taconite. Minnesotans are proud of their iron, which seems to seep into their character, giving them the steel to survive and even cherish their extreme climate.

I spent a happy two minutes gazing upon the gaping wound in the earth, accompanied by an unbelievably large crowd of fellow tourists. Minnesotans, it seems, like nothing better than big holes.

From Hibbing, Highway 73 heads due north, past the hills of the Mesabi iron ore belt and on through thick fir woods towards Canada. This is hunting, shooting, fishing country and every store sells worms and multitudinous walleye fish-flies that hang like ancient jewellery.

On the road I was surrounded by pickup trucks with bigger wheels than most cars I know. It's a wild and beautiful drive, past lakes and trees, and more lakes and more trees. The air chills, even in midsummer, and you start to feel like a nice hot cup of coffee.

Oh yes. A nice hot cup of coffee.

Very rarely in my life, on my various travels, I've encountered places, people, and things that I've known, without a shadow of a doubt, to have been unique. One of a kind. Superlatives without rival.

There's the world's most beautiful waterfall in Samoa. The most welcoming airport terminal in Cork. The world's scariest cave, Kitum Cave in western Kenya (where the Ebola virus is rumoured to have originated). And the best banana pancakes ever on the Thai island of Ko Tao.

And there's Simpson's Truck Stop on Highway 73 north, which serves the world's worst cup of coffee.

You couldn't tell just from looking at it. It seemed harmless enough, just another terrible American coffee in a polystyrene cup. I paid my sixty-five cents, ambled out to the car, drove on, sipped the coffee, and spat it all over the steering wheel.

The world's worst cup of coffee. The taste was indescribable, but I'll make an attempt. Imagine that someone has stewed diarrhoea-soaked pants for a week, then added mashed blue-bottles, battery acid and root beer, then boiled it down until only granules were left, and then added boiling rat urine.

It was so bad I kept it as a wedding present for Stan and Meg.

I crossed the Rat Root River, possibly the source of the water used in Simpson's coffee. After the garish road sign at Orr (pop. 251), which seemed to have been designed by a rustic Andy Warhol – a cartoon fish painted Pop Art green – I began to scent the aroma of wood pulp from the Boise Cascade paper mill at International Falls.

International Falls is not international and it has no falls. Right on the border with Canada, this is the most resolutely Middle American town in Middle America. It's none too complex a place: a main street of brick stores, Moose and Elk lodges, a 1,000-employee paper mill and a museum venerating its most famous son – the all-time All-American Football player Bronco Nagurski.

I popped in. He was a big lad, old Bronco, all 6 feet 225 pounds of him, with a 19½ inch neck. It's said that his NFL Hall of Fame ring was as thick as a baseball bat. Anyone that big deserves a museum. At the University of Minnesota ('Go Gophers, Go!'), Nagurski was the first and only athlete to be named an All-American athlete at two positions on the same team. He subsequently signed to the mighty Chicago Bears, becoming one of the original 'Monsters of the Midway' and leading the team to several national championships from 1930–37 and again in 1943.

'The only way to stop him,' said one commentator of the day, 'is to shoot him when he comes out of the locker room.'

'Humble and hardworking,' says the blurb in the museum, and you get the feeling these are two qualities much admired in Minnesota. Bronco seems to have been an athlete of the old school, as tough as granite on the field and as gentle as duckdown off it.

Not satisfied with demolishing large football players, Bronco also had a sideline as a professional wrestler (which, as Jesse Ventura shows, is a very Minnesotan career move). In 1937, the same year he won the Superbowl, he also became world wrestling champion in front of 35,000 fans. He stands in his photo, holding the belt aloft, smiling gently as if to say, 'Mine's a fairy cake.'

Upon post-war retirement Bronco subsequently ran a petrol station on the main street of his home town of International Falls. A local anecdote goes that one day he filled up a tourist car on its way south. After a few hundred miles, the owner stopped to refill, but couldn't loosen the petrol cap as it was screwed on so tight. It took two men and a wrench to open it.

The museum is crowded with pictures of Bronco in retirement, fishing, chopping wood, carrying his kids. Minnesotan pictures. Nice pictures. For some reason I had a tear in my eye as I left the museum, but it was probably just the fumes from the paper mill.

I headed east, passing another statue of Paul Bunyan, and on to the Thunderbird Lodge on the shores of Rainy Lake. It was ten at night, but the summer sun still filled the sky.

I presented Stan with my cup of Simpson's Truck Stop coffee.

'How bad can it be?'

'Try it.'

'It can't be that bad . . .'

'Try it.'

We heated it up in a microwave. Stan took a sip and turned purple.

'Jesus. That's awful.'

'Yep. It's your wedding present.'

Loons called into the dusk and the moon rose. The fairylights came on at the Thunderbird Lodge. Food was set up on the shores of the lake, and the guests who'd arrived early stood sipping cold crap beer and eating hot great burgers. Meg smiled, laughed and seemed wholly happy. Stan grinned from big ear to big ear. Their joy seemed to spread across the water with the moonlight.

It was a warm night by the lake, surrounded by dark silent sentinels, the fir forests that are the ancient guardians of this northland. Stan served thimblefuls of Simpson's coffee to his guests, and to my delight and pride they too found it inexorable.

I felt content. Here with two old friends who were about to be married, in the heart of a vast and still untamed continent. I was on the border of Canada, and somewhere, across the invisible line, stood, sat or lay Angie. She was breathing the same air (just). I wondered what she was doing – we must have been close to the same time zone.

Perhaps she was standing, sipping beer, looking at the same stars.

Instead of breaking my heart, this thought comforted me. I hoped, clearly and simply, that she felt happier now. I must have been drunk. I'm not usually this nice.

I wandered out on to the wooden jetty with a can of Old Milwaukee and sat watching shooting stars in the vast black night. All was silent, apart from the chatter of guests.

A couple walked down to join me. He, short, balding, thin-rimmed glasses that suggested a career in the media. Or dentistry. She, slim, black hair, a beautiful face. The lucky bastard.

'Hi.'

'I'm Todd.'

'Leah.'

'Jim.'

We toasted Stan and Meg, and Todd said he worked in TV in Minneapolis, and Leah said little but admitted she was doing a Ph.D. in nutrition at the University of Michigan. She had a soft, quiet voice, but said one thing that made me laugh out loud.

'Americans are fat. Is it all right to be fat? No, it isn't. It's unhealthy. I don't think it's right to say fat is good. It's like saying drug addiction is good or smoking-related cancer is good.'

She was vehement. Todd laughed, although he'd evidently heard it all before.

I liked Leah. She was slim and pretty and smart. I didn't like Todd, because he was with Leah.

That night Stan and I and a couple of his friends got drunk. His friends were both called Tim. I think. After too many bad beers and some worse bourbons it was hard to tell.

We sat at the end of the jetty listening to the intermittent howling of wolves in the far-off fir forests.

'Are they dangerous?' I asked, in a very European way.

'Some wolves ate a dog last year,' said Tim1. 'But they wouldn't take a human.'

'They'd eat a baby,' remarked Tim2.

'Oh yes. A baby. But not a human.'

The next morning I went into International Falls and had breakfast at Jim's Cafe ('established about 1935'), partly because the breakfasts were cheap and huge, but mainly because it had my name on it.

Jim's was packed with people wearing T-shirts and baseball caps, the American national costume. I shared a booth with an old couple called Bob and Wendy. Bob was seventy-three, Wendy a live-wire late sixties. They'd lived in northern Minnesota all their lives but, now retired, headed south for the colder months.

'Which are those?'

'September to June.'

Their passion during those nine months away was big-game fishing. Wendy loved big-game fishing.

'Caught a twelve-foot marlin in Ecuador last May,' she boomed. 'Wrapped it in brown paper and Fed-Exed the fish back here. Should have seen the delivery man walking up our drive.'

I asked them about winters in International Falls, a place US weather forecasters refer to as 'Frostbite Falls'.

'Oh, it gets cold,' said Bob.

'Yep. It gets cold.'

About minus forty they said. Such extreme temperatures require preparation and perseverance, tactical planning and cunning as life becomes one big battle against the elements. To keep their cars running some people light fires under their engines to thin the oil in order to start the car. Unfortunately this often results in their vehicles exploding. People try numerous tactics to thaw out their transport.

'Yep. Police arrested this drunk last year for urinating on a car, but he got off. His attorney said he was only trying to melt the frozen doors.'

'Yep. You throw a boiling cup of coffee into the air at forty below and it don't hit the ground. Vaporises, just like that!'

I was prepared to wager that Simpson's coffee would survive Bob's forty below test – the only worry being that if you dropped it on the floor it would burn a hole right through to China.

'Yep. Sometimes you just gotta leave the car running all night. It'll use up 'bout four or five gallons of gas, but it stops your dashboard from cracking. The logging guys leave their trucks running for weeks.'

'Yep. At forty below, you slam the car door shut, your windshield'll shatter.'

'Yep. Try moving your rear-view mirror, it'll come off in your hand.'

'Yep. Snowplough's no good at forty below. Steel just shatters.'

'Yep. Gotta be careful, human flesh'll freeze in a minute. Remember that guy who tried to pump gas without mitts? Lost his hand.'

'Yep. Sometimes it gets to fifty below. Now that's cold. Your house cracks and groans all night, sounds like gunshot. You don't get much sleep.'

'Yep,' nodded Wendy thoughtfully. 'You know, son, sometimes when we're in Arizona, I kinda miss the winters up here.'

I spent Friday afternoon with the two Tims at the Roadhouse, a bar that could only be American. From the outside it resembled a large barn. From the inside it resembled a large barn, only there was a bar at one end and some pool tables and a few grisly chain-smokers in worn baseball caps cannoning balls to the strains of Bon Jovi.

I sat in a corner, trying to write a best man's speech. It was hard. For an hour I pondered marriage, and why Stan and Meg were great for each other, and why Angie and I might have been great for each other.

Marriage, I hypothesised, is more about timing than love. Okay, love has a role to play, but it's timing that dictates. If each participant is at about the same stage of love, at about the same stage of life, at about the same income bracket, then marriage is possible, but this involves an alignment of careers, ages, continents and interplanetary systems. Angie and I, we'd never been properly aligned. There should be mechanics for this, as for cars.

'Relationship alignment. On the spot. Only $49.99, with a free libido change.'

Instead, we'd always been slightly out of sync.

When I thought about Angie, I felt sad, but the colours of this sadness were no longer as bright. The newspaper clipping of our relationship was yellowing. As it had to, if I was to go on.

I wrote a page of speech in forty minutes and went to the bar to drink kamikazes with the Tims. We played a couple of frames of pool, and for a few minutes I felt wholly American. Standing at a pool table at three in the afternoon, already a little drunk, with a wad of dollar bills in my pocket, listening to the Red Hot Chili Peppers.

'God bless America,' I said, missing the black.

'Yes brother,' said the Tims.

Our pool game was interrupted by two beer-toting women who challenged us to a frame. Sharon (large, tall, hair-lip, Levi's clutching backside like skin on a walrus) broke. Tim missed a red, and Rose (large, short, wart on nose, Levi's clutching backside like skin on a walrus) potted a yellow. Then missed. I needed a cue-bridge to make my shot and inquired if such a thing existed in the Roadhouse.

'Where do you think you are? Butthole, Eygpt?' barked Sharon. We blinked. She stared us down. I set up my cue-bridge shot and missed anyway.

'Butthole, Eygpt?'

The pre-wedding dinner took place at the lakeside. Once more burgers featured heavily on the menu. Tim1 was regaling a crowd with tales of Sharon and Rose.

'Where do you think you are? Butthole, Eygpt?'

There was laughter, but I felt bad. I'd liked Sharon, by the end. She'd never been further than Duluth (140 miles away) and had never even been into Canada, which was 2 miles away. For all she knew, Egypt might well look like a butthole.

'Your coffee was scary,' said a voice at my side. I turned. Leah stood cradling an Old Milwaukee.

'Thanks,' I said proudly.

'Probably toxic.'

'You really mean that?'

'Yeah.'

'Where's Todd?'

She smiled. She was pretty, under the northern sky. Under any sky. A prettiness that was strangely American – not fine, like French beauty, or tempestuous, like Spanish beauty, or chiselled, like Scandinavian beauty. Earthy beauty, which comes from bounteous food, exercise and generations of hard-working ancestors toiling the land. Oh, and plenty of skin-care products.

'Todd? Gossiping somewhere. He's such a woman sometimes . . . You know, he thinks you're cute.'

'He . . . he does?' A penny, slowly, hardly dropping. 'Todd's . . .'

'He's a good friend. Megan, Todd and I were at kindergarten together in St Paul. Todd was the first boy I kissed. Then he borrowed my skirt, hung out in the girls' washrooms. We kind of grew up together.'

I thought for a second of my friends, back home, if England

was still home. Which it would have to be. People I'd not seen, not talked to in months. I knew it was almost time to return. Almost. But not quite yet.

'I used to come up here with Megan for a few weeks each summer. You know, ever since she was a little girl she said she'd get married on this lake. Kind of scary, huh?'

And I saw Meg and Leah as little girls, daydreaming about the man they would marry. Had Angie done this with her friends, her sisters? Of course. Was I like the man she'd dreamed of? Probably not. He'd have been taller, broader, with olive skin, dark hair and a name like Guido.

Who would she marry now?

'I heard about your . . . thing . . . in Canada.'

I looked up, shaken out of fearful reverie. 'My . . . ?'

She looked at me. Eyes almost black. 'Drink?'

'I think that would be a good idea.'

I stayed close to Leah for the rest of the evening. I consumed ten cans of Old Milwaukee and felt a warmth at my core that came from a suspicion that Leah liked me. She'd glance over every so often, and when this coincided with my ogling at her (which it invariably did as I ogled at her a lot) she'd look away, vaguely embarrassed.

The excitement that comes from attraction. I hadn't really experienced this since . . . well, a long time. The electrics, the spark, the fizzle. Heart rate thumping, hands damp, pupils dilated. It might have been the Old Milwaukee, but it was more likely the twenty-nine-year-old Leah.

Which was why, when the wedding guests began to disperse and we applauded first Megan then Stan as they departed for one of the most sleepless nights of their lives, and when there were only a few of us left sipping warm beer by the lake, and Todd yawned and said, 'Goodnight, beautiful people,' and it was really just me and Leah and the moon, I coughed and said, 'Better get an early night . . . see you for the big day,' and clumsily, embarrassingly, stupidly, derangedly, stumbled up the path to the cabin I was sharing with Stan and the Tims, leaving Leah standing on the jetty with a middle-aged couple from Philadelphia who seemed bent on proving to each other and the world that they were still young by taking it in turns to consume a bottle of peach schnapps.

'Goodnight,' she said, softly, her Midwestern voice disappearing into the hush of the fir trees.

She didn't want me, anyway. I was convinced.

The wedding day was hot from the moment the sun lit the fir tops. The heat had been sucked into the middle of a continent and crept like steam through the forests, gaining strength and weight and body until it was a shimmering cloud resting on the water.

Stan woke early. He was nervous. I could tell by the way he cleaned his teeth six times.

'You're sure about this?' I asked in jest.

'I love her.'

We caught a boat out into Rainy Lake, the wedding party a hundred strong. Sunlight silvering. Ahead was Canada, but it looked like America, so I didn't feel too bad. And Leah was on the boat in a summer floral dress that did nothing to hide her slim figure. A nutritionist's figure. She smiled when she spotted me, but made no move to approach.

We crossed the invisible border and stopped at a tiny Canadian immigration post.

I stared down the Maple Leaf flag. It looked away.

'Citizenship?' asked the immigration officer.

The entire boat was American, apart from myself and an older woman from Norway. We raised our passports like refugees, which in this continent we were.

'Will you come with me?'

It was as hot as America in the office. On the window ledge was a Toronto Maple Leafs calendar. I stared it down. It stared back.

'So, you're no stranger to Canada?' said the immigration officer.

I shook my head.

'Seven times in the last . . . sixteen months?'

A tear welling somewhere deep and unexpected. Dry throat. 'I was dating a girl . . . It didn't . . . work out.'

The first time I'd confirmed this. Out loud. To an officer of the Canadian state. It was official.

He stamped my passport. 'Sorry to hear that. Well, thank you. Have a great wedding.'

Meg's island was tiny, 200 yards across. A wooden house, a few trees, rocks, lapping water. A place invented almost, in a children's storybook about a family who live in the middle of a lake and go fishing for mermaids every day.

I checked the rings in my pocket for the seventeenth time.

The service took place at the water's edge as Meg had always wanted, beneath a small bridal arch entwined with flowers. Stan stood, awaiting his bride, in his grey suit, looking like an insurance salesman, shifting from foot to foot. As a bald-headed eagle swooped, skimming the lake, an emissary from the American nation, Meg appeared from the house.

She looked like a dream. Stan's dream, displayed for us all. A simple white, 1930s dress, bobbed hair, bright red lips. Daisy from *The Great Gatsby*. An American vision, of understated wealth and assurance, on her very own island.

Stan stared, we all stared. Some cried. I fought the emotion-lump stalking up my throat, but a tear welled in my right eye and I looked to the lake to hide my reaction and even the eagle was weeping.

It was, as they say in the trade, a five-star wedding. The female minister, dressed in a soutane that seemed to have been designed by Jerry Garcia, gave good ceremony. I provided the rings on cue, and didn't drop them.

'. . . to love and cherish, honour and obey, from this day, forever . . .'

'I will.'

'I will.'

Two words, usually so slight, so weightless, so flippant, suddenly solid, vast, undeniable.

In the beginning there were the Words. And the Words became flesh.

The panic hit as soon as the service finished and the happy couple looked more than happy and everyone cheered.

The Best Man's speech. The worst form of torture in the Western world (other than Dan Ackroyd movies).

I embraced Now-Married Stan. 'How does it feel?'

'Sensational. God, Jim, I'm walking on air.'

I kissed Now-Married Meg. I didn't have to ask her how she felt.

I stood and looked at them both, arms linked, a phalanx, two as one. I thought of them both and couldn't imagine one without the other, which is some testimony.

I know women are supposed to get emotional at weddings, but these are modern times, and we modern men are big girls. I was not the only post-thirty, single man at the wedding, and I sensed we were all watching Stan with a drop of saddened jealousy in our hearts.

Imagine it. A beautiful woman who loves you, who has just signed a contract to stay with you forever, to have sex with you pretty much whenever you desire it, to bear your children, go to restaurants with you, dance with you in clubs even though you don't dance very well, laugh at most of your jokes and wake up beside you each morning whether you've shaved or not.

I ate one cheese biscuit during the wedding meal. It was a buffet and people took their food and sat on the rocks by the water. I found myself (okay I wandered there purposefully) by Leah, Todd and a few other of Meg's friends. Leah was eating chickpea salad.

Todd's hand on my shoulder. 'Got the speech ready, Superman?'

'No,' I said. Coolly, I thought.

*　　*　　*

10 p.m. 24 June

I am halfway to Drunksville, a small and incoherent town somewhere near Duluth. I've just finished my fourth hot-dog. And my tenth vodka and tonic. The sun is dipping below the firs, casting gold leaves across the lake. I feel warm, fuzzy and content, like a cheerful sherbet lemon.

The speech went okay. People came up and shook my hand with a smile on their face and it didn't seem like pity. I made a couple of jokes about Bill Clinton, one about the Queen, and got a little choky when talking about the joys of marriage.

'Behind every successful man is an astonished woman, and this is no exception. Megan, I know, is constantly amazed that anyone should employ Stan, not to mention pay him the six-figure salary he's conned the firm into paying. But he is a fine man, a man of integrity, a man of wisdom, taste, generosity and flair, who has recently revealed to me a warm feeling for James Coburn. And a man, who in his early twenties, dated a waitress at Hooters . . .'

As the sun glints one last time, a final burst of day before dusk strokes the forests, I waddle over to Leah and gauchly put a hand on her shoulder, but she doesn't flinch. She smiles, even.

'So, cowboy, feeling better after all those hot-dogs?'

'Yeah. Feeling good.'

I am. Diamond good.

'Will you escort a lady to her ship?'

I take her arm and it's warm and soft. We walk to where the boat is moored. I have to admit, I feel a little like I'm walking on air.

2 a.m. 25 June

There is dancing at the Thunderbird Lodge. Down by the lakeside, a bluegrass band, skipping, scratching, scrolling songs of lost and found love, hillbilly Irish mountain ballads of epic drinking and even more epic longing.

Fairylights in the trees, flickering candles descending to the shore. Meg and Stan, in each others arms like Jay and Daisy, and I watch them like stand-back Nick Carraway – happy yet sad, tall yet small, satisfaction yet yearning. The confused soul of the single wedding guest.

Then we dance. Leah's fingers tight on my arms, and in one instant she pulls me closer, her body against mine, smally insistent.

I have another burger. She watches me, smiling.

'Don't say anything.'

'I don't have to.'

'What's so interesting about nutrition anyway? It can't be good for you.'

She smiles again, igniting my heart like a temperamental boiler. 'I don't know. I guess I was brought up with cream, cheese, milk and more cream. That's the Midwest. Two uncles died of coronaries. My cousins were overweight by the age of six. So, QED, I became a nutritionist.'

Leah the nutritionist. Could she be good for me?

Somehow, more drinks later, we're stumbling along the lakeshore. Somehow, I'm taking off my shirt, slipping from my trousers (okay, stumbling from my trousers) and stepping from my shorts, taking a running jump into the lake.

Cold and delicious. Darkness, the rising light.

I break the surface. Leah rises at my side, quick, silent. Her arm brushes mine.

'Hey.'

'Hey.'

We swim out into the lake, the water as dark and thick as oil. Skinnydipping with a skinny nutritionist. I duck under and resurface to be baptised into moonlight, water dripping like mercury.

We sit, wrapped in towels, sipping bourbon. The American way. She's facing me, arms down, body relaxed. Her head is tilted up and her lips are parted.

I've read *Dating For Dummies*. I know what this means. And I've had enough vodka to respond.

* * *

243

'Just because you might fit into me,' she says much later, 'doesn't mean we have to. Or should.'

'Er . . . no.'

Silence. A wolf howl, maybe. Or just a dog. Or perhaps Butthole Sharon and a chain-smoking grisly.

The moon, massive but gentle; caresses of light on the tips of the firs.

'But then again, it might be fun to try.'

I woke in the arms of a woman. For those of you who do this on a daily basis, this might not seem like a big deal. But . . .

CHERISH IT.

IT IS A SMALL MIRACLE.

Outside I could see the trees tremble in the warm summer breeze. Lying in bed with a nutritionist in the heart of North America.

The careful simplicity of life. Of land and tree, of man and woman, ever before ever more.

We all said goodbye to the Now-Marrieds. They were going on their honeymoon to the coast of Maine. In America, it seems, couples most often go on honeymoon to America. Once again, the idea of crossing a border for pleasure is about as appealing to the American psyche as sharing your wealth, or losing.

'We speak the language, we know how to drive there, and we can pay in dollars. Anyway, the lobsters are the best in the world,' Stan had stated.

I waved them off next to one of their friends from Washington, DC, a thirty-year-old attorney who was fairly high up the legal food chain at the State Department, the government body that determines, shapes and executes American foreign policy and therefore runs the rest of the world. Simon admitted he didn't have a passport. Never had.

'I'd like to go to France one day,' he admitted.

Leah and I drove south TOGETHER towards Minneapolis and spent our last night in a motel off Highway 61. We walked out into farm fields as the sun dipped red like the stripes of the flag, behind a sky as blue as the star-speckled square. Cows munched happily in the field and beyond, by the forest's edge, deer nuzzled wheat.

There were no cars, no planes, just land. The beauty of rural America, a warm tranquillity.

Leah walked, her skin kissed by the setting sun, freckles and gold, health and vitality.

'I love coming back to the country,' she said, and I felt like writing a song entitled just that, with guitar twangs and Dolly Parton singing backing vocals.

We walked and talked and ended up amongst the wheat, America and England, a trans-Atlantic special relationship, and as I lay against the warm soft earth I thought this was how the New World was born and I was happy to be part of history, of tradition, of continuum.

In the bar near the motel, the aptly named Minnesota Tavern, old men in John Deere caps smiled at us and the barman with shaved head and wolf tattoos said, 'What'll it be, folks?'

We sat with weak beers and laughed and the men at the bar told stories to each other, stories that had evidently been told a hundred times and would be told a hundred times more.

'And Billy took the fella's money, tore it in two, and said, "That's what you git for chasin' wild turkey . . ."'

We drank more weak beer and Leah watched me eat a steak sandwich with disapproving but beautiful eyes, and as three old men walked out into the warm night, laughing and slapping each other on the back, I was overwhelmed by a sense of well-being.

America is a mixed-up crazy place, teeming with psychotic people bent on destruction. It's a superficial place where money rules and failure is not an option, where neighbours sue each other over lawn clippings, where white policemen kill unarmed black men, where Adam Sandler gets paid $20 million for farting on the silver screen. But America, at least in its rural areas – and don't forget most of America is a rural area – is still a wonderful land. These people in the Minnesota Tavern might not know where Kosovo is, even though their tax dollars bombed it, they might not believe in a national health service, but if you needed help one dark night in the middle of a frozen winter they would give it to you. And if you wanted a second opinion on whether you looked daft in a tartan suit, they'd tell you straight. 'Son, there ain't nothing wrong with a good old pair of blue jeans.'

As we walked back to the motel, I felt a pang of sadness to be leaving rural America. I envied its simplicity, its humanity. The old men who had gone to school together, worked together, drank together and would be buried together. Born into, living in, and buried into their land.

I had tried to forget Angie in the quick-dazzle of Las Vegas, LA and Florida, to reinvent myself in these Temples of Reinvention. For a while I had embraced the soft-hot flesh that is American hype.

But I didn't need to forget. I couldn't, shouldn't forget. I should appreciate and move on. Realise what is simple and unchangeable and human.

America, especially the wide open land, had taught me this. This wonderful expanse of alligators and pearl-white beaches, of crabs and golf-buggies, of cacti and God-hosting mountains, of Bronco Nagurski and his compassionate strength, of wolves and ice, grain and walleye, fir-tree and pumpkin patch, populated by straight-thinking, straight-talking people who still believed in God.

In the land of the brave I had learned that I could be courageous enough to fall in love again.

The badaboom was out there. All I had to do was believe.

Leah and I exchanged email addresses. She said she might be

in England sometime the following year. I said I might be by Chicago before long.

We kissed.

We parted.

I felt reborn.

9

Independence Day – New York City

I'm standing in the middle of Times Square. On a large Panasonic television screen, a twenty-foot-high President is saying sorry for sleeping with someone, or bombing someone, or not giving someone enough tax breaks. Above him, a giant illuminated Budweiser bottle seems to be pouring on to his head.

Yellow cabs hurtle past on either side, trying to give the illusion that they are transporting people where they want to go, but from the chaotic growling, honking, screeching brawl, it's obvious the cars are merely following their own, heated impulses. They want to fight, on this stinking hot, stinking fat day, and snarl at each other, like dogs.

Voices shout amongst the car barks, selling, promoting, preaching. Dirty young men handing out business-card invites to peek at women's bits in the remaining vice-dens off the square. A quarter-crazed wide-eyed black man whispering, 'Our Lord is with you to the end! Repent!'

'Burgers! Polish Sausage! Fa-la-la-fel!'

'Perfume, Armani, YSL, Calveeen Kleiiiiinnnnn!'

Men, women, children, cars, buildings, poodles in little pink bandannas.

It is as though the whole world has been condensed, like a scale model, into Times Square. A remarkably tall black woman by my side, as lofty as a lamp-post, a supermodel perhaps, or a man. An old sage stoops by with a plastic bag tied to his head. A woman shuffles past in a mink coat, despite the ninety-degree heat.

Above, neon flashes, bashing the senses, dashing up, down, across buildings, electric sweat.

Tourists stand bewildered, dazzled, bedeviled by the devil that is the fast hot July of New York City. They take pictures of themselves in the midst of Times Square, like people take pictures of themselves in haunted houses and hidden graveyards, to see if the developed negatives reveal unseen demons known to inhabit such places.

I stand in the midst of the world of Times Square and smile. Three and a half months ago, if I'd have stood in the midst of the world of Times Square I would not have smiled but thrown myself in front of a snarling yellow cab.

But today I'm standing still. I feel calm, tranquil, happy even. Not strong yet, but not weak either. I miss Angie. Of course I do. But in the same way we all miss the past. There's nothing, I think, I believe now, I can do to bring her back to me. I know, like a tectonic plate, I must move on.

There is still much healing to happen (in the background I hear Oprah singing 'Climb Every Mountain'), but I sense I have been set on the road to recovery, in part thanks to this endless, bounteous, welcoming, strange yet simple nation. GOD BLESS AMERICA.

Close by the subway entrance beckons, seeking, sipping, the dark damp and moist, the sex of the city sucking us in. I descend into the womb.

Beneath ground, it's not as hot as the temperature above, but the odour of body odour is impressive, as it should be in New York, the most impressive city on earth.

I love New York. It helps that I never came here with Angie. In many ways I consider it my city. I got to own it on my very first visit, en route to see her. I flew into JFK, had to transfer through Manhattan to Newark for a Continental flight to Buffalo (the closest airport to Niagara Falls).

I caught the bus into the Port Authority bus terminal, and from the moment we came over the Queensboro Bridge, my neck was craned to the skies. Or rather the tops of the buildings, which in

New York seem to take over from the sky as the top of everything, including outer space.

I walked along West Forty-Second Street, sure I was about to be mugged, and stumbled into Bryant Park and sat in the sun and munched a real New York pastrami sandwich, drinking real New York cwafee, feeling like the coolest guy on earth, which perhaps, at that moment, I was.

Two hours later I walked back to the bus terminal with a swagger that came from too much cwafee and not having been mugged.

New York made me feel strong. Confident. Buzzed.

So it was I made a habit of flying to Buffalo via New York, each time doing something different with my three-hour sojourn – the Empire State Building, Times Square, Grand Central Station (which entirely lives up to its name, being grand, central and undeniably a station), always eating pastrami on rye easy on the mustard, always drinking cwafee, always adding a few centimetres to my swagger.

It feels great to be back. Even though the man next to me on the Number Two subway line seems to be training for the National Perspiration Championships, held each year in Houston, Texas, and usually won by a man from Iowa called Big Len.

I get out at City Hall. Because I have a plan. On my last full day in America I'm going to walk across the Brooklyn Bridge.

Oh, didn't I tell you? I'm going home.

In City Hall Park office workers and municipal officials sit gasping for air like floundering carp. I pass along the gloomily named People With Aids Plaza and through the underpass on to the Brooklyn Bridge.

I've always wanted to walk across the Brooklyn Bridge. It seems, from afar, the most impressive viaduct in the city, and there is something cheerfully human about it, not least because its builders thought it would be a nice idea to construct a pedestrian walkway above the two lanes of traffic, right down the centre of the bridge. It's as though they were saying yes, cars need a route across the Hudson River, but humans, designed to be upright, putting one foot in front of another rather than sitting putting one foot to the floor, come first.

So it is I stride forth, above the cars, marching across the bridge with joyful disdain. To my right are the cliffs of downtown, a monumental alpine range, jagged and soaring. I know the skyscrapers are man-made, but somehow they seem eternal, organic, sentinels wise before their time, gazing down over human folly, sneering at the seething mass of honking cars. In their midst soars the immense sleekness of the Twin Towers, petrified like Giacometti sculptures in a half-menacing step up Broadway.

Manhattan, I find, brings out my most flowery prose.

The central footpath rises gradually, on to ancient wooden slats that are warm from the sun. Ahead Brooklyn shimmers. I breathe in the car exhaust fumes.

The Brooklyn Bridge was conceived as the biggest bridge in the world; 6,016 feet long, its construction was begun in 1869, four years after the end of the Civil War, a symbol of hope and advancement after four years of destruction.

Yet the bridge had a tragic birth. Its revolutionary designer, engineer John Roebling, hadn't even begun the building when, on a surveying trip near the Fulton dock, a ferryboat crushed one of his feet. Sixteen days later he died of tetanus. His mantle was passed to his son, Washington Roebling, who subsequently got the bends when exiting a compressed air chamber on the river bed and was paralysed. He directed the rest of the construction from a hospital bed until the bridge opened in May 1883.

I stop at the centre of the bridge and admire the four main cables above me, each 15 ¾ inches thick. This, by some strange coincidence, is the exact diameter of my neck, which makes me feel strangely pleased with myself.

On the far shore, a huge LCD temperature display reads eighty-six degrees Fahrenheit. And so I step onwards into the hot steamy funk of Brooklyn.

Brooklyn, on first sight, is more ramshackle, more mortal than Manhattan, a soulful riposte to the haughty serried ranks of towers across the river. Here there are warehouses, apartment blocks, rubbish dumps and smokestacks, repositories of shabby humanity unlike the airless office superstructures of downtown.

Brooklyn wasn't always so visceral. In the mid-1800s it was known as the City of Churches, thanks to the ingenuity of shrewd real-estate speculators, who offered free land to church congregations in order to build places of worship. The cunning developers then sold housing lots around the new churches that the faithful snapped up like communion wafers.

At the end of the bridge footpath I stop at the Celeste Restaurant Diner on Tillary Street because anywhere called the Celeste Restaurant Diner deserves custom. I sit in a pink booth as clean as a button while Stevie Wonder sings 'Part-Time Lover' and the waiter laughs into the heat, 'It's Wednesday, it's the hump of the week,' he says. 'Come tomorrow you'll be rolling. We'll all be rolling . . .'

I celebrate with another Coke.

Listening to Stevie Wonder in the Celeste Restaurant Diner in Brooklyn on a perfect summer's day.

Later I walk down Flatbush Avenue to Prospect Park. I'd heard about Prospect Park from one of the Tims, who said it was, in his humble opinion, much better than Central Park.

'Check out the Yummy Mummies, Jim.'

I'm not adverse to Yummy Mummies. I believe they are a fine invention.

I reach Prospect Park. It's hot and happy and as summery as suncream. And yes, there are thin sexy women in dark glasses gathering unto themselves babies, small children, pushchairs, prams and huge industrial-sized buggies.

As Tim had explained, 'You date in Manhattan, get married in Long Island and breed in Brooklyn.' Judging by the number of screaming infants in the park, falling sperm counts have yet to affect this part of the Big Apple.

Prospect Park has been known as 'Brooklyn's Backyard' since

its opening in 1866. At the time Brooklyn was the third biggest city in America, with a population of 500,000, and its Wise Men decided to commission a park to rival newly opened Central Park in Manhattan. Central Park's creators, Calvert Vaux and Frederick Law Olmsted, were headhunted by local businessman James Stranahan to do even better in Brooklyn.

'Prospect Park,' said Stranahan, 'must be the great natural park of the country . . . more varied and beautiful than that found within any city on this continent.'

They were at least partly successful. The park is undeniably varied. There are thousands of trees, with Brooklyn's (and probably New York City's) last slice of indigenous woodland, comprising maples, oaks, hackberries, ash, beech, larch, linden, plane, pine and yellow-wood that house squirrels as big as dogs. There are hills, ponds, caves and rivers. It's almost rural, 526 acres of undulating countryside 6 miles from Times Square.

Every Brooklyn child is brought up in the 'Backyard'. Many famous Brooklynites – of which there are hundreds, since being born in Brooklyn is to fame what being born in Afghanistan is to beards – recall formative moments as children in the park. Prospectophiles include Woody Allen, Spike Lee and Mae West, who experienced several rites of passage within the woods and meadows, stating, 'The Brooklyn I grew up in was still a city where gentlemen and deer ran wild in Prospect Park.'

Cars are allowed in the park, but only on the road around the perimeter, and it's easy to escape their angry voices. I head away from the north entrance and the statue of James Stranahan looking pleased with himself, towards a series of murky lily pools surrounded by oak trees. In the pools, vaguely gold fish swim in dim water, while old men sleep blissfully on sunny benches. Ahead a couple promenade, stopping every ten paces to link tongues (judging by the smattering of used condoms in the park, this is not all couples do here).

I leave them to it. Snogging couples no longer have the power to hurt me.

Prospect Park is not the tidiest of public spaces, but it has improved dramatically since the seventies, when vandalism and neglect led to the deterioration of many of the neo-classical landmarks. In 1976 the stone statue of Columbia crumbled and fell off the Union Arch at the park entrance just in time for America's bicentenary celebrations.

People stayed away in droves and it was not until Mayor Ed Koch created the post of Park Administrator in 1980 that the park was reclaimed. Today it feels like a friend's flat, or your brother's car – a little ragged, but very hospitable.

From the lily pools I head past Brooklyn Zoo to the shores of Prospect Lake. Skirting the hazy water I pass a man talking to a tree. In Britain he would be invited to dinner parties by Prince Charles. In New York City he's given a wide berth.

'Dodgers by five, Dodgers by five, go Brooklyn, go ...' he intones. So fervent is he, so focused and sincere, I'm tempted to walk from the park, find a betting shop and place my life's savings (not a staggering amount – I've spent most of them on my odyssey around America) on the next Brooklyn Dodgers baseball match.

Then I remember the Dodgers left Brooklyn in 1958 to become the Los Angeles Dodgers, in that pragmatic way American business has of putting profit before customer. So I, too, give the madman a wide berth.

I amble west to woody Lookout Hill and the monument commemorating 400 soldiers of the Maryland regiment, who sacrificed themselves to allow George Washington to escape the advancing British during the Battle of Long Island on 27 August 1776.

'Good God, what brave fellows I must this day lose,' said Washington to rally his young soldiers, before running away.

The British would never have been able to take the hill today. A noticeboard announces that gatherings of twenty people or more require a permit. You have to call at least a month in advance. 'No, sir, I'm sorry. I don't care if you are a member of His Britannic Majesty's Armed Forces, I don't write the rules but I do uphold them and it says here in plain English you have to apply for a permit four weeks in advance, so there's absolutely no way I can allow you to march up this hill, unless you want to do it in groups of nineteen. Here's a form, come back in a month! And next time read the sign, dummy!'

The park's pièce de résistance is undoubtedly Long Meadow. Calvert Vaux, English by birth, was greatly influenced by the style of Capability Brown, and created Long Meadow to resemble English country pastures – a mile of green grass that until the 1950s housed flocks of grazing sheep.

Sheep would have been nice. Who knows where they went – perhaps one day they just decided they'd had enough of munching heroin phials and used condoms and retired to Florida. Or maybe they were barbecued by the junkies who lurk in the park fringes. Today they're replaced by earnest little children playing soccer matches while their parents bellow like Olympic coaches on the sidelines.

I continue up the meadow, which, with its small rolling hills, resembles an expensive golf course. I pass Marvin's Juggling School (six people chucking balls at each other), two film students discussing a script and a man standing on his head beneath a spreading oak. As the sun lowers, light streaming through trees, Prospect Park seems a cauldron of creativity, a place of magic.

I stop and stand at the top of the Meadow, looking south. On this balmy, soporific summer's late afternoon, the world seems right and just. A couple of Yummy Mummies in skimpy shorts and tank tops are playing with their beautiful bouncing babies, their svelte shadows beginning to lengthen gently.

I wonder, almost out loud, if I'll ever end up with a Yummy Mummy, if the beautiful bouncing babe will ever be mine.

Maybe.

Just maybe.

Exiting the park is a shock. Suddenly I'm back in the concrete and noise of New York City. I cross Grand Army Plaza to the Union Arch. On the summit Columbia has been reinstated in her chariot, accompanied by copious eagles and bayonets. I sit for a while in the early dusk, watching the evening mums wheeling prams, and think that if I ever decide to breed, I too might well end up in Brooklyn.

The next day I say goodbye to the United States. I knew I'd get a last-minute ticket for this day, because it's the one day in the year you're guaranteed to get a flight out of America.

4 July. Independence Day.

As I sit in JFK Airport, an empty cavernous hall populated by straggling Europeans startled by the lack of Americans, I think, not for the first or last time, that life is a journey. Sometimes you lose the tickets and forget where you're going. Sometimes you lose the ticket stubs and forget where you've been.

I think that my journey around America has got me back on track. It's quite likely I would have been saved by other countries, but there is something – and this might sound controversial here, but not as controversial as some of my other opinions such as The Beatles weren't very good and Andie McDowell is a talented actress – but there is something simple, honest and caring about America, especially rural America, which means it is not a bad place to go if you're feeling a little low.

The plane takes off from JFK into a hot treacle night. As I press my nose to the glass, fireworks ejaculate towards me, bursting forth in a climax of red, white and blue. All over the city little orgasms of colour spurt happily, a great fizzling orgy of pigment. Golden showers, red flashes, orange spurts. A nation giving thanks and praise for being American.

I too give thanks and praise, in my half-empty 747.

I've survived. And I'm going home.

CONTINENTAL DRIFTER

Tim Moore

Financed by a bet with a Yeovil linen draper, court jester Thomas Coryate's 1608 journey to Venice and back was an unlikely template for the Grand Tour.

Almost four hundred years later, Tim Moore put on a ridiculous velvet suit and set off in Coryate's tracks at the wheel of a senile and incontinent Rolls-Royce. Treading an uneasy line between Coryate's turnip-stealing frugality and the bawdy self-indulgence of the later Grand Tourists, Moore's confrontations with Continental croupiers, nudists, sugar-beet farmers and offshore welders are a grotesque blend of Baldrick and Blackadder.

While charting the decline of the Grand Tour from sombre academy of cultural betterment to the Club 18–30 of the 1830s, Moore also resurrects the reputation of Coryate, whose reward for introducing the fork to Britain and coining the word 'umbrella' was ridicule, poverty and an almost unbearably poignant ending in India.

Abacus

0 349 11464 1

CORNUCOPIA

Paul Richardson

Food, once the shame of the British nation, is now the object of our shameless interest. A revolution is afoot, and never in the field of human nutrition have so many people eaten so well.

So, at least, we are led to believe. But in the course of a dyspeptic journey around the eating places, the fine-food producers, the markets and supermarkets of Britain, Paul Richardson found out that the truth is more complex and much more amusing.

Tasting everything from deep-fried Mars Bar to bull's wazzel, *Cornucopia* answers the question: what is the state of our national cuisine?

'Stylishly written, seasoned with unobtrusive learning, laced with tempting recipes, *Cornucopia* is a hugely entertaining guide to the good, the bad and the emetic in British gastronomy. I'd recommend it as a bedside book, except that it will probably have you raiding the fridge between chapters' *Independent*

'[Richardson's] amusing, wry, perceptive account of his travels in search of good British food provides delicious, even nourishing insights into the way we live now, as well as the way we cook and eat' *Sunday Telegraph*

Abacus

0 349 11132 4

FEEDING FRENZY

Stuart Stevens

Feeding Frenzy finds Stuart Stevens on a mission to eat his way across Europe's greatest food temples, accompanied by his friend Rachel 'Rat' Kelly, her frisky golden retriever Henry and a 1965 cherry-red Mustang that is anything but reliable. That wouldn't be so bad, except that time is something of the essence: for if Stuart and Rat dine in all twenty-nine of Michelin's three-star European restaurants in just twenty-nine days, then Rat's boyfriend will pick up the tab . . .

'A mad-cap dash filled with adventures and misadventures, encounters with star chefs and snooty maitres d'. The book's strength is the undoubted attraction of Steven's sharp American wit . . . a funny read' *Independent on Sunday*

'A quirky fun read, it makes a change from more deeply philosophical travelogues. There is only one catch; it may not make you want to travel, but it will make you want to eat' *Wanderlust*

'A mixed dish of chaos, frivolity and expanding waistlines in a funny and original travel book' *Books Magazine*

'A fun read and a cheap way to enjoy some of the best restaurants in Europe' *Literary Review*

Abacus

0 349 11423 4

PARK AND RIDE

Miranda Sawyer

Forget the Britain that is green and pleasant, urban and dangerous, historic and scenic: this is the rest of it, the vast swathes of inbetweeny land, the multiplexed, motorwayed, mind-your-manners Great British Experience. And it may well be where you live . . .

'A Mike Leigh screenplay for the *Changing Rooms* generation' GQ

'The sheer pungency of her almost apocalyptic account of Britain's thriving suburban castles lends exceptional zest to a series of sharp, well-aimed, acid toe-capped kicks . . . Such annihilation has been performed before. John Osborne did it. Sid Vicious was there. But this is prime stuff' *Independent on Sunday*

'A travel book on the real Britain without the patronising asides . . . Sawyer is Bill Bryson for people who don't read the *Daily Mail*, and she's not afraid to get her hands dirty' *Mirror*

'As excellent as we expect from this most talented young person' Julie Burchill, *Guardian*, Books of the Year

'Miranda Sawyer has done for Wilmslow what Jilly Cooper did for polo' *Cheshire Life*

Abacus

0 349 11319 X

Now you can order superb titles directly from Abacus

☐ Continental Drifter	Tim Moore	£10.99
☐ Cornucopia	Paul Richardson	£7.99
☐ Feeding Frenzy	Stuart Stevens	£7.99
☐ Park and Ride	Miranda Sawyer	£6.99

───────────────── ⬭ABACUS⬭ ─────────────────

Please allow for postage and packing: **Free UK delivery**.
Europe; add 25% of retail price; Rest of World; 45% of retail price.

To order any of the above or any other Abacus titles, please call our
credit card orderline or fill in this coupon and send/fax it to:

Abacus, 250 Western Avenue, London, W3 6XZ, UK.
Fax 020 8324 5678   Telephone 020 8324 5517

☐ I enclose a UK bank cheque made payable to Abacus for £...........

☐ Please charge £........... to my Access, Visa, Delta, Switch Card No.

Expiry date   Switch Issue No.

Name (Block Letters please) . . . .

Address . . . .

. . . .

. . . .

Postcode . . . . Telephone . . . .

Signature . . . .